W9-ARH-936

Robert L. Barker
Douglas M. Branson

Forensic Social Work
Legal Aspects
of Professional Practice

Second Edition

Pre-publication
REVIEWS,
COMMENTARIES,
EVALUATIONS . . .

"**F** *orensic Social Work: Legal Aspects of Professional Practice* gives social workers the understanding and tools they need to function in a litigious society and within agencies that carry out society's legal mandates. It contains a number of useful chapters for professional social workers, including how to testify in court, be an expert witness, and avoid malpractice; how laws and professional aims may collide;

how to conduct a professional review and prepare written contracts, and finally the legal underpinnings of social work credentialing. This book is a wonderful resource for all social work practitioners and would be an excellent text for social work courses in social policy, ethics, and social work practice offerings that deal with the interface of social work and the law."

Frederick L. Ahearn Jr., DSW
Professor and Former Dean,
National Catholic
School of Social Service,
The Catholic University of America,
Washington, DC

WITHDRAWN

NORTHEAST COMMUNITY COLLEGE LIBRARY

More pre-publication
REVIEWS, COMMENTARIES, EVALUATIONS . . .

"**F**orensic Social Work provides readers with a very efficient summary of a wide range of compelling issues in practice. Social workers will appreciate Barker and Branson's succinct overview of practitioners' diverse and challenging roles in legal settings. This book is chock-full of practical information and advice pertaining to such topics as courtroom testimony, prevention of lawsuits and ethics complaints, and clinical documentation. Using extensive case material, the authors have produced a user-friendly and practical introduction to forensic social work that professionals can use to protect clients and themselves."

Frederic G. Reamer, PhD
Professor,
School of Social Work,
Rhode Island College,
Pawtucket

"**B**arker and Branson, with this new and enlarged work, once again provide essential, practical information to every social worker who may ever be involved, in any way, with the legal system, especially those who appear in courts of law. Of particular interest are the newer topics raised, including the National Organization of Forensic Social Workers, *Jaffee v. Redmond* (U.S. Supreme Court), recovered memories of child sexual abuse, and the need for alternatives to law courts."

Sol Gothard, JD, MSW, ACSW
Judge, 5th Circuit Court of Appeal,
State of Louisiana;
Board member,
National Organization
of Forensic Social Workers

The Haworth Press, Inc.

NOTES FOR PROFESSIONAL LIBRARIANS AND LIBRARY USERS

This is an original book title published by The Haworth Press, Inc. Unless otherwise noted in specific chapters with attribution, materials in this book have not been previously published elsewhere in any format or language.

CONSERVATION AND PRESERVATION NOTES

All books published by The Haworth Press, Inc. and its imprints are printed on certified pH neutral, acid free book grade paper. This paper meets the minimum requirements of American National Standard for Information Sciences-Permanence of Paper for Printed Material, ANSI Z39.48-1984.

Forensic Social Work
Legal Aspects of Professional Practice

Second Edition

Forensic Social Work
Legal Aspects
of Professional Practice
Second Edition

Robert L. Barker
Douglas M. Branson

344.73
B255f

The Haworth Press
New York • London • Oxford

© 2000 by The Haworth Press, Inc. All rights reserved. No part of this work may be reproduced or utilized in any form or by any means, electronic or mechanical, including photocopying, microfilm, and recording, or by any information storage and retrieval system, without permission in writing from the publisher. Printed in the United States of America.

Cover design by Monica L. Seifert.

The Haworth Press, Inc., 10 Alice Street, Binghamton, NY 13904-1580

Library of Congress Cataloging-in-Publication Data

Barker, Robert L.
    Forensic social work : legal aspects of professional practice / Robert L. Barker, Douglas M. Branson. — 2nd ed.
        p.   cm.
    Includes bibliographical references and index.
    ISBN 0-7890-0867-X — ISBN 0-7890-0868-8 (pbk.)
    1. Forensic sociology—United States. 2. Social workers—Legal status, laws, etc.—United States. 3. Evidence, Expert—United States. I. Branson, Douglas M. II. Title.
KF8968.7.B37 2000
344.73'0313—dc21   99-39464
                                                                                          CIP

CONTENTS

ABOUT THE AUTHORS

Robert L. Barker heads a consulting organization to help social agencies write and administer grant proposals and raise funds. For twelve years Dr. Barker was Professor of Social Work at the National Catholic School of Social Services, The Catholic University of America, in Washington, DC, and Co-Director of the Potomac Psychiatric Center in Maryland and Washington, DC, where he specialized in marital and family therapy, group therapy, and group work. He has worked as a social worker in juvenile courts, family courts, and frequently as an expert witness, especially in family custody legal disputes. He is the author of twenty-one books, including *The Social Work Dictionary, Social Work in Private Practice, Treating Couples in Crisis,* and *The Green-Eyed Marriage.* He received a master's degree in social work (MSW) from the University of Washington, and holds a doctorate (DSW) from Columbia University.

Douglas M. Branson is Professor of Law at the University of Pittsburgh Law School and visiting Professor at law schools in Spain, South Africa, and Australia. He is the author of over ninety articles and four books, including the major textbook, *Corporate Governance.* A legal consultant to various social activist organizations and professional societies, Dr. Branson is a member of the American Bar Association, the Washington Bar Association, the Pennsylvania Bar Association, and the American Law Institute. A graduate of the University of Notre Dame, his law degree (JD) is from Northwestern University, with postdoctoral studies at the University of Virginia Law School.

Preface and Acknowledgments

As society increasingly looks to the legal justice system for solutions to its myriad problems, many professions have been called upon to assist the law profession in dealing with these issues. More than ever, social workers have participated in this movement; their presence in courtrooms as expert and fact witnesses is becoming commonplace, as is their participation as lobbyists for lawmaking groups and proponents for various changes in the legal system.

Reflecting the trend, social workers have begun to embrace the new specialty known as "forensic social work." It is a field that requires considerable knowledge and practice experience, particularly inasmuch as it draws not only on the knowledge base of the social work profession, but that of the law profession as well. However, not until recent years had much been written about forensic social work; the need for more information about this field, presented in a practical, relevant, and concise way, was becoming increasingly apparent.

When the first edition of this book was published in 1993 it was immediately well received among social workers as offering one of the first extensive and systematic inquiries into this new field. It was widely adopted as a textbook in newly emerging courses in legal aspects of social work practice, and as a supplement to existing social work courses that wanted to provide more attention to this emerging field.

In the next few years, many social workers and lawyers who read and used the book wrote to the authors; they provided valuable suggestions for expanding and improving the text. Moreover, since publication of the first edition, many laws and court decisions affecting social work practice have been established. Since then, all the states in the nation have passed laws creating public boards to regulate social work licenses and practice. An expanded and updated second edition of *Forensic Social Work* was needed.

Because forensic social work is a specialty that exists at the interface between the two professions, this book is the result of collaboration by its authors—a social worker and a lawyer. We have also drawn on the knowledge of many of our respective colleagues. Many social workers and lawyers have provided us with valuable information, examples, resources, and advice in the production of both editions of this book. They include Jackson Rose, William Oltman, John and Sally Watkins, and Judge Thomas Larkin. Social workers who are widely recognized for their expertise on social work ethical and justice issues and who have provided useful suggestions and information include Geoffrey Greif, Jill Doner Kagle, Carlton E. Munson, and Frederic G. Reamer. Valuable input came from several social work educators who are also lawyers, including John Michael Seelig, Lloyd Johnson, and Lorrie Greenhouse Gardella. Judge Sol Gothard, who is a social worker, lawyer, and eminent jurist, was especially supportive, knowledgeable, and instructive in all stages of the development of this book. Donna DeAngelis of the American Association of State Social Work Boards also provided valuable information and insights about the current issues pertaining to social work regulation.

Bill Cohen's team at The Haworth Press has, as always, been very supportive and highly competent. Those deserving of special thanks include Peg Marr, Linda Mulcahy, Donna Biesecker, Andrew Roy, Dawn Krisko, and Yvonne Kester. Finally, we appreciate the support and patience of our families, especially Dr. Mary Elizabeth Donovan, and Clare and Annie Branson.

Robert L. Barker
Douglas M. Branson

Chapter 1

Forensic Social Work in a Litigious Society

Forensic social work is a professional specialty that focuses on the interface between society's legal and human service systems. It includes such activities as providing expert testimony in courts of law, investigating cases of possible criminal conduct, and assisting the legal system in such issues as child custody disputes, divorce, nonsupport, delinquency, spouse or child abuse, mental hospital commitment, and relative's responsibility.

Social workers with clinical orientations have for decades been central figures in the legal-psychological processes of adoption, termination of parental rights, eldercare, disability rights, mandated treatment, juvenile and family courts, criminal justice, probation and parole (Roberts, 1997; Cole and others, 1995; Ezell, 1995; Miller, 1995). Clinical social workers also make significant, though often unacknowledged, contributions to social justice (Swenson, 1998). Workers with public policy and social change orientations have been active with legislators, political leaders, and lobbying groups to help make laws and human rights more just and equitable for all (Witkin, 1998; Haynes, 1998; Litzelfelner and Petr, 1997; Weismiller and Rome, 1995).

As contemporary society increasingly seeks to resolve its conflicts and other problems through its legal justice system, professional social workers are compelled to learn more about this system and to participate more fully with those who implement it (Kopels and Gustavsson, 1996; Hutchison, 1993). The relationship between social work and the legal system is growing closer (Schroeder, 1995; Johnson and Cahn, 1995).

Meanwhile a growing number of people claim that American society has grown too litigious, wanting to settle all its disputes legalistically through courts of law and threats of suits (Pflepsen, 1997; Smith, 1997). They point out that there has been an explosion of civil litigation to accompany the growth industries of criminal law and resulting prison building (Schlosser, 1998; Olson, 1991). The law profession itself has been subject to increasing criticism; some claim it is engaged in manipulation of people and social institutions "to provoke litigation artfully and unnecessarily" (Hearn, 1999, p. 2).

Social work and other professions are caught in a crossfire of seemingly contradictory laws and ethical standards. For example, they now must balance their ethical principles of confidentiality against mandatory reporting laws (Dickson, 1998); they must turn in clients they think may be engaged in antisocial conduct but risk being sued for slander and libel when they do so (Gambrill and Pruger, 1997; Hutchison, 1993). Laws pertaining to social workers and other professionals now spell out when they must, and when they cannot, perform specified actions (Polowy and Gorenberg, 1997; Alexander, 1995).

Social workers and social work agencies are being sued with increasing frequency, often for dubious claims (Marine, 1998a; Kurzman, 1995). The pressure has mounted on the profession as a whole to protect itself from its own incompetent and malevolent members; it is doing so with a profusion of new credentials, competency certification procedures, tighter codes of ethics, and stricter licensing laws (Reamer, 1998b).

In the context of this emerging trend, it is more important than ever for social workers to know about the law, how to use it for oneself and one's clients, how to minimize legal difficulties, and how to serve it better in its quest for social and civic justice. It is a propitious time for the development of the specialty known as forensic social work (NOFSW, 1999; Solomon and Draine, 1995; Schultz, 1991).

THE PURPOSE OF FORENSIC SOCIAL WORK

Forensic social work seeks to educate law professionals about people's human and social service needs; it also educates social work colleagues about the legal aspects of their work. Forensic social workers use their skills to assist law authorities in a variety of ways:

they interview crime victims and witnesses and provide the information to investigators and to courts of law; they consult with lawyers about the kinds of juries that would be optimal to their cases; they work with other mental health experts to determine if clients possess enough mental competence to stand trials; they are frequently fact witnesses or expert witnesses in trials (Gibelman, 1995).

The specialty is also oriented to helping social workers avoid becoming defendants in malpractice suits, or when that is unavoidable, to help one side or the other achieve the best possible outcomes. Finally, forensic social work is interested in the legal regulation of professional practice, including professional licensing and credentialing, and other provisions for public accountability.

Such activities are of growing interest and importance for social work. The reasons are obvious. They include the trend toward litigiousness in American society, the increasing likelihood and expense of malpractice litigation, the issuance of laws and court rulings affecting the practice of social workers and other professionals, the confusing and apparently contradictory nature of some of these laws and rulings, and the fact that social work is legally regulated in every jurisdiction in the nation.

In the past decade, social workers as well as members of all other professions have been sued for malpractice with increasing frequency and escalating costs. They have been named in suits for major and minor violations of their ethical codes and licensing requirements, but also in cases where they were only tangentially involved or had no alternative course of action. For example, social workers who provided consultation to colleagues have been sued by the colleagues' clients. Workers have been successfully sued for disclosing client confidences even when laws compelled them to do so; other workers have been sued for not revealing client confidences when that information could have prevented crimes.

Schools of social work have been sued for discrimination for not admitting grossly unqualified students and for passing over well-qualified faculty members to promote less qualified colleagues. Social work supervisors have been sued for the malpractice of their subordinates, and social agencies have been sued for the actions of their employees, sometimes even when off duty. Examples of such actions have been described in the literature (e.g., Grabois, 1997-

1998; Madden and Parody, 1997; Houston-Vega, Nuehring, and Daguio, 1996; Mullaney and Timberlake, 1994; Hutchison, 1993; Alexander, 1993).

Laws and courtroom rulings involving professional practice have changed dramatically in recent years, especially regarding confidentiality and the legal requirements to control one's clients. Court decisions, especially the cases known as *Tarasoff, Ramona,* and *Jaffee vs. Redmond,* have placed limits and requirements on social workers that seem confusing, contradictory, and unresolved.

And in this climate of legal change social workers have seen professional licensing come to every state in the nation (Biggerstaff, 1995). Legal regulation of social work practice has been necessary for the profession to maintain credibility and remain eligible to provide mental health services and receive insurance reimbursement for it—but it also means that the public scrutiny of social work is more intense than ever (Whiting, 1995).

These trends require social workers to be more involved in the legal aspects of their professional practices. Forensic social work is the specialty that has newly emerged within the profession to systematically address these concerns.

LAW IN THE ORIGINS OF SOCIAL WORK

While forensic social work itself is a recently identified specialty, many of its activities are as old as the profession itself. At the beginning of the twentieth century social work emerged in large part to fulfill many legal functions. The earliest social workers investigated families to determine if parents were abusing their children or otherwise not meeting their children's developmental needs. They reported the findings of their social investigations to the media and law authorities and testified in courts about their findings (Richmond, 1898; Addams, 1899).

The earliest social workers were oriented to changing society and its social injustices. They led political movements to change laws and to pressure the legal system to enforce existing laws with more rigor. They led successful campaigns to change or enact child labor laws, obtain legal rights for women, improve laws that would better protect workers and consumers. This social activism was largely motivated by their direct exposure to the problems of poverty and their work in prisons and crime-ridden neighborhoods (Axinn and Levin, 1992).

Many of the people who created the social work profession and its employing organizations were lawyers. For example, attorney Robert Weeks deForest (1848-1931) was a founder and the principal leader of the Charity Organization Societies, the early social agencies where social workers were first employed and given their present name (Quam, 1995a). He also founded the first school for social workers (now known as Columbia University School of Social Work). Robert deForest also organized the Russell Sage Foundation, the philanthropic foundation that financed many of social work's first organizations, educational facilities, and publications. The Foundation published most of the first major social work textbooks and the *Social Work Yearbook,* which evolved into today's *Encyclopedia of Social Work.*

Lawyer Florence Kelley (1859-1932) is also considered a founder of the social work profession. Her law background led to her work as head of a government agency to enforce its labor laws, which later developed into her crusade against child labor and exploitation of the working poor. She helped create the National Consumer's League and the United States Children's Bureau. Realizing that these organizations and others with similar goals at the local level required competent, trained, staff to be effective, she encouraged and obtained funding for training programs for a new professional group (Edwards, 1995).

Another pioneer in the creation of social work was lawyer Sophonisba Breckinridge (1866-1948), who brought social work education into the university system and led the movement to include legal courses in the social work education curriculum. She helped develop the graduate program now known as the University of Chicago School of Social Service Administration and was its long-time dean. She also helped create the influential social work journal *Social Service Review* and was a founder of the organization that became the National Association of Social Workers (Quam, 1995b).

Many of the other founders of professional social work who were not lawyers, nevertheless spent considerable energies working with the law. Jane Addams (1860-1935) devoted much of her life to social activism and lobbying lawmakers, from local aldermen to national and international leaders (Addams, 1902). She organized and led political parties and became the first woman president of the National Conference on Charities and Corrections (Bryan, Slote, and Argury, 1996; Lundblad, 1995).

Mary Richmond (1861-1928), who now is widely considered to be the progenitor of the clinical side of social work, was actually also very much involved in legal work and social activism (Longres, 1995). She helped establish child labor laws, juvenile courts, and legislation for deserted wives. Her early books, especially *Friendly Visiting Among the Poor* (1898) and *Social Diagnosis* (1917), contained extensive discussions about how workers should engage the legal system in efforts to help the disadvantaged.

EARLY AFFINITY OF SOCIAL WORK AND THE LAW

With such a foundation it was natural for social work to have close ties to the law and legal justice system. Almost every new professional school included law courses. Field placements were in family courts, prisons, legal aid offices, and even private law firms. Upon graduation, many social workers became probation and parole officers and court investigators. They were often asked to evaluate the merits and risks of keeping an offender in the community and to prepare "Pre-sentence Investigation Reports (PSIR)" (Isenstadt, 1995, p. 71). Those who worked in welfare offices, settlement houses, and charity organization societies encountered the victims of crime and injustice and reported their findings to law authorities (Tice, 1998).

During its first thirty years social work was closer to the law than it is now to the health and mental health fields. Most early social workers belonged to the National Conference on Charities and Corrections (founded in 1879), and many of its other members were law officials. The nation's juvenile court system avoided the adversarial procedures of other courts by employing social workers to advocate for the child, family, and state simultaneously. Then the worker would act as probation officer for the judges' sentences of juvenile cases (Ezell, 1995).

The major employers of social workers were public welfare offices and child welfare organizations, and much of their work involved investigating and reporting to the legal authorities the conditions to which children and the disadvantaged were subjected (Trattner, 1999). Many social workers found themselves testifying in courts almost as frequently as they were working with clients. Recognizing that this was becoming a major social work function, the schools of social work increased their offerings of courses in legal aspects of professional practice and encouraged more students to study such offerings.

DIVERGENCE BETWEEN SOCIAL WORK AND THE LAW

It was not until the mid-1930s that social work began its turn away from a legal orientation toward its emphasis on mental health and humanistic concerns. The poverty and economic problems seen in the Great Depression (1929-1941) drew the interests of many social workers away from the law and more toward economics and sociology. The new philosophies of Sigmund Freud (1856-1939) and other psychoanalytic theorists influenced many other social workers toward an interest in the mental processes of individuals (Specht and Courtney, 1995).

Many professional schools of social work replaced their curricular offerings in the legal and justice fields with more courses with psychosocial orientations. Field placements in law settings were replaced by those in mental health clinics. Even though the social work profession recognized and advocated closer relationships with law professionals, few practical steps were made in that direction (Schroeder, 1995; Brieland and Lemmon, 1985; Sloane, 1967).

As social workers pursued other interests, prisons, juvenile courts, and the probation system could no longer find enough workers to fill most of their jobs and had to turn to members of other disciplines . (Miller, 1995). Reflecting the schism between social workers and the justice/corrections system, the National Conference on Charities and Corrections split into two groups. The *Gault* decision in 1967 gave children the same legal rights in courtrooms as adults, and soon social workers were replaced by lawyers in the juvenile court system (Manfredi, 1998; Singer, 1996). In public welfare and child protective service agencies, investigations of potential abuse were carried out increasingly by individuals who had not been trained as social workers.

As social work moved farther from the legal institutions, it also seemed antipathetic toward legal regulation of professional practice. By the mid-1960s only three states had social work licensing laws (DeAngeles, 1993). Efforts to license social workers in other jurisdictions were minimal and ineffective.

Many influential social workers argued against licensing (Flynn, 1987). They claimed that it was anathema to the values of the profession, that it would only encourage elitism, and that it would drive everyone but clinical social workers out of the profession. And most important, they said, it was unnecessary; the profession did not need to be legally regulated because it had two safeguards that were supposedly more reliable. One was the profession's system of controlling its workers by closely supervising them in their agency employment. The other was the widespread assumption in the profession that the worker's behavior would be unassailable because of social work's high moral principles and values (Vigilante, 1974).

The view that licenses were unnecessary changed, perhaps more for economic reasons than high-flown moral ones. Insurance companies, which became increasingly important to all providers of social and health care services, began to refuse reimbursement to professionals who were not licensed. Clients who had insurance would seek only the services of licensed professionals; social workers wanting to serve these clients would have to find a psychiatrist willing to supervise their work.

Most social workers continued to shrug off the insistence on licensing by insurance companies. They believed, for awhile, that it would affect only private practitioners, who were not very popular in the profession anyway (Barker, 1992). After all, most clinical workers were employed in social agencies, and their funding was paid for by taxes or donations and programs such as United Way.

However, the social agencies themselves found they too were affected. For all but government agencies, funding from private donations and fund drives remained static as costs mounted. Clients who had insurance went to licensed professionals. The more affluent clients who paid larger portions of their co-payment costs were gone, and the agencies could not see many clients who could pay little or nothing for their services. The agencies also needed the insurance company money. They wanted to hire only licensed professionals.

The change came dramatically fast. In little more than a decade, by 1992, every state had established licensing or legal regulation of its social workers (Landers, 1992). Once licensing was established, social workers could become recognized providers of mental health services at the local and state levels. The movement was spearheaded by individual social workers in each state, along with help from professional associations, agencies, and consumer groups, as well as lawyers and lawmakers. They overcame opposition from within the profession and from other professional disciplines, notably psychology and psychiatry. Their opposition was based largely on concerns about losing market share of the mental health care "business" (Whiting, 1995, p. 2428).

Of course, the victory for social work is a mixed blessing. Legal regulation may mean more jobs, income, opportunities to serve all clients, and public acceptance; it also means more scrutiny and higher risks. Social workers became subject to the same controls that the public exercises over other professions—at a time when the public has grown increasingly litigious.

GROWTH OF THE LITIGIOUS SOCIETY

While social work sought to become legally regulated, American society as a whole grew into the most litigious society in history. Professionals in all fields are scrutinized more heavily than ever; to an unprecedented degree they are held accountable, not only to their employers, but to their clients, their professional colleagues, and to the general public.

In the current climate of litigiousness, laws and rulings have been created to protect citizens against virtually every risk (Priest, 1990). When the risks have unhappy outcomes, professional practitioners are often named in lawsuits for malpractice. Social workers are not excluded from this circumstance; social welfare organizations, nonprofit social agencies, and workers are now being sued with regularity (Reamer, 1995b).

This trend began in the early 1960s with President Kennedy's message to Congress. He proclaimed the existence of four basic consumer rights. These were: (1) the right to safety (protection against the marketing of goods or services hazardous to one's health); (2) the right to be informed (protection against fraudulent advertising or misleading information about products and services, and the right to be given the facts needed to make an informed choice in the marketplace); (3) the right to choose (reasonable access to a variety of producers and services); and (4) the right to be heard (assurance that consumers will get sympathetic hearings by all government agencies and that consumer laws will be enforced).

The consumer movement resulted in major changes in the way the helping professions provide their services. Professionals started advertising and overtly competing for clients. The various professional groups worked hard to define their respective turfs and proclaim exclusivity within that realm. All the professions helped legislators develop more stringent licensing laws.

Social workers left social agencies and the supervision of experienced colleagues and entered private practice where the only controls on their practice were through licensing and peer review. The omissions and commissions of public agency social workers, especially in making recommendations to legal authorities about clients, were intensely scrutinized by the legal system. Workers involved in child abuse cases, adoptions, custody disputes, marital mediation, parole, and commitment procedures were frequently challenged in courts. Mental health professionals were being held accountable in courts for failing to accurately predict violent behavior in their clients, even though there was little evidence that they had such prescient powers (Otto, 1994).

SOCIAL WORK'S RENEWED INTEREST

In this climate, social work is renewing its interest in the law. More social workers have entered specialties that involve the legal and justice systems (Gibelman, 1995). More graduate schools of social work are adding curriculum content about legal and ethical issues (Kopels and Gustavsson, 1996). More social workers with social policy orientations are becoming lawmakers throughout the nation (Haynes, 1998). Even clinical social workers are increasingly involved in activities to achieve social justice wherever oppression occurs (Swenson, 1998).

Social workers are reentering fields that involve law enforcement, the justice system, and lawmaking activities (Gendreau, 1996). They have created a variety of specialties, including police social work, social work mediation, assault victimization specialties, juvenile probation, and other fields, in addition to forensic social work.

Their involvement in the traditional fields of work with the poor and disadvantaged or the mentally ill has led many social workers into closer relationships with legal institutions as a part of their work. For example, Solomon and Draine (1995) point out that it is actually difficult to distinguish between community mental health workers and forensic workers in incarceral settings, given the high arrest histories among inpatient and outpatient mental health program clients.

Police social work is a professional specialty that has become increasingly important, especially in the larger cities of this nation and Europe (Treger, 1995). Law officers have found social workers to be valuable when called upon to deal with domestic conflict problems, rape victimization, hostage and suicide threats, potential riots, and in interpreting psychosocial behaviors in the effort to locate offenders, victims, and missing persons (Brown, Unsinger, and More, 1990). More social workers have been employed to help police with victim and witness assistance programs; this movement is partly in response to community complaints that the rights and comforts of offenders seemed more important to police than those of ordinary citizens.

Because the basic methods and philosophies of police officers and social workers have been at variance, not many social workers have entered this field to date. Few of those in the specialty are themselves uniformed police officers, and many more are employed by police on a contracting-out basis, when special needs for their services become apparent.

A similar social work specialty is found in the auspices of county prosecutor's or district attorney's offices where social workers are employed to help deal with the widespread problem of domestic violence, rape victimization, and child abuse. Law authorities acknowledge that social work mediation can sometimes offer a swifter and more personally meaningful outcome than that of the courts (Severson and Bankston, 1995). Social work mediation has been used in child protective cases in many communities in the United States and Canada, where a majority of cases have been successfully mediated before resorting to court action (Wilhelmus, 1998).

Many clinical social workers in agencies or in private practice have recently been called upon by law authorities to establish and maintain mandated treatment programs (O'Hare, 1996). In lieu of incarceration or extended parole, judges are requiring offenders to participate in community based correctional programs for specified periods of time or until the professional has indicated that the treatment goals have been reached.

The social workers and other professionals who maintain these programs must coordinate their efforts closely with the law authorities; they offer programs that help the client and assure the authorities that the client has been in compliance. Social workers provide these services especially in cases of alcohol abuse, drug abuse, dangerous driving, domestic violence, sexual offenses, and shoplifting.

WHAT SOCIAL WORKERS MUST KNOW ABOUT THE LAW

Social work's renewed interest in the law and legal institutions has made many social workers aware of the need for more knowledge of jurisprudence. They need to know more about how laws are made, changed, interpreted, and enforced. Knowledge about courtroom procedures is also essential. Social workers should know more about general procedures in courtrooms, grand jury settings, judges' chambers, and law offices. They need to know the roles of the various personae involved in trials, and this knowledge should be based on serious study rather than watching television courtroom dramas or serving on jury duty.

Regarding information that they give to legal officials, social workers should have a better idea about the admissibility of evidence, that is, what information can and cannot be used in trials. In this context the worker must know how to obtain accurate information from clients, legally and ethically, so that it can be considered as admissible evidence. And, of course, more social workers should be knowledgeable and polished as to the presentation of effective testimony.

All social workers also need to know about malpractice exposure. They need to know its causes and all the behaviors that a worker can perform which have led to lawsuits. They need to know how to avoid such behaviors and to minimize the negative consequences of legal action, for their own sakes and for the well-being of colleagues or clients whom they are helping in such actions. Social workers may serve on either side of malpractice cases, so they need to know how to present their viewpoints in ways that strengthen their cases.

In dealing with clients in a litigious society, social workers need to know how to maintain relationships that meet the client needs while minimizing risks of misunderstandings or conflicts. Contracts that spell out the goals and procedures of the therapeutic relationship can be prepared for the signatures of both client and worker.

Social workers should also become knowledgeable about what the law requires of them in their work with clients. Workers are not always fully informed or aware of legal requirements or changed laws. Some social workers still do not know, years after such laws were made, that they may be required to report their suspicion of child abuse or threats their clients make to harm others.

Social workers need to know about the legal regulation of their profession and other forms of accountability. Licensing, peer review, third-party review, and professional scrutiny and sanctions are all increasingly important considerations in social work practice. When workers have problems with reviewers or licensing regulators, they are likely to seek the services of colleagues who are knowledgeable about such matters.

THE EMERGENCE OF FORENSIC SOCIAL WORK

As social work becomes part of the American trend toward a more legalistic society, the development of its forensic specialty is overdue. With such a historical, if interrupted, alliance it is surprising that such a field has so far remained underdeveloped. But forensic social work may be about to emerge as a major component of the profession. More workers have entered the field; they are testifying in court as expert witnesses and helping lawyers present cases more effectively. The National Organization of Forensic Social Work was created to help develop the speciality. Professional conferences have increased their presentations and workshop offerings in legal aspects of social work practice.

The available literature reflects this growing interest. The *Journal of Law and Social Work* has been publishing exclusively on this topic throughout the 1990s, and many other social work journals have devoted significant space to legal aspects of social work practice. Several worthwhile books about social work and its relationship to the law have been published in recent years including Dickson, 1998; Schroeder, 1995; Fontana and Besharov, 1995; Sagatun and Edwards, 1995; Reamer, 1994; Thyer and Biggerstaff, 1989; and Brieland and Lemmon, 1985.

This book seeks to add to this knowledge. Its purpose is to introduce social workers to the activities of forensic social work and to other legal aspects of their profession. It describes how forensic social workers become established, work with lawyers, and testify in trials. The book also explores many other legal issues facing all social workers, including malpractice, licensing and credentialing, and peer review. It discusses how social workers must conduct themselves in this legalistic society to practice within the law and conform to the rules of society as well as to the ethics of the profession. It discusses contracts with clients and presents prototypes of written contracts that social workers use with their clients.

At the end of the book are several resources that may be helpful to any social worker interested in the legal aspects of the profession. These include a glossary of the legal terms used in this book and frequently used in professional practice by social workers. Also included in the appendix are the names and addresses of all the social work licensing boards in the United States. The bibliography contains the essential literature of forensic social work.

Chapter 2

The Practice of Forensic Social Work

The specialty of forensic social work will remain underdeveloped until more practitioners learn what the field is all about. They need to know answers to the following questions: What do forensic social workers do? How do they do it? How do they learn to do it? Why should they want to do it? How do they get into the field? What credentials must they have to be forensic social workers? What special knowledge must they possess, and how do they acquire it?

Then they will have more practical questions to answer: What are the benefits and liabilities of the job? Who hires them? How much does it pay, and who pays them? How do they become known to those who will hire them? How do they get "new business"? How do they establish and maintain connection with other forensics experts? Once they are established as forensic social workers, how do they develop and refine their skills? Answering these questions is the focus of this and subsequent chapters.

WHAT DO FORENSIC SOCIAL WORKERS DO?

Forensic social workers fulfill at least ten major functions. First, and perhaps most central, they testify in courts of law as expert witnesses. In this job, the worker provides requested information in general about the human welfare needs of individuals, families, groups, and communities. For example, the worker might disclose what usually happens to the personalities of children or wives who are abused. Expert testimony is also given to legislative committees and lawmakers so they can decide if people need new laws or not.

Second, the forensic social worker systematically evaluates individuals so that the resulting information can be presented in court or to legal authorities. These evaluations are conducted to answer many questions that the court needs to know, such as the following: In what way has this person been psychologically and socially damaged by the defendant? Why did this person behave this way? Is this person responsible for his or her actions? What happened in this person's background that helps explain that current behavior? Is this person competent to stand trial?

Third, the forensic social worker investigates cases where criminal conduct has possibly occurred and presents the results to judges, juries, and other law authorities. For example, the worker testifies about visits to the home of a family whose child has been physically and sexually abused.

Fourth, the forensic social worker recommends to courts of law and other legal authorities ways to resolve, punish, or rehabilitate those found guilty of crimes or negligence in civil actions. For example, after evaluating a defendant to see how he is likely to react to various punishments, the worker delineates to the court various needed community service projects that could be fulfilled by the defendant that would be useful in his rehabilitation.

Fifth, the forensic social worker can facilitate the court-ordered sentence for the convicted person. This happens in many ways but primarily involves monitoring the person and reporting any progress to the court. It also happens by providing treatment to the person or advice to those who work with the person. For example, the worker can actually supervise the convicted person as he or she carries out a community service sentence, or give advice to the staff at the site of the sentence on how to deal with the person. Social workers also function in the formal role of probation or parole officer in many jurisdictions.

Sixth, the forensic social worker mediates between individuals and groups who are involved in disputes or conflicts that might otherwise require extensive intervention in the courtrooms. Many people, especially couples with marital problems, want to avoid the adversarial nature of legal proceedings and do so through professional mediation services. This has become a burgeoning field in which social workers are very active, especially in those states that encourage the mediation process. Mediators must be well versed in the law as well as in aspects of human nature in order to help disputants find fair and enduring resolutions to their conflicts.

Seventh, the forensic social worker testifies about the professional standards of social work to facilitate cases of possible malpractice or unethical conduct. When a social worker is sued for malpractice it is necessary to establish in the court what the standards are that were violated. Both the defendant and proponent attorneys might call upon social workers to describe specified elements of the profession's code of ethics and other professional standards. Social workers might also be asked about whether certain practices are the most efficacious or safe and whether other procedures might have been preferable. Such information might also be sought in peer review investigations and when the professional organization has a committee on inquiry to determine if a worker has deviated from professional standards.

Eighth, forensic social workers devote considerable attention to educating their colleagues about the influence of law on their profession. They teach courses and give workshops on the legal aspects of social work practice. They provide consultations to agencies and individual workers about how to provide professional services within the law and with respect to the risks of liability. In a variety of formats they inform colleagues about the causes of malpractice and professional sanction. They also inform lawyers and other legal officials about social welfare and the social work profession.

Ninth, forensic social workers facilitate the development and enforcement of licensing laws to regulate professional social work practice. They help develop these laws, educate the public and the profession about them, and help ensure that they are continuing to meet the needs of the public, the clients, and the members of the profession.

Tenth, and most important, forensic social workers maintain with their own clients relationships that uphold the letter and spirit of the law and the ethical principles of their profession. In this respect at least, every ethical and competent social worker is a forensic social worker.

MOTIVATIONS FOR FORENSIC SOCIAL WORKERS

Why would anyone want to be a forensic social worker? The motivations for entering the specialty remain elusive at best. Most social workers who have been called to court to offer testimony know this; many have not had entirely pleasant experiences, and they would like to avoid it if at all possible. For those who have not testified in court, the benefits are uncertain, but the challenges and difficulties are guaranteed. Only a small proportion of all social workers would find they have the interest and patience to engage in such work, much less the personality, knowledge, and skills.

So far, forensic social workers do not enjoy great prestige. Even though they might get introduced in court as being world-renowned social workers, the jurors, judges, counsel, and spectators will be less impressed than if introduced to a world-renowned forensic psychiatrist. And if their credentials and experiences are extolled by one side, the opposing attorneys will do everything possible to diminish those accomplishments. Opposing attorneys will challenge the social workers' claims to expertise. They will have to answer that they are not medical specialists, and have little expertise in psychiatric diagnoses, and cannot dispense drugs, and belong to the mental health specialty which, compared to psychiatry and psychology, has the least stringent requirements to practice. Finally when the time comes to answer the questions about the case, one's self-confidence might well be shaken.

An important factor that motivates social workers for anything they do is the satisfaction derived from helping people in need. And people involved in legal issues are surely in need. Thus, one supposes that when forensic social workers do well in their testimony they feel good about helping someone. This is only partly true. The problem is that the nature of the forensic social work is confrontational; to help one person win a legal case is to help another lose. The forensic worker's testimony that helps one person distresses another. If the help is appreciated at all by one side, it is likely to be highly resented by the other.

PAYMENT FOR FORENSICS EXPERTS

How much money do forensics specialists get paid and who pays them? The amount varies considerably, depending on the specialty, the particular case, and the amount of time required to fulfill the task. Recent news articles (Collins, 1997) suggest that some specialists have received several hundred thousand dollars for work on single cases. Many forensic psychiatrists are said to charge $200 to $350 per hour and other experts are paid even more. Some experts, such as appraisers, charge over $300 per hour, but many also receive percentages of the value of the objects they evaluate.

Most forensics experts, including social workers, are paid much less. Experts do not generally charge much more for their legal services than they receive in their regular jobs. There are two reasons for this. The forensics professional associations consider it unethical and in violation of the spirit of the scientific and objective provider of information to help bring out the truth. Also, when experts go to court, they are usually asked by opposing attorneys how much they are being paid for their testimony. If the answer is exorbitant, the credibility of the information being provided may be called into question. These people would be less effective in their testimony and thus would not be called by other attorneys.

Most forensic social workers and members of other professional disciplines charge an hourly rate, including travel time from their offices. If they practice far from the courtroom, they also receive travel expenses. If they are private practitioners they are thus unable to charge their regular clients for the time gone, so their financial situation is not measurably improved if their rates are about the same. And some expert witnesses have found it difficult to collect the fees they were promised, especially if the outcome of the case is unfavorable, or if the expert's presentation in court did not go as well as anticipated.

POSITIVE INCENTIVES

If the incentives do not include great prestige, fully satisfying experiences, or significant financial gain, why would social workers want to be involved in forensics if they could avoid it? No doubt, the motivations are unique for each worker. Some are interested in the challenge, the chance to fight for some other cause that has an imminent resolution. Others seek some variety in their work experience, a chance to get away from the routine of their offices and usual clients and bureaucratic conflicts. Money might attract some workers, if they are employed in universities or agencies that pay them even when away, or if they are private practitioners who have too many empty hours in their appointment books.

Perhaps the incentive for most social workers is more noble than these; it is to serve the cause of justice and human rights wherever possible. Courts of law are like all the other sites where social workers engage in this struggle. In presenting expert testimony, experienced social workers believe they fulfill their professional function of facilitating social justice, maintaining the benefits of the social order, and helping to eliminate social problems.

Through this role they also help protect vulnerable individuals, and they enhance their own profession and the other mental health professions by revealing to law authorities what the standards of good care are. The cases adjudicated in these courts of law involve people with problems, and it is the social workers' duty to help the legal system solve them.

FORENSIC SOCIAL WORK
AS A PART-TIME OCCUPATION

Most forensic social workers and other professionals are part-timers. Typically, they are engaged in courtroom and other legal activities only as ancillary activities; they are called away from their normal professional responsibilities when their unique services have been requested by law officials. The part-time forensics expert seems to have more credibility to judges and juries than does the specialist whose sole occupation is providing expert testimony. Jurors will wonder just how reputable a person is who doesn't have a real job other than providing expert opinions for money. Critics have called these people "whores of the court" (Hagen, 1997).

Anyone who devotes a career exclusively to testifying will almost inevitably be challenged in cross-examination as one whose expertise is for sale and whose information may be altered to suit the highest bidder (Roser, 1994). This contention is probably untrue, but the opposing lawyer usually tries to call into doubt the worth of any unfavorable testimony or the motives of one who presents that testimony.

The part-time forensics expert, on the other hand, can be presented to the court as a person who already has an important professional position and one who takes time away from these other serious duties to assist the jury in understanding complicated elements of the case (Oates, 1993).

Forensic social workers are no exception; most of them are also part-timers. They keep their jobs in social agencies, universities, institutions, or private practice, and provide forensic services on an ad hoc or consultative basis when their special expertise is wanted. Most social workers who do part-time forensics work prefer it this way; retaining their primary jobs lends prestige and gravitas to their testimony in the courtroom (Schultz, 1991). One study of the career activities of forensic social workers found that nearly all those in the representative sample had full-time jobs in fields other than forensics and that over 75 percent worked as clinicians, mostly in agencies (Hughes and O'Neal, 1983). A social worker who has spent years in a child protective agency, for example, can offer testimony in a child abuse case that might be more effective than if the information came from a social worker who did nothing else but testify at such trials.

Those who are also employed as university professors in schools of social work are fortunate in combining credibility and enough time for this activity. Private practitioners are another credible group, if they are well known for providing clinical services to specific client groups, i.e., those clients who have problems similar to the case being adjudicated.

Social workers who are social/political activists can also be successful forensics experts if, in the course of their professional activity, they have developed extensive knowledge and expertise in the problem being tried and if they can make their presentations objectively. Indeed, social workers in every specialty can become forensic social workers if they achieve high levels of expertise and are well recognized as having the knowledge needed and the ability to present it well (Solomon and Draine, 1995).

STEPS TOWARD A FORENSICS SPECIALTY

How do social workers get started in this field? Three steps are essential. They must acquire superlative knowledge within their realm of expertise, the ability to communicate it, and they must become known to those who would employ them.

The first and most important step by far is the development of expert knowledge. One need not have a great width of knowledge in the area of expertise, as long as the investigation and testimony is confined to that narrow realm, but depth is crucial. Nowadays, this expertise in nearly every field is built upon a foundation of extensive formal education, followed by considerable experience.

Experts in a very few fields are still being developed without considerable formal education, but these are rare. For example, handwriting and photographic analysts are not required to have college degrees, nor are specialists in such forensics fields as the techniques of burglary, automotive damage appraising, and fire safety and arson investigation. However, even they have competitive disadvantages when attorneys seek their services, because there are experts in their fields who have the experience and formal education credentials. The expert without formal training will more likely be challenged and impugned. Some experts, in some fields may overcome this deficiency, but only if they have compensating attributes such as great experience, personal charisma, or unique communication skills.

While the lack of formal education may be overcome by some forensics experts, the lack of experience is insurmountable. Lawyers would be highly reluctant to call upon, as an expert witness, anyone fresh out of school, no matter how prestigious the school or how high the grade point average. Those who try to become established as forensics experts before they have developed considerable experience are more likely to impede their progress toward this goal by prematurely offering opinions that may not be sound. They damage their reputations and take longer to undo the damage than if they had started later.

Those who do become experienced courtroom expert witnesses usually start as assistants or helpers of recognized experts. They assist with the investigations and give oral and written factual data and opinion to their chief, who then makes the presentation in court. Eventually this assistant provides some testimony in court as a highly specific supplement to the chief's overall presentation. Eventually the assistant testifies to a wider range of information until assuming the role of the chief expert witness. By the time this role is assumed, the witness can truthfully claim to have appeared in court as an expert witness on many previous trials.

The second step toward a forensics career is being able to present expert testimony clearly and effectively to laypersons. The ability to communicate without resorting to pedantics, jargon, or "psychobabble" is essential (Melton et al., 1997). The effective communicator can convey the desired message in a way that is understandable to juries, judges, and all other parties in the procedure. This is a talent that is mostly learned, although some people seem to find this learning process much easier than others.

It takes practice for anyone to become an effective communicator in presenting expert testimony. Frequent public speaking and, especially, public debate are good ways to acquire this practice. It is also helpful to speak to lay groups and students about the complex subjects of one's expertise to help develop the needed skills.

The third step—to get hired—is often the most difficult for academically oriented people. It is difficult because it takes an unfamiliar kind of skill and personality for academics—salesmanship and self-promotion. Being invited to testify in court does not just happen to people who are highly knowledgeable and excellent communicators. It only happens when those who do the hiring—lawyers, law officials, and lawmakers—know that the expert is available and willing. The witness has to become known.

HOW EXPERT WITNESSES BECOME ESTABLISHED

Ultimately, the most effective way experts are called upon to assist in presenting legal cases is through word-of-mouth. Lawyers who have been happy with the work of their experts will call them again when the need arises. They will also inform their colleagues. When lawyers seek presenters of expert testimony their first and most reliable recourse is to talk with other lawyers who have successfully presented cases with similar issues. The experts who are most in demand no longer need to market themselves because they have become well known in the network of lawyers who hire them. But they were not always well known. The obvious next question is, "How did they become known originally?"

No forensics specialists are an "overnight discovery." They gradually evolved into it, usually in the course of their regular jobs. Some forensics specialists began by supervising novices in their field, consulting with colleagues, and teaching courses in local universities. Some became known in their fields after giving talks about their work to local civic groups. Giving presentations at professional conferences and writing papers and books in the field also helped solidify the recognition for expertise. Typically, the knowledge and communication skills of some experts became recognized through the presentation of professional speeches or the publication of books and articles in professional journals.

Frequently, forensic experts first started to be recognized by lawyers by appearing in court as fact witnesses, usually for cases involving their own clients. For example, a social worker would testify on behalf of a client to show that the client has made efforts and progress toward improvement, with the hope of a more favorable courtroom judgment. Recognition as a possible expert witness also occurs through testifying to lawmakers on social problems or the need for new laws. When the expert becomes so well known in the community for knowledge about a certain issue that he or she is asked to testify before lawmakers, testifying in courts is more likely to follow.

Using the media is another way some experts became known to lawyers. Some started by writing popular articles for their local magazines and newspapers, describing some of the issues and problems of public concern that are dealt with in their jobs. Some specialists came to the attention of lawyers after being interviewed for news reports; some wrote letters to editors correcting errors or elaborating on issues within their realms of expertise.

A prominent but highly questionable method of getting media attention as one who purports to some expertise is by discussing the psyches of celebrities (Grinfeld, 1999). In the tabloid papers and television shows, social workers and other mental health specialists have been willing to describe the apparent personality defects of political leaders, sports celebrities, and movie stars based not on personal interviews but on what they read in other tabloids. Even if their sources of information were reliable, to disclose personal information to the public is highly unethical.

REFERRAL-BUILDING ACTIVITIES

Some forensics experts take even more direct and assertive approaches to getting the lawyer's attention (Feder, 1993). Self-marketing is appropriate and, if done tastefully, is expected. Those who don't promote themselves are either so well established that it is unnecessary, or they remain underemployed. Making the law community aware of one's willingness and abilities is an important part of the work of most forensics specialists, no matter how experienced and successful they have been. An apparent reticence to show that one is motivated for such activities usually implies passivity and indifference, characteristics that are not highly prized in expert witnesses.

One referral-building activity is advertising. This may be done by distributing pamphlets to the specific law community specifying the type of service one has to offer, and the qualifications, credentials, and experience for doing so. Forensics specialists also run similar ads in legal journals and newsletters. Since the target group is relatively small, the costs are not prohibitive; however, many specialists find that because there are so many competitors who are also seeking the lawyer's attention, they have to use numerous follow-up materials.

Another referral-building method is to cultivate professional relationships with lawyers who have litigated cases within the areas of one's expertise. Most lawyers, themselves, become specialists in one or another kind of practice, e.g., family practice, divorce, adoptions, malpractice, consumer liability, personal injury, and so forth. It is fairly simple and often appreciated to mail the attorney published information that could be used in understanding or presenting aspects of his or her typical kinds of cases.

A reprinted article or published clipping, especially one that the forensic expert has written, may be presented. It could be attached to a card or pamphlet, indicating the type of service one has to offer, and the qualifications, credentials, and experience for doing so. The expert's pamphlet may appear more tasteful, credible, and effective if it indicates the individual is part of a firm or organization that provides expert testimony.

Some forensics experts initiate direct, personal contact with lawyers who may be involved in cases that require the expertise that they provide. Some of these people write or call with specific suggestions on what the lawyer needs to do to effectively present the case. They might list some relevant expert textbooks or articles, or even give such publications to the lawyer. If they cannot connect with the lawyer directly, they seek out the people who do see the lawyer, such as secretaries, other lawyers, private investigators in the area, and clients.

Professionals who are forensics experts and also psychotherapists sometimes have the opportunity to establish and cultivate relationships with lawyers when they refer clients for needed legal services and then maintain communication about the progression of the case. This is not to imply that the therapist would make the referral primarily to establish such a relationship; if that were the intent, making such a referral would probably be for one's own self-interest rather than for the best interest of the client. Instead, the referral activity would be done only when the client is in actual need of the lawyer's services and explicitly requests referral information from the worker.

Of course, the therapist would not then serve in the role of expert witness in the case. But in subsequent communications these therapists might have the opportunity to reveal to the lawyers what their forensics interests and abilities are, for future reference. Most forensics experts, however, find these approaches somewhat distasteful and akin to "ambulance chasing." They prefer to affiliate themselves with groups and organizations who act, essentially, as agents for their services, and let these organizations do the marketing.

FORENSIC MARKETING ORGANIZATIONS

Most forensic experts are affiliated with, and listed by, organizations whose purpose is to provide expert resources. These organizations maintain data banks of experts and provide the relevant information to lawyers, insurance companies, government agencies, and businesses. Hundreds of these organizations are found throughout the nation in every major city; some provide services to lawyers within a single metropolitan area, while other organizations have a national and international reach.

The larger of these organizations maintain files on thousands of experts representing every issue where legal actions might be involved. For example, the organization that publishes the *National Directory of Expert Witnesses* has a subject index listing nearly

4,500 entries; each entry is followed by dozens of narrow specialties of expertise.

A few of the subjects include engineering, real estate, accident reconstruction, safety and disasters, accounting, finance, appraisal and valuation, environmental, construction, hazardous materials, photography, agriculture, animals, identification, chemistry, juror profiling, and of course health care, including psychiatry, psychology, nursing, physical therapy, dentistry, and social work.

Within each of these subject areas the specific types of issues are covered. For example, under the subject of engineers are over ninety specialties of expertise, including automobile safety design, industrial air quality, earthquake preventative measures, acoustical design, hazardous waste, and structural defects. To find the most suitable experts in the desired location, the lawyer would merely search the data bank, locate the names of the experts within the needed specialty, and call the expert directly.

The organizations receive their compensation primarily from the experts whose name and credentials are listed in their data banks. The expert pays an annual fee (often in the $200 to $500 range) and is usually listed under one or more entries. Most experts have skills that fit more than one of the subject areas so they can be listed in all the categories where it is appropriate. If they offer their services in more than one geographic region they can also be listed wherever they are willing to go to provide their services. Their fees go up, of course, for each listing they require.

Lawyers and others who seek the experts' services usually do not pay the organizations, except when they purchase a published book listing the names and credentials of the experts. Many companies even provide these books to lawyers without charge, as an advertising strategy.

Hard copy publication of these materials is rapidly giving way to the use of the Internet. The Internet makes it possible for the organization to keep the information up-to-date and for the customer to use cross-referencing tools to locate a small pool of the experts who fit most of the criteria sought. Most of the organizations make their listings available to lawyers or nearly anyone else who has reason to access it.

Once the expert is contacted by the lawyer, the listing organization is usually no longer involved. Any negotiations about fees, payment, or time considerations is made entirely by the forensic expert and the lawyer. Organizations that seek a percentage of the money negotiated for the services rendered are considered the least desirable element in this field. Reputable companies are well compensated for their work already through fees for listing paid by the experts.

It should also be noted that these companies do not generally assume responsibility for the veracity of the experts they list. They stress that this is the responsibility of the person hiring their expert; however, they are certain to drop anyone who is determined by a lawyer or anyone else to be misrepresenting himself or herself. Another kind of organization, the professional alliances of forensics specialists, are more careful that their members meet specified standards.

FORENSIC PROFESSIONAL GROUPS

Expert witness professional associations have the same goals as other professional associations: primarily to develop and maintain high standards among their members and to provide opportunities for the members to exchange and share knowledge. They sponsor conferences, publish newsletters and journals, and maintain codes of ethics to which their members are bound. They represent virtually every human endeavor that could be found in a courtroom dispute. Some of the larger associations of this type include the National Association of Real Estate Appraisers, the Association of Construction Inspectors, the Environmental Assessment Association, the National Association of Document Examiners, and the National Association of Medical Examiners.

One of the most well-established and well-respected organizations of this type is the American College of Forensic Examiners and its constituent specialty board groups. These include the American Board of Forensic Accounting, and American Boards of Forensic Dentistry, Engineering and Technology, Medicine, Nursing, Law Enforcement Experts, Psychological Specialties, and the American Board of Recorded Evidence. A social work group is in its formative stages. ACFE was founded in 1992 when several of its specialty groups combined; it is based in Milwaukee, Wisconsin, though many of its specialty board groups are headquartered in other cities.

The American College of Forensic Examiners stresses that its members endorse the "objective science model of forensic examination" (ACFE, 1999, p. 1). That is, the examiners should conduct their examinations and consultations and render objective opinions regardless of who is paying their fee. ACFE's professionals should only be concerned with establishing the truth and are not advocates. They are obliged to not intentionally withhold or omit any findings during a forensic examination that would cause the facts of a case to be misinterpreted or distorted.

Each specialty board within the ACFE has its own criteria for membership and for becoming Board Certified "Diplomates," "Fellows," or "Life Fellows." Members qualify by application, graduation from accredited schools, having at least three years experience in their fields, and having completed certain courses including those in ethics, law, forensics, evidence, judicial procedures, and a moot court course. These are offered under the sponsorship of ACFE or other approved associations. Most of the boards will eventually require passing specialty examinations as well.

There are, of course, many other professional associations of experts, each of which has their own high standards, qualifications for admission, and benefits, especially in reaching out to lawyers who might want to employ them.

Most of the reputable professional organizations sponsor annual or quarterly meetings throughout the nation to help inform members and maintain the group's high standards. One of the largest and most well-established of these annual meetings occurs under the sponsorship of the *Expert Witness Journal*. This seminar draws expert witnesses from all fields, as well as the trial attorneys who employ them, to discuss aspects of expert witness testimony and trial techniques.

Participants receive theoretical and practical information for succeeding as expert witnesses and litigators; the program usually includes lectures, mock trials, and discussion groups. Presentations often include topics such as the following, from the 1998 seminar: "What the Expert Witness Can Do to Protect Against Being Impeached," "Presenting Persuasive Courtroom Graphics," "Expert Witness Bloopers," "Trick Questions and Trial Tactics."

FORENSIC EXPERTS IN RELATED FIELDS

Many of the fields closest to social work seem to be in greater demand as expert witnesses. This is evident by the fact that all these fields, including medicine, psychiatry, psychology, nursing, sociology, and anthropology, have had established organizations to promote themselves in the forensics field longer than social work. Moreover, their members are represented in much greater numbers in the lists of expert witnesses that are offered by the organizations described above. The professional journals of these groups seem to have many more articles about the experience of testifying as experts than is found in the social work literature; nearly all of these fields have at least several more textbooks on the subject than social work.

Psychiatry and other medical specialties have been especially active in this work. It is tempting for every defense attorney to justify a guilty client's criminal conduct by indicating that some mental dysfunction is the actual culprit. Psychologists too have been used extensively by defense attorneys to help in making such pleas. Social workers have been prominent in some cases involving alleged mental impairment, but they have been called upon more as fact witnesses than as professionals whose opinion was considered in establishing whether the client is mentally ill or not.

Of the hundreds of specialty areas that require experts in courts listed by expert witness organizations, dozens are in areas that could well be served by social workers. Some of these specialty areas include child and elder abuse, alcohol and drug testing and treatment, life care/elder care, discrimination, juvenile violence, pension benefits, child custody evaluations, and divorce mediation. Medical doctors, especially psychiatrists, are listed by the forensic marketing associations as providing expertise in every one of these fields. Psychologists are almost as frequently listed. Other disciplines, including nursing, economists, and anthropologists, all have greater representation than social work.

This underrepresentation should be viewed not as a tragedy, but as an opportunity. Forensic social workers have great opportunities to become known in these fields and will not have much competition from their own colleagues, for awhile.

What does it take to get more social workers into this field? They need more role models, more organization, more instruction in the possibilities and how to do it.

NATIONAL ORGANIZATION OF FORENSIC SOCIAL WORKERS

The social work organization most closely identified with this field is the National Organization of Forensic Social Workers. NOFSW was created to foster the development of this specialty and provide a vehicle through which practitioners can share ideas and experiences. The organization sponsors an annual meeting featuring presentations and workshops of interest to social workers interested in and engaged in legal issues; they also issue a regular newsletter and other publications and facilitate opportunities for specialized training.

Among other objectives of NOFSW are to help establish standards of practice where social workers are involved with the law, to develop training programs, encourage research, and provide information to the public about the interface between social work and the law. They also examine and certify practitioners of forensic social work for their competency in the field.

In 1985 NOFSW established its professional certification program, known as the Diplomate in Forensic Social Work. A certified diplomate is one who is a member of NOFSW, who meets all its standards, and passes competency criteria.

Thus far there is little evidence that NOFSW has had a great impact among social workers or among the consumers of forensic social work services. No doubt as the work of the NOFSW becomes more widely known in the field, its ideals and programs will be revealed as immensely useful in the profession.

CONCLUSION

Getting hired and connected as a forensic social worker is crucial, but even more important is knowing how to provide the services that the legal system desires. Testifying in courts of law, as an expert witness or even as a fact witness, are the essential activities of the specialty. These are the subjects of the next two chapters.

Chapter 3

Testifying in Courtrooms

Providing useful and relevant information to judges, juries, and other legal officers is an important role, not only for forensics specialists, but for all social workers. Workers are trained to possess and acquire information that judges, juries, and lawmakers can use to make fair decisions and good laws. The information is presented in courts of law when a social worker testifies in the witness box. After being sworn to provide all the relevant information, the witness makes the presentation through an oral question-and-answer format, dealing with the questions asked by the opposing attorneys in the case.

There are several kinds of witnesses in courts of law, depending upon the type of information to be presented. When social workers are called to testify they may come as "fact (or lay) witnesses," "material witnesses," "character witnesses," or as "expert witnesses."

TYPES OF COURTROOM WITNESSES

A fact witness is one who has been a direct observer of aspects of the events being presented in the case. For example, a Child Protective Service social worker who investigated a home where an occurrence of child abuse was alleged, reveals to the court what actually was seen in the child's home and what facts were learned from interviews there with the child's family. In this case the worker could have been called by the prosecutor of the case, or by the attorney for the defendant who was accused of committing the abuse, depending on which side believes the worker's testimony is most favorable.

One type of fact witness is the "material witness," who possesses information that is so essential to the case that it cannot be concluded without it. If the CPS social worker actually saw the child being severely beaten and was the only person to have seen it, the worker would be a material witness in the case. Social workers testify much less frequently as material witnesses, because their observations are more commonly circumstantial. An abuser is unlikely to beat a child in the worker's presence, but might well leave indications of abuse that the worker in a home visit could describe to the jury.

"Character witnesses" are usually more peripheral in the trial. They tend to offer information about the general personality and accomplishments of someone involved in the case, usually the defendant. For example, a social worker who administers an alcohol treatment program might testify that a client seems highly motivated to continue working in the program and has shown a high degree of determination to correct behaviors that originated in the trial. In this case the worker is not presenting direct evidence about the alleged wrongdoing or about the defendant's actions in that act. Social workers have tended to be called as character witnesses as much or more than any other courtroom role.

The expert witness is an individual who has no direct knowledge of the specifics of the case being tried, but does have specialized information that provides context in which to better understand the case (Anderson and Winfree, 1987). Experts work for the attorney who calls them. After the court establishes that they indeed possess this specialized but general knowledge, they describe how things should be, and what are deviations from this standard. They are allowed to offer opinions within the range of their expertise. Experts are often asked to evaluate evidence or interview participants in the trial to assist in uncovering additional evidence.

There may be overlapping roles between these different kinds of witnesses, although the court generally tries to preserve the distinctions. It is, however, the attorney's job, and that of the judge, to maintain these distinctions, and not the witness. In the case of all four witness roles, the witness's sole concern is to tell the truth.

ROLES OF THE SOCIAL WORK FACT WITNESS

In the normal conduct of their jobs, social workers are called to court to describe their direct observations and personal encounters with the people and problems at issue. The cases that most often require their presence in courts include alleged child neglect, child abuse, child custody disputes, juvenile justice issues, involuntary placements, and disputes over entitlement payments. They also facilitate decisions about adoptions, foster placement, elder care, divorce settlements, and probation/parole. On some occasions social workers testify about their colleagues and other professionals.

Social workers sometimes testify about their investigations about housing deficiencies, welfare problems, health care issues, and workplace problems, especially sexual harassment, discrimination, and employee impairment. They may conduct and report on their pretrial investigations in such cases as substance abuse problems, and on alternatives to incarceration that might be helpful to the client (Jenkins, 1995). They prepare comprehensive social histories on defendants which may show mitigating circumstances that can influence sentencing decisions (Andrews, 1991).

Fact witnesses testify on behalf of the prosecution or the defense (Brieland and Lemmon, 1985). When appearing for the prosecution, often in the role of petitioner, the social worker helps show that allegations against the defendant are valid. For example, a social worker employed by the Department of Child Protective Services investigates a home where child neglect has been reported; in court the worker reports observing a very unkempt home and hearing admissions from parents that they are absent much of the time. The worker does not tell the court that the children were obviously being neglected, but lets the facts speak for themselves.

Workers also appear for the defense when their information favors that side. For example, a worker operates a treatment facility for people convicted of DUI ("driving while under the influence of substances that impair") and reports to the court that the defendant attended all sessions and has not been in recent trouble. The worker does not tell the court the defendant is no longer a driving risk, but merely what has happened since the last courtroom appearance.

As fact witnesses, social workers also appear in courts in ancillary roles. They provide details for one side or the other that help allow the case to be made, but which are not conclusive by themselves. For example, a worker testifies about the general character of the defendant and the motivations the defendant has recently shown to overcome problems relevant to the case. They frequently serve as "character witnesses" for clients, colleagues, agencies, or causes they support.

When social workers are on the stand as fact or lay witnesses they do not render opinions; but when they are called on as experts, opinions are expected from them. Any worker who is called to testify must know the differences between the fact and expert witness roles if they want to be effective in either. The two witness roles have different goals, methods of presentation, and rules of presenting testimony.

DISTINGUISHING FACT AND EXPERT WITNESSES

When social workers are asked to testify, it is sometimes unclear whether they are to be fact witnesses or experts. The expert witness is supposed to answer hypothetical questions that are closely based on the case's actual facts and which the expert will have carefully examined. The fact witness is supposed to answer questions about what was actually seen or experienced. In court a professional cannot be both in a given case; however, some professionals try to do both jobs before the trials begin.

Those who have tried to be both therapist for a client and an expert witness in that client's case may encounter difficulties for themselves, for the clients, and for the legal system. Even so, some writers describe how they have succeeded in providing both services for clients (Linhorst and Turner, 1999). Other researchers, however, indicate that the roles of the therapist and expert witness are incompatible (Strasburger, Gutheil, and Brodsky, 1997) or that combining the roles is unethical (Appelbaum, 1997). The most cautious position is for the social worker to decline an invitation to serve as an expert witness if the worker has had anything to do with the client in any other capacity.

This position may not be as convenient for social workers to follow as for members of other professions. Social workers may be more vulnerable to the blurring of these roles than many other professionals who are asked to testify. Most forensics experts are able to examine evidence that is removed from the place it was gathered and see it in relatively pristine environments. Medical examiners look at specimens in labs; forensic accountants review a company's financial records outside the company's offices; forensic engineers examine blueprints. Even experts who are psychiatrists and psychologists are more frequently asked to review the notes or reports of others in assessing clients.

Social workers, however, in the very nature of their work perform their jobs in a social systems context. They usually go to the site of the issue being litigated and conduct interviews with participants of the case. They observe ongoing relationships and the environments where these relationships occur. Their findings, if taken in a clinical vacuum out of social context, would be inadequate and not representative.

But when they go to the home of the defendant, for example, and interview residents, they come close to being a participant in the case—a fact witness rather than an expert witness. In court, the worker could then be asked about what the subject said or did during this examination rather than being asked for a general opinion about the subject.

Social workers have not always been successful in keeping these two roles apart. In fact, researchers have reported that cases have been thrown out of court because it was not clear whether the social workers were acting as expert or as fact witnesses (Mason, 1992). For example, a social worker was asked to interview a child who was said to have been sexually abused, and the worker testified as to the child's veracity. Later, the ruling in the case was overturned on appeal because the worker had not been qualified as an expert witness as to the credibility of sexually abused children, and should have been treated exclusively as a fact or lay witness.

Courts have generally accepted social workers as expert witnesses in child sexual abuse cases but it is clear that they, like all other professionals, have to go through the court process of being qualified as an expert before testifying.

This is not as easy as it appears in the abstract. Consider these examples: In a child custody case a social worker who has treated the family is called to testify on behalf of the mother. The mother claims she is the one who could provide the best home for the child and best meet the child's needs. As a fact witness, the worker would only describe the mother's characteristics and motivations that were observed in the treatment sessions. If the worker had been qualified as an expert witness the worker might be able to offer opinions as to what children need, and what characteristics a mother might have that could meet those needs. However, having treated this family, the worker would be crossing an important boundary by assuming a role as an expert. The worker could not effectively testify as an expert in this case.

For another example, a social worker is asked to testify in a civil action in which a colleague is being sued by a former client. The client alleged sexual exploitation and other forms of professional misconduct. The worker had served on a professional review board that had expelled the colleague for sexual misconduct with the same client. On the stand the worker is qualified as an expert because of the need to understand what the profession's practice standards and ethics are. The court finds that the worker is an expert on these matters and is thus allowed to offer general opinions. The worker is asked about these professional standards, how long they have been in force, and what the profession does about those who do not live up to them. Finally, the worker is asked if certain hypothetical behaviors could be said to conform to the standards. Thus far, the worker is clearly within the boundaries of an expert witness.

However, the attorney begins asking questions about the review board, and the reasons for its decision regarding the defendant. If the answers are allowed, the boundary between expert and fact witness is breached. The judge would probably have to throw out either the worker's facts or opinions, if not the entire case.

THE SUBPOENA

One sure way workers can know what their role is to be, is to receive a subpoena. A subpoena, of course, is the legal document informing the individual of an obligation to appear in court at the specified time. They are for fact witnesses only. Experts appear at court hearings of their own volition, while other witnesses are compelled by law to appear. When the subpoena is formally presented the witness absolutely must be present at the courtroom at the time indicated. Failure to appear is a serious crime. The judge presiding over the case has the right to declare the absent witness in contempt of court, and can impose a fine or jail sentence.

Frequently social workers, and other officials such as police officers and government workers, receive less formal verbal requests to appear as fact witnesses at trial. When prosecuting attorneys or defense attorneys are sure that the witness will appear at the scheduled time, they may forgo the trouble and formality of obtaining the subpoena and having it delivered. In such cases, however, the witness should recognize that this is merely a professional courtesy and that the obligation to appear still exists. When witnesses fail to appear after these verbal understandings were made, they may not be held in contempt of court immediately. However, they are more likely to be issued formal subpoenas thereafter, and probably won't be granted the extra courtesies normally given to cooperative witnesses.

When a subpoena is issued to a social worker it is commonly initiated in the prosecuting attorney's office. The defense attorney may also arrange to subpoena the worker, if it is believed that the worker's information will be more beneficial to the defendant. The obligation to appear is just as strong if it comes from one or the other.

Rarely does a subpoena come as a surprise if it is issued in the worker's professional capacity. The attorney would want to know well in advance if the worker has information that would be useful for one side or the other. Frequently it comes after the worker is deposed through an interview in the attorney's offices and has disclosed most of the information that is to be presented on the witness stand.

The worker who is required in court by subpoena is not there to provide expert opinion; in fact, the opposing attorney may object if the worker is asked to offer any professional opinions, especially those that are unfavorable.

Social workers who are required to testify as fact witnesses cannot, of course, charge a fee or expect to be paid for their appearances. It is considered their professional duty or their obligation as citizens. A few lawyers of dubious ethics may seek the professional expert witness services of a social worker without paying for it, by attempting to blur the roles of the two types of witnesses. They may imply to the worker that they need information about the worker's direct observations. They ask if it is necessary to go through the formality of a subpoena. The worker promises to appear without the subpoena. However, once the worker is on the witness stand the lawyer begins the process of qualifying the worker as an expert.

Only the most foolhardy or ill-informed lawyers would do this, if for no other reason than that they cannot be sure of what the reaction of the witness will be or what information will be given. They run the risk of learning about unfavorable information during the trial. Social workers can minimize this possibility by taking several precautions. They should not commit to anything until it has been made clear what the purpose of the testimony is and what the role of the worker is. The lawyer should be asked specifically if the role is as an expert or a fact witness. To be sure that the roles are not blurred, the worker can begin negotiating about fees, or requiring a subpoena. Even if an expert has personal knowledge of a case and is subpoenaed, if in court the lawyer qualifies him or her as an expert, the witness is entitled to a fee. It is, however, difficult to collect under those circumstances.

PRESENTING TESTIMONY EFFECTIVELY

Not all social workers, of course, are equally effective in their presentation of testimony. Those who are most effective have thoroughly prepared themselves in advance and have given considerable thought and care to the way they want to make their presentations. While they cannot know specifically what questions the lawyers will ask, or manner of the questioning, they can be fairly certain about what general information is sought and the way that information will fit in with the rest of the case. Therefore, it is important to have a thorough knowledge and solid memory of these facts.

Most workers who testify effectively go over their case records carefully prior to the court day. They review relevant dates, diagnoses, and all the facts that justify the diagnoses. If the records have any inconsistencies or subsequent revisions, the worker should clarify any discrepancies in his or her mind. An additional page of notes that addresses and clarifies these discrepancies can be added at the end of the case file if it is clearly noted when and why these additions were included. It is inappropriate and dangerous to alter the case records once the notice to appear in court arrives. This could be seen as tampering with evidence, and at best can only weaken the points the witness is espousing (Anderson, 1996).

After reviewing the records and rethinking the course of treatment with the clients involved in the case, the worker might find it helpful to write down all the questions that could be asked in court. Then the answers can be thought through and rehearsed aloud. Rehearsals can be made more effective in role plays if colleagues or family members can be enlisted to pose the questions and try to intimidate or confuse the witness. This process is not likely to get at all the questions and answers that will appear in the court, but it should help the worker become more comfortable, confident, and accurate than would otherwise be the case.

When social workers present effective fact witness testimony, they are aware that more than their words are being evaluated. Their nonverbal behaviors are also considered, including style of dress, posture, tone of voice, level of confidence and comfort, and their ease at retrieving the right facts from their minds or their case records. For most purposes, social workers should appear in court in conservative business attire, with a respectful manner, and a tone that suggests cooperation and willing participation.

They are familiar enough with courtroom protocol that they need not be directed in everything they do. They know where to go when called to the stand, and where the judge and jurors are located, and where to go when dismissed. Social workers who have not yet become familiar with this protocol would do well to attend several court hearings in person.

When asked a question, the worker thinks through the answer and responds in a clear, well-modulated tone. The answers are presented to the judge and jury, rather than to the attorney who is asking the question. Good eye contact with jurors, and an amiable manner will enhance the level of communication. A short pause after each question is usually helpful in keeping out any slips or undesired information. Responses should be strictly confined to the questions asked; no other information should be volunteered. If an attorney objects to a question, the pause precludes any hasty answers that may not be allowed. If the objection has been made, the worker should not attempt to answer the question until the judge has ruled on its admissibility. The answers should be given in words that are easily understandable, no matter how tempted the worker is to use clinical jargon or display an excess of sophisticated knowledge.

The social worker may bring the case record to court and keep it while in the witness box; however, opening it and looking around for relevant information in answer to questions is distracting and ineffective. If the worker had prepared carefully, it would not normally be necessary to refer to the record. For the most part, when it is opened, it should be to locate specific dates or times of events, or other minute data. Unless the subpoena has explicitly required that the record be brought, the worker may choose to leave it in the office. If it is not referred to in court, it is less likely that it will have to be publicly scrutinized by the lawyers.

RESPONDING TO DIRECT EXAMINATION

When answering questions as a fact witness the social worker is not necessarily expected to be as detached, objective, or knowledgeable as an expert witness. (In fact, the worker may be even more knowledgeable than an expert witness, but that is not the appropriate role in this context.) Instead, it is rather expected that the worker is appearing on behalf of one side or the other. The goal of telling the truth remains the same, but what is really wanted is that aspect of the truth which favors the side who called for the witness.

In that context, the worker can expect to be asked very different questions by each side, and in very different tones of voice. The lawyer in direct examination will ask easier questions in a more friendly and respectful manner because the worker is, hopefully, providing answers needed to make the case. They should be easier to answer because the lawyer and witness will have discussed the questions beforehand and rehearsed different ways of presenting the truthful answers. More of these questions will be open ended, permitting somewhat more latitude in responses, rather than questions to be answered in a strict yes or no format.

Lawyers, in direct examination, are not permitted to ask leading questions. Leading questions are those that suggest the answer the questioner desires, and those that elicit responses that are advantageous to the questioner. For example, this question would not be allowed: "When you entered the room, did you see the defendant hitting the child?" But this question would be permitted: "When you entered the room, what did you see?" Often the direct examiner will want to discuss answers beforehand so that the witness will know where to go with the nonleading questions. This is to avoid irrelevant answers. For example, without a prediscussion, the witness might say in answer to what was seen in the room, "Oh, I saw lots of toys and a bed and a small desk and. . . ."

RESPONDING TO CROSS-EXAMINATION

Immediately after concluding the direct examination, the witness is subject to cross-examination by the opposing lawyer. The procedures and rules of examination are almost identical in direct and cross-examinations, the major exception being about leading questions. If a direct examiner asks, "What did you think when you first saw the bruises on the child's back?" the question would probably be disallowed. If, however, the same question were asked in cross-examination, it could be permitted. This is because the goal in cross-examination is not to reveal what the witness knows, but to test the accuracy with which it has been described. To do this, the lawyer will probably ask the same question repeatedly, but in different ways. When several different answers have been given, the lawyer can point out any real or perceived discrepancies and thus discredit the entire answer (Bailey, 1994).

If an attorney objects to a question as leading, the judge will decide if it can be allowed. If not allowed the direct examiner will be required to rephrase the question or ask a new one. The witness should answer such questions only when it is required by the judge.

The lawyer in cross-examination will ask harder questions and usually in a suspicious, confrontational manner. The questions will be harder because the worker does not quite know what to expect, or what the underlying purpose is for the question. One is always wary of some trap that intends to expose falsehoods or incorrect interpretations. Usually the cross-examiner will purposely look skeptical and repeat answers in a disbelieving, sarcastic tone. The purpose is to confuse the witness and possibly uncover discrepancies; the behavior also attempts to convince the jury that the answers are not credible and the information presented is worthless and should be disregarded.

Lawyers, especially in cross-examination, can sometimes cause difficulties for social workers when they ask long, rambling questions. If the witness responds in a manner that appears confused or uncertain the lawyer has succeeded. Witnesses can counter this tactic. They can calmly wait for the opposing attorney's objection. If no objection is made, the witness can ask for the question to be clarified before attempting any answer. Often these long questions are "mini-speeches" disguised as questions, and may be disallowed if they are recognized as such by the judge. Sometimes the attorney follows the long statement with a short question that must be answered with a yes or no. The answer then implies that it applies to the sense of the whole speech rather than to the last question. The witness can respond either by asking the lawyer to repeat the question, or by answering yes or no and repeating the question, as in, "Yes, I did think it was a strange thing to do."

The cross-examination is likely to include questions the witness cannot or does not want to answer. Of course the witness cannot object; only the opposing lawyer can, and if the judge overrules the objection, the question must be answered. At this point, the effective witness will not try to evade the answer but respond truthfully and not begrudgingly. To do otherwise gives the appearance that the witness is less than candid and is more an advocate than a witness to the facts.

HAZARDS IN PRESENTING TESTIMONY

The opposing attorney can help make the witness's testimony appear weak or worthless, but sometimes workers do it without help. The seven worst traits of ineffective witnesses, which are conducted without the help of opposing attorneys are as follows: (1) the witnesses are so nervous they appear suspicious and guilty; (2) they speak so quietly or softly they cannot be heard, and when requested to speak up they sound high-pitched and unpleasant; (3) they cannot articulate facts or diagnostic data without resorting to technical jargon, and otherwise cannot explain in a comprehensible manner what information they want to impart; (4) their body language and verbalizations give an impression of uncertainty and nonconfidence, especially about the truth of their information; (5) they ramble in their answers, not staying precisely with the questions, and giving too much irrelevant information; (6) they forget important dates and other information and spend court time rummaging through files in search of it; and (7) they present their information so pedantically and colorlessly that they lose the attention of the jurors, even when the information is inherently interesting.

If these traits occur in direct examination, not much effort is needed by the opposing attorney to impeach the witness in cross-examination. If, on the other hand, the social worker gave a credible presentation on direct, the skilled cross-examining attorney has many techniques to weaken it. One approach is to cause the witness to become defensive or argumentative through questions that seem condescending and skeptical. Or the questions are parsed so finely that the only responses possible seem to contradict earlier testimony. If the worker responds as planned, by acting irritated, angry, or indignant, or by strongly insisting on a further explanation or additional details, then the lawyer can sternly demand that the witness is to be controlled. The jury sees the witness as overly sensitive and too strident to be trusted.

Social workers who are experienced in courtrooms know not to take personally the manner of the opposing attorney. It is this attorney's job to call the testimony into question, and he or she is not otherwise inclined to attack the worker's integrity.

TESTIFYING AGAINST CLIENTS

Some issues that lead social workers to court have become so controversial that every worker should think about them carefully before embarking on any professional involvement with the legal . system. One issue concerns giving testimony about children, or assisting children with their testimony in court. Another issue concerns the current controversy about client's memory, and whether those memories are "recovered" as some therapists claim, or "implanted" as some lawyers and other experts claim. Another issue concerns the dilemma of a social worker testifying against a client.

The most common way workers are compelled to testify against clients is when they see as a unit members of a family or group, and later one of the members of this group initiates a legal action against another. Social workers also testify against clients who have made threats to harm others during sessions, or who have admitted to committing serious crimes or planning such crimes.

Usually the workers do not enter this situation willingly; they are compelled to appear by subpoena and are then required to disclose what they know about, and have been told by, the client. Because social workers still hold their confidentiality principle in high regard, it is difficult for them to deal with the laws that require them to do otherwise. Nevertheless, the law has affirmed that there is no alternative; they must answer the questions about the client, truthfully and fully, and usually in the client's presence nearby in the courtroom.

The worker in this position will feel like a traitor, and will wonder about how this will affect the client's emotional well-being in the future. The worker will also be concerned about the professional consequences, if this will lead to a malpractice lawsuit or some other hostile response from the client in the future. And the worker will be concerned about the immediate problem of presenting the testimony effectively while withstanding the cross-examination that will surely attack the worker's honor and credibility.

As the direct examination begins, the worker may be tempted to "sugar-coat" the answers, in an attempt to keep his testimony from seeming so critical of the client. For example, the worker might say, "Well, yes, he did say he planned to kill his boss during the Christmas party, but it seemed like he was just kidding. He has a subtle sense of humor."

Such attempts at obfuscation are ill advised. For one thing, the judge probably would not allow such statements and would probably admonish the witness. For another, the attempt would be used against the worker by the opposing attorney. That is, if the worker says something to soften the testimony against the client, or otherwise tries to appease the client with positive remarks, the opposing lawyer, during cross-examination, would use the remarks to weaken the case that the worker is espousing.

To deal with this difficult situation, the worker acknowledges that there can be no further helping relationship with the client and that, therefore, the case should be treated as any other. The social work witness would answer all the questions dispassionately and especially with no show of regret or remorse. Although understandably the client will not like it, but any other response will ultimately have even worse consequences.

THE TESTIMONY OF CHILDREN

Social workers and members of other psychotherapeutic professions are often called upon to facilitate the testimony of children in the courtroom. Sometimes they do it by helping the officers of the court to conduct interviews with the child outside the courtroom atmosphere. Sometimes they interview the child and appear in court to describe and interpret what the child revealed. When therapists discover situations where children are being neglected, abused, or in the middle of family custody issues, they may be called to court to help present the case from the perspective of the child's interests, or to help the child do so directly. The professionals in this position must become very knowledgeable about the nature of these problems and how to present the appropriate information in law courts. Excellent recent publications that provide most of this information include Besharov (1998), Ceci and Hembrooke (1998), Sattler (1998), and Fraser (1997).

Considerable debate occurs about how to protect children from the strange and frightening experience of courtroom testimony (Karger and Stoesz, 1995). Everyone would prefer to keep children from having to describe these events, but all too often they are the only witnesses. They may even be too young to talk, and are distressed enough to want to avoid thinking about it. Many questions remain unanswered: How much credibility can be placed in the child's testimony? How much or little pressure should be put on children to compel their answers? How can the court know whether the child has been influenced in her answers by parents, social workers, or other authorities? How much stock should be put into the child's wishes about which parent to live with? Perhaps there can be no all-purpose answer to questions of this type; each child's testimony will have to be judged individually (Sagatun and Edwards, 1995).

Social workers have been involved in many high profile cases involving children who have had to testify in courts (Costin, Karger, and Stoesz, 1996). Workers have been accused of prodding children into claims of sexual abuse in child care centers and of ignoring other children who showed signs of parental neglect. Workers have taped interviews of children for pretrial hearings and have thereby been accused of improper influence over the children or of misinterpreting their disclosures. No doubt many of these criticisms are valid; no doubt many others are merely attempts to salvage the case for the accused person, and it is more effective to attack the social worker than an innocent child.

In either case, the social worker's duty is to the truth, not to advocate for the exclusive rights of one or the other party in a dispute (Fontana and Besharov, 1995). Social workers must constantly remind themselves that children can be influenced to give the answers they think the questioner wants to hear rather than the truth. Children want to please adults and might easily agree with everyone, each parent, the day care teacher, the social worker, the judge, the attorney, and the opposing attorney. On the other hand, when children are in the middle of adult disputes, their rights can easily be overlooked. The zealotry of some social workers in seeking to protecting those rights is understandable, if not legally defensible.

RECOVERED OR IMPLANTED MEMORY

Finally, another controversial issue that often involves social workers in courtrooms concerns the so-called "recovered memory syndrome" (Madden and Parody, 1997). The issue has pertained mostly to adult clinical clients with the anxiety symptoms of post-traumatic stress disorder. In this psychiatric condition, the client suffers stress, depression, phobias, and other symptoms, which seem derived from horrible events in the past. Often clients with this disorder do not remember the trauma; a treatment method for them is to bring it to conscious awareness where it can be dealt with more rationally (Hyman and Pentland, 1996).

The specific trauma that has led to the disorder for many social work clients has been childhood sexual abuse. Many of these clients were victimized while they were very young children; others were older, but so distressed by the event that all memories of it were pushed out of consciousness. In the course of therapy where child-hood experiences are described and reanalyzed, many victims came to realize what had actually happened. As adults they want to over-come their trauma and also to bring the perpetrator to justice. The event is reported to authorities, and eventually there is a trial. The client, and usually the social worker, testifies for the prosecution. The defense argument usually is that the alleged occurrence did not happen.

To make their argument stronger, the defense attacks the client's memory and suggests that it was the therapist's influence, and not an actual experience, that led to the accusation. The defense brings in witnesses to attack the client's stability and credibility; then expert witnesses testify to show that the memories of this type can be "implanted" rather than "recovered." It is difficult to win a conviction, unless the charges are corroborated independently of the client and the worker.

Social workers who have been on the losing side of such cases may be nearly as frustrated as their clients. They are sure they are right, but have no way to prove it in court. No doubt there have been many cases of childhood sexual abuse in which the person who committed the act was acquitted; it is also possible that in some cases workers did implant false memories in their clients. There is significant evidence that false memories have been created through repeated questions and discussion about the subject (Roediger, Jacoby, and McDermott, 1996). Mental health professionals recog-nize these possibilities and advise therapists and examiners of these clients to adhere to strict and high standards for evaluating alleged victims (Oberlander, 1995).

Conscientious and ethical social workers will want to exercise great caution in their treatment of clients who come to believe they were molested as children (Stocks, 1998). It is ethically indefensi-ble to accuse people of such horrendous acts based on questionable memories (Mersky, 1996). The cases are too easy to lose, and the parents accused of past sexual abuse will almost certainly fight back (Whitesell, 1996). Social workers should study more about the uncertainties of memory, especially where it concerns traumatic events. In the course of therapy with clients who eventually make these accusations, workers should discuss the treatment progress with supervisors, colleagues, or consultants to be sure they are not, in fact, unfairly encouraging the client to develop such "memories." And they should be aware of, and make their client aware of, the great difficulty in winning cases of these types. Even for "winners," the courtroom experience, the charges and counter-charges, and the public airing of the family's "dirty linen" can be almost as traumatic as the painful memory itself.

But if, despite these precautions, the client and worker are certain that the memories are valid, it may be their painful duty to proceed in the legal system. Those who molest children deserve to be judged, and society has the right to see that their actions are punished and prohibited. In this case, as in all cases where social workers are called on to testify in court, their major obligation is to bring out the truth as effectively as possible.

TEN GUIDELINES FOR THE EFFECTIVE WITNESS

In conclusion, social workers who want to present themselves as effective witnesses should adhere to the following guidelines:

1. Always answer every question truthfully, including those for which the correct answer is, "I don't know."
2. Answer the questions succinctly, clearly, and confidently.
3. Avoid emotional responses or overreactions to hostile questions.
4. Do not answer anything other than the question asked; do not volunteer additional details or irrelevant facts.
5. Do not take personally the examiners' questions, brusque manner, or hostile approaches. They are just doing their jobs.
6. Before answering any question, pause to deliberate about the answer; avoid getting caught up in the examiner's rapid-fire questioning, which can lead to confusing or inaccurate responses.
7. Do not prolong the time before answering; undue delay will seem like uncertainty or dishonesty.
8. Pause briefly after each question to permit the attorney to object without revealing information that would not be admissible.

9. Stop immediately when an objection is made; proceed there-after only when the judge rules on the objection and/or pro-vides instructions to continue.
10. Always remain calm and polite with both lawyers, judge, and all others present; never argue with anyone about their ques-tions, procedures, or rulings.

Chapter 4

Testifying As an Expert Witness

The expert witness presents to the court and to attorneys background information about the issues being debated or adjudicated. This information is not about details of the specific case but about general facts and educated opinions about hypothetical situations relevant to this type of case. For example, the social work expert may describe to the court the latest scientific findings about the effects of removing a child from a home of one divorced parent and into the home of the other (Klein, 1994). Or the expert may describe the ethical and professional standards of the profession and what treatment methodologies would be most appropriate for a given type of condition.

Court decisions or laws are rarely reached solely as a result of the expert witness's testimony. Rather, this information is used to establish the context or framework within which to view the actions of the individual(s) being tried. Most malpractice and other civil suits, and many criminal cases, utilize expert testimony this way. The expert witness's knowledge is derived from specialized, formal education, study, and experience. The role of the expert witness is to explain, to teach, and to elucidate matters beyond the ordinary layperson's ability to understand.

Increasingly, courts of law are accepting social workers who have been qualified as expert witnesses (Pollack, 1997). However, their expertise is frequently challenged by opposing attorneys. Some solace exists in the fact that the expertise of psychiatrists and psychologists is also frequently challenged (Campbell, 1994).

Lawyer-social worker Mary Ann Mason (1992, p. 31) reported that in the child sexual abuse cases she studied, "The majority of the decisions are accepting of and even enthusiastic about social workers as expert witnesses." She goes on to mention that the characteristics mentioned most frequently as qualifying the social worker are experience and education (especially the MSW degree). Characteristics that were mentioned with lesser frequency were recognition in the field, training in the relevant area, providing lectures or writings on the subject, being well read in the literature, exposure to conferences and seminars, and licensing as a clinical specialist.

Effective performance as an expert witness is challenging and complex. Doing it well requires considerable knowledge, experience, and social skills. The requisite knowledge includes courtroom procedures, admissibility of evidence, and the roles of the participants in court cases, as well as the specific information requested. Experience usually enables the worker to respond to the examiner's questions in ways that are most helpful to all concerned. Social skills are important in giving the worker the ability to clearly communicate the information without being diverted or distressed by the manner of questioning.

PRETRIAL NEGOTIATIONS

When the attorney asks the social worker to participate as an expert witness, the worker considers many issues before deciding to serve or to decline. One is to understand clearly what the lawyer actually wants from the witness. The worker needs to know if the lawyer really wants and will accept unbiased, objective expert testimony or only something that is biased in favor of the client (Hess, 1998). If biased testimony is sought, the decision to decline is easy for ethical forensics experts. Their codes of ethics explicitly state that their testimony is to be objective, truthful, and based solely on the evidence presented, regardless of which side is employing them (American College of Forensic Examiners, 1999).

Obviously, many people who are called upon as expert witnesses do not live up to this standard. Legal writers and scholars are well aware of the "hired-gun" syndrome, in which experts can be found who will say almost anything that favors the argument of the lawyer who employs them (Hanson, 1996). Experts who begin serving as "hired-guns" soon find they have chosen a difficult path in their lives. Those who engage in "character assassination" are finding they are now losing testimonial immunity and may be sued in certain situations for their remarks (McDowell, 1997). Some expert witnesses have been sued for malpractice when their courtroom conduct proves to be unethical (Richmond, 1993). Their reputations as experts become tarnished; lawyers will avoid hiring them for reputable cases; and, henceforth, if and when they are asked to provide testimony, it is generally in support of ignoble goals.

Many social workers and other experts who take this path end up being used by zealous lawyers of borderline scruples. They are most commonly called upon to help justify the misconduct of clients, usually on the basis of questionable theories. For example, many workers have perpetuated "the abuse excuse" in which the client's criminal behavior seems mitigated by having been mistreated at an earlier, more impressionable age (Dershowitz, 1994). Social work experts have been used by lawyers to document their assertions that their clients had been molested as children. Others have helped develop "novel" criminal defenses based on the "toxicity of the social environment" (Falk, 1995).

Many of these accusations are undoubtedly valid; however, many experts have presented "scientific" data of dubious worth in courtrooms and as a result have contributed to serious injustices. Oberlander's (1995) study showed that there was wide divergence among mental health experts, including social workers, in their views about how to best conduct and interpret these investigations, showing that there are serious limits to expertness. More experienced and knowledgeable experts recognize these limitations, perhaps better than do lawyers, judges, and juries. But many less experienced experts do not; they believe in the veracity of their opinions and their scientific basis, even when no such basis really exists. Because the role of expert witness is relatively new to most social workers, their challenge is to learn more about these limitations and to be cautious in how their findings are presented in courts (Schultz, 1991).

Even if the social worker is convinced that the lawyer wants only objective, truthful, unbiased testimony, there may be other reasons to decline participation. If, for example, the worker feels strongly that the ruling of the case should justifiably go against the lawyer's client, for whatever reason, the most honorable action is to decline. It might be too hard for the worker to remain objective and professionally detached. In such instances, the role of expert is replaced by the role of advocate, and the judge will not accept such testimony, or it will be strongly challenged by the opposing lawyers.

Another reason to decline occurs when the required expertise is outside the range of the worker's knowledge. Many lawyers are not familiar with what social workers know and do, and may seek their services based on misinformation (Solomon and Draine, 1995). It is important before an agreement to testify is made to establish the worker's specific range of expertise. If it is anticipated that questions will be coming from beyond this range, then declining the invitation to testify is the wisest response.

When social workers decide they can offer competent and ethical services, the next step is to make a firm agreement with the lawyer. The lawyer is hiring the worker to perform a service, so the worker needs to know the conditions of employment. The worker must know what information will be sought, how much time it will take, how long the case is expected to endure, and how the fees will be paid. Experienced forensics experts usually do not agree to serve as witnesses unless these points are established clearly and in writing.

NEGOTIATING PAYMENT

Experts are hired by the attorney and paid by the attorney. The amount to be paid is negotiated in advance of any service provided and should be in writing. Experts who are wise and experienced usually insist on payment before testimony begins unless they are on close and good terms with the lawyer.

Generally, the fees for forensic social workers' services are based on the amount of time they devote to the cases; the actual amount is the same as or close to the amount they receive for their normal working time. Thus, the initial agreement might indicate that the specialist, whose regular income is $150 per hour, is paid $200 per hour of time spent on this case. Of course this includes not only time on the witness stand, but also the time waiting to be called and the time spent in getting to the courthouse or lawyer's office. It also includes the time spent on research, interviews with those involved in the case, pretrial rehearsal time with the attorney, and testimony planning.

The written contract signed between the lawyer and the expert witness should spell this out. The contract will show agreement to pay the witness's hourly fee plus other expenses in connection with the case including costs of travel, food and hotel accommodations, and related secretarial costs. The experienced worker maintains careful expense records and diaries to document these expenditures, both for the employer-lawyer and for the tax accountants.

It is not unheard of that forensics specialists have had difficulty collecting the amount they were promised by the attorney who called them (Minan and Lawrence, 1997). Sometimes these attorneys want the expert witness to wait until their law firm is paid. If the case is a contingency case, as it usually is in civil litigation, such payments may not come for years in victorious outcomes, and never when the case is lost. Experts who are wise and experienced usually insist on payment before testimony begins. The payment should be made by the attorney and not the client, since it is the attorney who is the employer.

Some attorneys have tried to circumvent this payment procedure with promises to increase the fees if the witness can wait until the lawyer is recompensed. Of course it is unwise for the expert to make such an agreement; it is also professionally unethical, risky, and distorts the nature of the purpose for providing the testimony. Some lawyers may attempt to delay payments by appealing to the witness's sense of justice or sympathy for the lawyer's or client's plight. However, the lawyers themselves usually require advance payment from these same clients in criminal or divorce proceedings. In contingency civil litigation they justify receiving one-third to one-half the receipts when they win by subsidizing the costs of the case and waiting for a long time to collect, if they ever do. The expert witness, properly, is not part of the potential for large paybacks, so he or she should also not be expected to be part of the subsidization, the risk, or the long wait.

Some unscrupulous lawyers try to avoid paying expert witness fees by suggesting that a subpoena will have to be issued if the expert does not come voluntarily. A naive social worker might agree to testify in order to avoid the subpoena, forgetting that experts cannot be compelled to come to court. Subpoenas will not be issued for them because expert witnesses have no special knowledge about the facts of this particular case.

A few lawyers have tried to avoid paying the witness because of dissatisfaction with the outcome of the case. They say to the expert witness, "We didn't win, so we have no money to pay you." "We settled out of court so you didn't testify and thus you shouldn't be paid for something you didn't do." "Because your credibility was challenged and the judge refused to hear your testimony, you didn't deserve payment."

To avoid such problems the experienced forensics specialist never agrees to payment contingent on the outcome of the case. Not only would this be an unwise and unnecessary economic risk but it would destroy the witness's appearance of, and claim to, professional objectivity should the opposing attorney bring that fact out in cross-examination or deposition.

Instead, the contract or letter of agreement should indicate that fees will be paid on an ongoing basis within thirty days after the bill is submitted to the attorney. Some experts require payment of a retainer or engagement fee in advance. Periodically, specified amounts are deducted from the retainer for the amount of time spent on the case. Some experts specify in their contracts that they are entitled to keep all or a portion of the retainer if the case is settled quickly, before the witness testimony would have been needed.

If the expert's services are no longer needed at any point during the case, often because of settlements, the fees incurred up to that time are to be paid immediately. Even without actually making a court appearance, the expert's presence is often influential toward getting the opposition to agree to a settlement. In any event, the worker should seek all payments due prior to sharing the findings and certainly before entering the witness box.

PREPARATION AS AN EXPERT WITNESS

It is the competent lawyer's job to make sure the expert witness is well prepared for the job of presenting expert testimony (ABA Journal, 1999). Part of this preparation includes going over the relevant part of the case that the expert will discuss on the witness stand. The attorney and the expert usually confer about the facts of the case, the kind of information sought in the expert testimony, the procedures and personalities of those involved in the case, and any other pertinent information. The lawyer usually also helps the expert obtain access to whatever evidence is to be examined. Throughout the examination the lawyer may discuss the findings and their possible interpretations with the expert in order to know in advance how best to present this part of the case (Berger, 1997).

The expert prepares by learning as much as possible about the specific case. The worker may investigate the case thoroughly by reviewing all relevant documents, previous decisions, and relevant legal actions. If the worker is being asked to interview a subject of the trial, professional ethics apply to the interview procedure just as much as to any other professional work with a client. Whenever possible these interviews should be videotaped, beginning with the initial contact. This is to show the court, when necessary, that the information gleaned from the subject was not due to the interviewer's influence.

It can be useful for the worker to prepare notes about the case and include therein such factual data as relevant dates and places, names of the important people involved, and information about any diagnoses, symptoms, and historical data. This material usually will be brought to the trial and referred to if the worker has any difficulty remembering it. This is in contrast with the case records of the social worker who is a fact witness; while the expert will always bring the records, the fact witness may choose not to, in order to keep irrelevant confidential information out of the public domain.

Experienced expert witnesses do not rely only on the lawyer-employers to become prepared. They also prepare themselves mentally for the challenge of the experience in the witness box, and also for the inevitable, mundane aspects of the trial.

One of the most unpleasant aspects of the expert witness role, according to many who have performed it, is the long waiting, often in relative isolation (Chesler, 1998). Much more of the expert's time will probably be spent waiting to testify than actually doing so. Expert witnesses are frequently sequestered from other witnesses or participants in the trial in order to ensure that their testimony is not influenced by others. Witnesses must be available to go on the stand at any moment, but no one can predict when that moment will come. The witness cannot watch the trial so it is usually necessary to wait in hallways or witness rooms.

Most cases are settled out of court, often just before the trial begins, so much of this waiting appears to serve no purpose. The social work expert will probably need to set aside a considerable amount of time away from the regular job to accomplish no other function than being immediately available for the actual court appearance. Most experienced witnesses take books or some work so that the wait can be somewhat more productive.

The other form of self-preparation is for the social worker to become as familiar as possible with general courtroom procedures and especially with the law of evidence. Knowing what type of evidence can and cannot be admitted is helpful. Even though the opposing attorney and judge will prevent the witness from presenting inadmissible evidence, it is easier and more comfortable to avoid such disclosures in the first place than to have to be frequently interrupted and corrected. This knowledge helps one know how to frame answers during examinations by counsel. This knowledge is acquired in advance of work on a specific case by reading and reviewing testimony given by other experts, attending trials and legislative committees, and talking with experienced attorneys.

REHEARSING EXPERT TESTIMONY

Many expert witnesses help prepare themselves by rehearsing what they will say in the trial, often with the lawyer-employer's assistance and prompting. After reviewing the case and discussing with the attorney the questions they will be asked, they write out all possible questions and answers. Then they try delivering these answers orally, duplicating as much as possible what and how they intend to present themselves in court.

Often the lawyer or a colleague in the law firm will play the role of opposing counsel and attempt to rattle the witness or to show where the information is incorrect. The purpose is to locate flaws in the argument so that it can be presented better, or avoided. Or it is to help the witness become more resistant to attacks or ridicule by opposing counsel.

Going through this experience a few times can be very helpful if it results in gaining confidence for dealing with the real opposing attorney in the trial. However, for others rehearsal can be contraindicated, especially if it causes so much anxiety that the witness is uncomfortable long before entering the courtroom.

In most cases which are not high stakes, many lawyers do not rehearse so carefully with expert witnesses (Schlichtmann, 1998). Either they don't believe it is an efficient use of their time, or they think that much rehearsal would result in weaker testimony. They believe that well-rehearsed testimony more often than not looks stilted and insincere. Or they are concerned that if the witness has answers almost memorized, the opposing attorneys can easily trip them up by posing unexpected questions or asking questions in unexpected ways. Lawyers who are most effective will usually make this determination based on the particular needs and personality of the witness.

Finally, in getting ready to testify, it is especially important for both the expert witness and the lawyer to know the limitations of the witness's expertise (Vandenberg, 1993). If these limitations are recognized and acknowledged before the trial, it is easier for the attorney to shape the inquiry toward the witness's strengths and away from the limitations. If the witness attempts to go beyond the information possessed, the attorney's case can become derailed. Moreover, it is usually discovered during cross-examination, causing the entire presentation to lose much of its credibility.

VOIR DIRE: QUALIFYING AS AN EXPERT

When it finally comes time for the expert testimony, after the oath to be truthful is administered, the initial procedure is to qualify the witness. In order for the expert's knowledge to be presented in court, the lawyer producing the witness must establish that the witness is qualified as an expert. Only those who have been qualified as experts can provide the court with opinions, inferences, and conclusions about matters within their realm of expertise. Voir dire is the process of examining this witness to establish the extent and limit of the witness's expertise.

The lawyer who has called for the expert also must establish that this particular case requires the use of expert testimony. This requirement occurs when the fact finder (frequently the jury but in many cases also the judge) needs assistance to understand or evaluate the evidence.

Expert witnesses can only be asked for opinions concerning matters within the area of expertise for which they have been qualified. In other matters they must testify, as any other witness, only to facts that they have personally observed. For this reason it is important for the lawyer to show that this witness indeed possesses this relevant knowledge.

The expert can be excluded from testifying when it is determined that the judge and jury do not need assistance to understand or evaluate the evidence. The expert's testimony can also be excluded if it seems to supersede the judge and jury's established role of reaching the ultimate conclusions in the case. For example, if the jury is to determine if a defendant was criminally negligent in the operation of an elder care center, the expert may not be permitted to describe how the defendant's operation failed to meet established elder care center standards. This is true even though modern evidence rules may permit testimony as to ultimate facts or conclusions, at least in theory. Judges, however, may resist. They naturally resent the expert whose testimony attempts to wrap up the entire case for one side or the other.

When expert witnesses are finally called and sworn in, they begin by first identifying themselves, their occupations, and the nature of their expertise. This is the procedure known as "qualifying the expert" or "laying a foundation." Ideally, at this point the attorney may formally move that the court accept the social work professional as an expert. This is done if the opposing lawyer concedes that the witness is qualified.

Some adversary attorneys may want to concede this even before the credentials of the expert witness are presented. However, in some jurisdictions this is not permitted; the adversary cannot prevent the jury from hearing the expert witness's credentials by conceding that the witness is qualified. If the opposing attorney wants to contest the qualifications of the proffered expert, it is done by objecting to the first question that seeks to elicit the witness's opinion. The objection is made on the ground that the witness is not qualified. This opens a debate that continues until the judge makes a ruling.

The judge's ruling about the witness's qualifications as an expert is a preliminary matter of fact. The court considers such factors as formal education, degrees, special training, professional experience, authorship of publications, professional society memberships, credentials, and reputation. These factors are usually deemed necessary but not sufficient. The court must also find that the expert has some level of special knowledge beyond that of a well-informed layman. Thus, a social worker's opinion about how spouses should treat each other is insufficient to establish expertise; however, opinions about why people in certain stressful life situations often treat their spouses as they do is an expert opinion.

There are many reasons why an opposing lawyer might want to challenge an expert's qualifications, even if the end result is not expected to be actually preventing the testimony (Campbell, 1994). Since it is presumed that the information to be presented will not be favorable to the opposing attorney's case, any damage to the credibility of the witness before opinions are offered can be advantageous. The challenge can make the witness feel and look guarded, unnatural, stilted, insincere. The challenge might cause the witness to be somewhat less sure of the veracity of the information to be presented.

The challenge might come in the form of hostile or sarcastic questions about the witness's profession. A frequent tactic used on social workers is when the opposing lawyer asks such questions as these: "You are not qualified to prescribe medications are you?" "You aren't legally permitted to practice psychiatry in this state, are you?" "Are social workers required to have college degrees?" "Why are social workers involved in this case? Isn't their job to help poor people get money from the welfare department?"

Some workers, especially those who don't understand this as a courtroom tactic, become angry or defensive and thus lose the aura of expertise before they have even begun. Experienced social work experts learn to take this in stride and even feel bemused by the attempt. They recognize that the attack is not personal and that the attorney is merely doing the best job possible.

PRESENTING EXPERT TESTIMONY

If accepted by the court for the information they have to present, experts are first questioned in direct examination by the proponent (the lawyer who employed them) and then by the opposing lawyer in cross-examination. Sometimes after the cross-examination, the proponent may ask additional questions (redirect examination), followed by recross-examination, or surrebuttal. After the testimony is completed, the court may allow the witness to remain in the public gallery if there is no further need for testimony. Otherwise, the worker has no further involvement in the case.

The expert witness will have some influence on the case outcome depending upon the amount of credibility (i.e., believability) established. To be a credible witness, the worker should appear to be confident, comfortable, and knowledgeable about the case and respectful of the court and its procedures. The worker should be dressed appropriately (usually in a business suit) and act in a professional manner. Showing respect for both attorneys as well as the judge and jury is important as is presenting an appearance of objectivity, impartiality, and recognition of one's limitations. One should never convey disapproval of the judge's rulings either in verbal or physical expressions.

Answers to the lawyers questions should be stated as simply and jargon-free and slang-free as possible. If the responses are presented so technically that it remains beyond the jurors' comprehension, it is nearly worthless (Schutz, 1997). Answers should be concise, responsive, and relevant specifically to the question asked. It is essential to listen carefully to the question asked and to be sure that the question is understood before an answer is offered. Some experienced witnesses make it a practice to always pause before answering, even to the extent of mentally counting to three before speaking. The witness should avoid to the extent possible any vague responses, or personal/ emotional conjectures such as "I think that. . ." or "I feel. . . ."

DIRECT EXAMINATION OF THE EXPERT

The most congenial part of the process usually occurs during the direct examination. The witness has probably become more relaxed, having taken the oath and established credentials. The attorney, wanting to confer the utmost amount of authority on the witness, is respectful. The questions in direct examination are familiar and the witness has already been prepped to answer each question effectively. Any notes to be used are readily at hand and the witness has examined them thoroughly so there is no awkward time of searching for documentation or trying to decipher shaky penmanship.

Many experts attempt to give long, overly complicated answers. They might want to explain their findings as they would explain to colleagues, or to students, or to other experts. Jurors rapidly become bored and indifferent to such presentations. It is more effective to keep answers short and precisely related to the question. It is also effective to use verbal or written illustrations. Presenting statistics can add to the presentation, especially if done sparingly.

Another potential problem during direct examination is an expert's occasional loss of the appearance of neutrality. The witness is more familiar with and comfortable with the lawyer conducting the direct examination and usually wants to be helpful. But if this wish becomes too evident to the judge, jury, and opposing attorneys, it can be counterproductive. An appearance of neutrality and some detachment from the particulars of the case is more effective.

Expert witnesses should try to present their candid opinions without considering whether it is helpful or harmful to their attorney. If the expert's opinion is considered harmful, the lawyer would not have asked for that testimony. The greatest harm by expert witnesses during direct examination is to slant testimony so it seems biased in favor of the direct examiner's case. Such testimony becomes easy to attack during cross-examination and the whole testimony ultimately becomes more of a liability than an asset.

The expert witness can sometimes run afoul of the issue about "hearsay evidence." Because the witness may be asked about what others have said or revealed, there may be debate between attorneys about whether the information is admissible. Hearsay evidence is legally defined as an out-of-court declaration sought to be admitted into evidence to prove the truth of the matter asserted by the declarant. Generally the hearsay rule says that evidence is not admissible unless it comes directly from the declarant in court.

Hearsay evidence is excluded because the subject did not make the statement under oath and is not available for cross-examination. Furthermore, the statement may have been made in a different context than the use to which it is put in the court. Nevertheless, there are numerous exceptions to the hearsay rule. These should be discussed thoroughly with the lawyer prior to testifying. Because the lawyer must establish a basis for attempting to include such information into the court record, the worker will not bring it up without having worked it out with the lawyer first.

CROSS-EXAMINATION OF EXPERT WITNESSES

The cross-examination phase of the testimony is usually the most difficult experience for many workers in the expert witness role. The opposing lawyer's basic objective is to challenge the credibility of the information presented. This is done by continuing to question the witness's credentials, pointing out inconsistencies in the testimony, revealing gaps in the witness's knowledge, trying to show that the witness is not reasonable or objective, and by asking questions that compel the witness to talk about issues unfavorable to the opposition.

Less experienced expert witnesses in the adversarial system of justice may find the sudden role shift disconcerting. At one moment witnesses enjoy being respected authorities; suddenly they are thrust into the dramatically different and unfamiliar position of having their integrity and professionalism challenged.

Some expert witnesses respond by acting defensively or indignantly. They are offended that their reputations are questioned and they want the court to know it. Gradually, they begin to assume the role of adversary instead of neutral and objective professional. They have fallen into the opposing attorney's trap; their behavior becomes an aid to the opposition. Opinions expressed with anger or vehement advocacy have little credibility.

Skilled cross-examining lawyers use an arsenal of additional techniques to undermine. They often use intimidating countenances and sarcastic tones of voice. Some lawyers favor attempts to intimidate the witness by affecting tones of hostility, ridicule, extreme skepticism, or by formulating questions that suggest some witness impropriety.

Every effective trial lawyer has a set of favored tactics for use with expert witnesses; the more skilled lawyers detect the witness's greatest vulnerabilities and use only specific tactics that best exploit those vulnerabilities. The skilled expert witness knows these tactics and has already developed an effective defense.

TACTICS TO IMPEACH EXPERT WITNESSES

Attorneys may begin their cross-examinations of expert witnesses with the question, "How much are you being paid for this testimony?" The implication is that the information is not valid because it is being bought. However, judges and juries know and expect that esteemed professionals are being compensated. They do not construe it as suspect unless it is for an such an excessive amount that it seems like a bribe. Usually the purpose of the question is to rattle the witness and possibly cause some feeling of defensiveness to be detected by jurors. The answer should be given easily, truthfully, and without guilt or apology. Some writers recommend an answer like this: "I am being paid nothing for my testimony, because it is the truth and that is not for sale; what I am being paid for is my time, which is at the same hourly rate I receive in my regular job."

A similar question, asked for the same intentions, is this: "What were you told to say in the courtroom today?" The cross-examiner wants to imply that the information offered by the expert is not based on expert findings but on the demands of the other side. The question, however, is not often used by experienced attorneys because it is a slow pitch down the middle of the plate. The answer provides an opportunity for a home run when the witness responds, "I was told only to tell the truth, and that's what I have done."

Lawyers in cross-examination commonly try to show jurors that the witness is not really that knowledgeable by asking unanswerable questions. The expert and the lawyer may know they are not answerable, but often members of the jury may not. For example the lawyer asks such questions as these: "What is the cause of a personality disorder?" "How can you be sure that the patient was always telling the truth?" "How soon will you experts have a cure for Alzheimer's disease?" The witness's best response is to briefly indicate what the latest studies show and indicate that these experts also cannot be sure yet.

Some lawyers attempt to impeach the witness by pointing out inconsistencies between the testimony already given and what the professional literature says about the same thing (Lawson, 1998). If a textbook can be produced and quoted to show that other authorities have views that are diametrically opposed to the views of the witness, the testimony may be damaged. Lawyers find it relatively easy to quote passages from authoritative textbooks or journal articles that appear to contradict the witness. And because the witness does not have ready access to the publication, it is difficult to show that the quote was taken out of context or misinterpreted.

The lawyer begins this part of the cross-examination by asking if the witness knows about this author. If the answer is no, the lawyer can show incredulity and convey that the expert must be ignorant of important information in the field. If the answer is yes, the lawyer can find quotes which seem to contradict the views of the witness. Sometimes these quotes refer to exceptions to the major point made in the publication; in any event, the witness can be made to appear to be presenting debatable assertions as unopposed facts.

The witness can deal with this most effectively with a fair knowledge of the publications most likely to be cited. Many publications, especially in the mental health field, are unauthoritative or are written by "common-sense" laypersons or people antipathetic to the field. If the witness is unfamiliar with an author, it is best to say so because many publications could be of this type. An effective response is to say something like, "The most relevant new literature by authorities on this subject is by Wilson and Jones. I don't recall any citations to your authors, but if you have copies I'd be glad to review it during the next recess."

To indicate that a publication is authoritative in the field is fraught with danger. If unfamiliar with the writing or the writer, the witness may honestly say so, and add that "there are many authors in the field and most support the view I've just described." On the other hand, if the witness does know the publication well, and can explain any discrepancy between the testimony and points in the publication, the witness's credibility is greatly enhanced.

Some expert witnesses have difficulty when confronted with their own writings that contradict their current testimony. Famous trial lawyer F. Lee Bailey advises attorneys to carefully examine everything an opposing expert witness has written on the subject related to the trial. "There is nothing more devastating to an expert," he wrote, "than having something he himself has uttered used against him" (Bailey, 1994, p. 132). Conversely, this tactic can be dangerous for the cross-examiner if the witness can show that the quote was taken out of context or misinterpreted.

A common tactic in cross-examination is to demand a simple "yes" or "no" response to a question that cannot responsibly be answered that way. The questions are usually of the "have you stopped beating your wife" variety. Often the information to be provided by expert witnesses requires explanation and elaboration for it to be an accurate depiction of the truth. For example, the lawyer asks, "Is it your testimony that small children can't be induced to make up stories about their fathers molesting them? Yes or no?" The witness may try to respond with an elaborate answer, but may be required by the judge to give the one word reply. The most reasonable responses include: "It depends." "I'm not sure." "I don't understand your question." "Sometimes yes, sometimes no."

Most judges will not permit a lawyer to demand a simple "yes" or "no" under these circumstances if the opposing lawyer objects. So the optimal strategy for the witness is to pause after each question of this type is asked, to give the lawyer a chance to make the objection and rescue the witness.

CONCLUSION

Social workers are being called upon increasingly to serve as expert witnesses, especially as lawyers and law professionals become more aware of the contributions they are able to make. Professionals who are most effective as expert witnesses have recognized that the job requires considerable knowledge and skill. They prepare for it with as much effort and study as they would for any other social work specialty. For most, the effort is worth it to help ensure that the justice system works for all.

Chapter 5

Malpractice and How to Avoid It

Malpractice occurs when a professional person causes harm to a client through improper performance of duties. It does not matter whether the professional's conduct is intentional or occurs through carelessness or ignorance. A competent and ethical social worker might think, therefore, that the risk of malpractice will be minimal. Social workers assume that if they adhere to the highest standards of the profession, conform to the professional code of ethics, conduct treatment competently in accordance with the traditional methods of the profession, and always achieve what are considered successful therapeutic outcomes, there would be no problems with malpractice (Abbott, 1995).

A worker who believes this nowadays is naive. Most competent professionals would be hard pressed to say they have always been able to accomplish these results. But even if they did, they could still be vulnerable, as seen in the following examples.

SOME MALPRACTICE EXAMPLES

A nineteen-year-old man has just been medically discharged from the U.S. Army for depression, after three months in a combat zone. He returns to his parents' home and they urge him to seek treatment. He seeks help with the Veteran's Administration but finds that the waiting list for help is too long. So he begins working with a social worker at a family service agency. After four months of therapy he shows signs of improvement. He gets a job, makes new friends, and many of his depressive symptoms are diminished. He then decides he wants to get a place of his own. He decides to stop therapy to save money.

The worker advises against it, saying that the depression is likely to return, and the therapist and agency even agree to reduce fees to ensure continuing treatment. The man does not keep the next few scheduled appointments. The worker calls several times and is told by the young man that he no longer wants to come. The therapist never sees him again. Three months after the last session the young man commits suicide. His parents, feeling that the therapist did not do everything possible to anticipate or alleviate the suicidal tendencies or either keep him in treatment or get him hospitalized, seek compensation from the worker though a lawsuit.

* * *

A middle-aged woman is a victim of the "learned helplessness syndrome." Married to an abusive alcoholic for eighteen years, she has a high-paying job and is the family's sole source of support and stability. She has been unable to get her husband to work on his problem or to stop his abuse. Nor has she been able to get out of the marriage, primarily because of severe problems of self-destructiveness and insecurity. At the encouragement of her Al-Anon group, she enters psychotherapy.

The therapy helps her to become self-confident, less self-destructive, and determined to improve or end the marriage. After presenting an ultimatum to her husband to get help or get out, the marriage comes to an end. The husband then explains to his divorce attorney that the therapist caused the breakup of the marriage and ended his source of livelihood. The therapist is then sued for the loss of income and other harm he has allegedly caused the husband.

* * *

A woman has been in a private social work practitioner's group therapy for several months. She is an attractive, young mother of two, in treatment because of conflicts about her sexuality. She confides to the group that she recently broke off a secret affair with a married man. Another group member is very interested in the woman's revelations. He has severe characterological problems and has had various troubles with the law, difficulties holding jobs, unsuccessful relationships with women, and deep-seated resentment toward authority.

Even though everyone in the group is admonished to honor and respect one another's confidentiality and to not see one another outside the group, the man secretly starts following the woman to her home after group sessions. He calls her on the telephone. She rebuffs him and calls the group therapist. The therapist contacts the man and reiterates the group rules about confidentiality and no outside contacts. The man becomes enraged at the therapist and refuses to continue his sessions. The woman also refuses to return to the group, despite the therapist's attempt to get her to continue.

The man now begins calling the woman and harassing her. He threatens to reveal her secret to her husband and to her ex-lover's wife if she does not meet with him. When she still refuses, he writes letters to both families. This results in a considerable conflict between spouses. They all seek legal assistance and attribute much of the blame for their troubles to the group therapist. They contend that the therapist should not have included the man in the same group with her and should have exercised more control over the man. The therapist was forced to defend against threats of litigation from two parties.

* * *

It is easy to see how the most well-meaning and competent social worker can become enmeshed in malpractice litigation. In all of these examples the workers were capable and experienced, yet they had to defend themselves against blame for events over which they may have had little or no control. As is true of most malpractice cases, all of these were settled before reaching the courtroom. Nevertheless, the workers had to expend considerable funds, time, and energies to defend themselves, and their reputations could never be fully restored.

RESPONSIBILITY FOR THERAPY OUTCOMES

These cases became malpractice issues, not because the workers' behaviors were incorrect, malevolent, or unusual, but primarily because the outcomes were so unhappy. Yet many clients do not achieve successful results no matter how competent the therapist is or how reliable the methods usually are. The first case illustrates the difficulty of predicting the risk of suicide. While professionals can identify the signs that are most commonly associated with suicidal ideation, many people who take their own lives do not show such signs in advance (Jacobs, 1998). Moreover, even when they do, it is not possible to hold people against their wills for long.

The second example illustrates that some people might be unhappy with the consequences of the therapy even when the outcome is "successful." It is not uncommon that therapy leads clients to make changes in their lives which negatively impact others. If these others perceive that they have been harmed by the professionals' work, they can initiate legal actions.

The last case illustrates the vulnerability of professionals who are sometimes seen as being responsible for client behaviors. If the client causes harm to another, those harmed wonder why the therapist did not do more to prevent such actions. This view has become so prevalent in our society that laws now compel professionals, in certain circumstances, to take actions to protect others from their clients (Cooper, 1995).

While society increasingly holds professionals responsible for the behaviors of their clients, the authority of professionals to control their clients is diminishing. Mental health professionals, including social workers, have been successfully sued for holding clients inappropriately in mental institutions against their wills (Wilk, 1994). It is rarely possible to keep clients in therapy or custody against their wishes, no matter how much they might need it. The social trend is to protect the rights of mental patients against the actions or controls of therapists. Therapists cannot make clients take their needed medications, cannot have clients incarcerated when the clients do not seem imminently lethal, and cannot accompany them through their lives to protect those with whom they interact.

Yet, when they fail to exercise the controls that would be necessary to prevent harm, judges and juries have found them at fault. When they try to exercise the controls, they have been seen as interfering busybodies or as cruel power-mongers (Szasz, 1998). When they do nothing they have been found at fault for not preventing serious injury or death. They have even been sued, successfully, for malpractice, not by their own clients, but by family and associates of the client.

ALLEGED CHILD ABUSE: TO REPORT OR NOT?

One of the most difficult dilemmas currently facing social workers involves the legal requirement to report suspected child abuse. The law in every jurisdiction in the nation is clear: the worker is required to report it to the appropriate authorities (Stein, 1998). The consequences for not doing so can be severe; many judges and juries have imposed heavy penalties on social workers who knew, or should have known, that children in their purview had been abused. Thus, if a worker sees a child with suspicious bruises or other signs of physical injury, or if the child describes (directly or obliquely) being abused, the professional responsibility is determined.

The procedures for reporting are also well established. The personnel of most hospitals, health care centers, schools, child care centers, and social agencies that work with children are told what kind of clues to look for and who to call with the information (Besharov, 1998). Usually, when these reports look serious, the information is given to specialists in the county prosecuting attorney's office. This puts the claim in the public domain. Thus, the worker or whoever initiated the report has publicly charged an individual with a horrendous act of wrongdoing.

In some states, the person who initiates such charges may be immune to lawsuits from the accused, but only if the evidence tightly conforms to specific guidelines, and only if the procedures for reporting this evidence have been scrupulously followed (Bullis, 1990). In the Supreme Court's 1989 *DeShaney* decision, social workers were not held liable when a child in their charge was severely abused by his father (*DeShaney vs. Winnebago County,* 1989). However, the case specifically did not grant immunity to workers in all states under all circumstances. Thus, in many other jurisdictions, there is no immunity at all for the worker who initiates the report. The worker had better have very good reasons for initiating the report and good documentation of all subsequent actions relevant to it.

When a client's appearance or verbalizations lead the worker to conclude that abuse has taken place, a serious decision has to be made. Failure to make the right one can result in malpractice litigation or criminal charges. Studies show that many therapists are likely to have certain biases and act accordingly (Garb, 1998). For example, some workers have been inclined to notify authorities when there is even a remote suggestion that abuse has taken place; other workers have failed to give notification even when there is substantial evidence that the client is being victimized. It is these cases of overreacting or underreacting that most, but not all, legal conflicts about alleged abuse take place (Karger and Stoesz, 1995).

It is reasonable to see how a worker could react one way or the other. On the one hand there seems to be an epidemic of abuse cases. One of the biggest selling self-help books of the past decade was written for adult victims of childhood sexual abuse; *Courage to Heal* (Bass and Davis, 1994) and its sequels have sold over 300,000 copies, nearly all, presumably, to people who have confronted this tragedy.

On the other hand, workers who react overly cautiously also can justify their actions. One of the most common causes of malpractice suits now is making a false accusation about someone based on a client's statements while in therapy. A major controversy, which is nowhere near to being resolved, involves the efforts of mental health therapists, particularly social workers, who have tried to help clients recover memories about childhood sexual abuse (Stocks, 1998).

Many professionals believe that victims of abuse frequently cope with the trauma by suppressing the memory of it. Supposedly, with it out of their daily thinking they can get on with their lives. However, as with many suppressed conflicts, many behavioral dysfunctions and other symptoms are the residue. A skilled therapist works with the client to get in touch with these memories. The controversy is, however, whether this uncovering process is valid, as many claim, or is merely evidence of "implanting" false memories. Children and victimized adults may be highly suggestible and easily manipulated into unconsciously or consciously fabricating the idea of having been abused. The most prominent litigation to decide the issue is the *Ramona* case.

THE RAMONA *CASE*

Ramona was the nation's first notable "false memory" trial (Brody, 1999). In 1994 Mr. Gary Ramona, a wealthy business executive in the Napa Valley area of California, successfully sued a therapist for malpractice. The therapist had been treating Ramona's daughter, a young woman who, in recounting childhood memories, told of episodes of sexual abuse by her father. At the therapist's invitation, with the daughter's consent, the father came to one of the sessions to participate in a confrontation.

The daughter made her accusations, which the father denied. Unconvinced, she later relayed her accusations to the district attorney's office. Her father was arrested and then prosecuted for criminal assault and incest. Before the case went to trial, Mr. Ramona was fired from his high-paying job, and his wife filed for divorce. But then, after a widely publicized trial, the jury acquitted him of the charges.

Ramona blamed the therapist for his troubles and sought damages in a malpractice lawsuit. Even though his daughter, and not the therapist, reported the allegations, Mr. Ramona contended that this wrongful accusation would not have occurred without the therapist's aggressive influence. Moreover, since he came to a session, and paid for it, he claimed he was thereby a client and entitled to the same protections as any other client. The major focus of the courtroom testimony and argument turned on whether "recovered memory therapy" was a valid procedure and concept. Many experts were found to support both sides.

The jury in the malpractice case found for Mr. Ramona, and he was awarded $500,000 damages. The money was not for emotional distress, as he demanded, but for the wages he lost upon being fired, the direct result of the abuse allegations (Ayres, 1994). The case left unresolved whether memories were recovered or implanted by the therapist.

The outcome of *Ramona* has sent a chill through the already beleaguered ranks of the psychotherapy professions. It has been followed by a series of lawsuits alleging that therapists have manipulated their clients, "implanting" memories in their minds about episodes of childhood sexual abuse that did not occur (Ceci and Bruck, 1995).

The community of mental health experts remain divided about the process of human memory (Oberlander, 1995). Some say that the influence of the therapist, often through hypnotherapy, free association, catharsis, or other therapy procedures, helps clients uncover and rediscover emotional crises events from their pasts (Brown, Scheflin, and Hammond, 1998). Others say that the painful stories related by clients are too detailed and too realistic to have been imagined. It is difficult, they claim, to convince children or adults to describe experiences of sexual abuse in great detail if they did not actually happen.

Most honest and unbiased social workers and other psychotherapists acknowledge that there simply is not yet enough scientifically obtained data to support one view or the other. Each case must be evaluated on its individual merits, rather than saying that everyone who makes such allegations must be believed or disbelieved. False memories may be "implanted" in some cases, and in others the client is helped to uncover experiences that occurred but that are now buried in the unconscious (Madden and Parody, 1997).

Another chilling aspect of these cases is that they suggest that therapists are to be held responsible not only for their clients, but also for those who are associated with client. Therapists may be held responsible for people they do not know if harm comes to them. And the blame may extend beyond the therapists, to the therapists' supervisors or employers; they would share responsibility under the *respondeat superior* doctrine (Clark, 1997).

If these laws were to be worthwhile and serve the purpose for which they were intended, some way to protect professionals from defamation suits had to be found. Otherwise the charges would not be filed, and many molesters would go unchecked. If the accusation came from someone who did not even remember the trauma until therapy, the chances of conviction would be doubtful. And if the major evidence came from a young child, one who would eventually have to testify in court about it, the prospects of a guilty verdict would be even more remote (McGough, 1994).

Thus, several states and jurisdictions passed laws to provide immunity for those who reported suspected abuse. The laws were upheld by various courts, including the U.S. Supreme Court; professionals were granted some limited immunity from lawsuits (Alexander, 1995). The courts found they were merely carrying out their legal duty in filing the reports, even if the accusation could not be legally sustained.

The relief for professionals was short lived. The laws and court rulings proved to be so limited they could be circumvented (Bullis, 1990). Lawyers representing the people accused of child abuse found a way around any claim of immunity. They could sue the therapist who reported his or her client by alleging that the therapist implanted the memories. The aggressive action in manipulating the client to make the false accusation could make the therapist liable for malpractice. The therapist would be put on trial for compelling a client to disclose an event that had not happened.

The "implanted" or "recovered" memory controversy is only one of the issues that nowadays places therapists amidst a field of legal land-mines. Whatever paths they take to remove themselves from malprac-tice dangers are uncertain, even with their best efforts to be competent and ethical. The most likely, but not guaranteed, route to safety is a good knowledge of how malpractice claims are brought about and a willingness to practice defensively to avoid those circumstances.

CRITERIA FOR MALPRACTICE LIABILITY

Of course most malpractice cases occur as a result of a worker's actions that are clearly outside the standard of professional conduct and are directly harmful to the client. Malpractice occurs when a professional causes harm to the client through a lack of care or skill. Unlike the ordinary person on the street, a professional is held to a certain minimum level of skill or competence. The law holds that the professional should bring to the task at hand that amount of skill and knowledge possessed by the typical professional within the same discipline in the same or similar communities.

To recover damages in any malpractice action, the plaintiff must prove four elements: (1) that the professional owed the client a duty to conform to a particular standard of conduct, (2) that the therapist breached that duty by some act of omission or commission in the professional practice, (3) that the client suffered actual damage, and (4) that the professional's conduct was the direct or proximate cause of the damage (Houston-Vega, 1996; Reamer, 1994).

To win a malpractice case, the plaintiff has to establish that all four of these elements existed. The first element is the most clear cut. A duty of care is established if a worker/client therapeutic relationship has already begun, especially if verbal or written contracts have been made and fees have been paid for the service.

Establishing the third element, that the client has suffered actual damages, is also clear cut, although more complicated. It is difficult to show emotional damages as a result of what social workers and other mental health professionals call "talking therapy"; it is not so difficult when the client develops health problems, commits suicide,

NORTHEAST COMMUNITY COLLEGE LIBRARY

is improperly incarcerated, or harmed physically. The plaintiff's attorney will attempt to establish damages by documenting the client's health and circumstances prior to and after the therapy. The documentation will probably include medical case records, physicians' testimony, and other witnesses' testimony about the client's condition before and after the professional's intervention.

Most malpractice disputes center on the other two elements, whether or not the worker's care met established standards and, if not, was that substandard care related to the damage. To ascertain this in court, the plaintiff's attorney will call on expert witnesses, members of the defendant's profession if possible, to explain what the standard of care requires for cases of the type experienced by the plaintiff. This may include testimony from social work practitioners, educators, and members of the professional association and licensing authority.

The evidence presented most certainly will include a review of the social worker's code of ethics. Behaviors by the social worker which are at variance from the code of ethics will be noted. The plaintiff will be less likely to prevail if the defendant can show clearly that the practices were in accord with professional standards or that the professional made an acceptable choice of treatment alternatives from a range of acceptable choices. However, most cases of this type do not reach the courtroom when the defendant can show that these standards were reached. Many plaintiffs gain de facto victories when defendants settle out of court, paying sums to avoid the considerable inconvenience and notoriety that would be faced by contesting the case in court.

If the court determined that the worker's care was substandard and that the client was damaged, it theoretically becomes necessary to link the two. In practice, however, the plaintiffs' attorneys are sometimes successful when they simply establish that damage was done and that the worker's care deviated from standards. It is easier to get a jury to make the connection, as its members tend to sympathize more with a damaged client than with a successful professional.

PREVENTIVE AND DEFENSIVE PRACTICES

To rebut proof or inference of proximate cause, the defense could attempt to show that some other person's action superseded any alleged negligence by the defendant. Thus if the plaintiff had gone to other professionals after working with the defendant, it becomes more difficult for the jury to decide where any negligence might lie.

Although there are no guarantees against losing malpractice cases nowadays, the practitioner's best hopes are in always adhering to professional standards of conduct. This means that the worker must first know what those standards are. Ignorance of the standards is in itself practicing at a substandard level (Jayaratne, Croxton, and Mattison, 1997). Next, the worker must choose to meet those standards. Most of the known claims against mental health professionals have been made in situations where the professional knew what was appropriate and inappropriate conduct but chose the inappropriate action anyway.

Unquestionably, the best defense is to avoid going to court at all, by convincing the plaintiff or the plaintiff's lawyers that they cannot win a favorable judgment and will not receive a favorable settlement. Preventive practice, while not guaranteeing the avoidance of litigation, can reduce its likelihood to the extent possible.

To achieve this goal the worker needs to maintain an explicit rationale for every action taken. This rationale should be documented in writing in the client's case record. Then, when the plaintiff's lawyer reviews this record and finds a full explanation and justification for the course of action taken, the plan to proceed with the case becomes very daunting for the plaintiff.

CONDUCT LEADING TO MALPRACTICE CLAIMS

Hundreds of cases of social work malpractice have been heard in court, and many more have been settled prior to reaching court. The major insurance companies, including the American Professional Agency (primarily for members of the National Association of Social Workers) and the Interstate Insurance Group subsidary of the Fireman's Fund Insurance Company (primarily for members of the Clinical Social Work Federation) have spelled out the types of behaviors that most frequently have led to legal actions.

The major causes of malpractice, specifically, are incorrect treatment, sexual impropriety, exploitative dual relationships, breach of confidentiality, improper child placement, improper diagnosis or faulty assessment, defamation, improper death of a client, failure to properly supervise the client, bodily injury to clients, violation of civil rights, countersuits due to fee collection practices, assault and battery, false imprisonment, breach of contract, failure to warn of the client's dangerousness, and failure to achieve promised or implied results in treatment.

In nearly all actions and threatened actions, the complaint tended to allege more than a single unprofessional act. For example, if a complaint alleged that the worker's action led to improper imprisonment, it would also almost certainly allege violation of the client's civil rights and incorrect treatment. By counting as a separate "case" each act of allegedly improper conduct, rather than each worker who is sued, the insurance companies may be a little disingenuous. They are perhaps implying that they are having to deal with many more actions than is actually the case. The companies are somewhat vague about the number of claims they handle, possibly to justify their increasing premiums.

Nevertheless, the insurance companies have been busy enough with social workers in malpractice trouble for their misconduct (Bullis, 1995). Whenever a worker is contacted about a possible malpractice issue, the company is sure to be called. And they have been paying out growing sums of money when they lose in courts and in settlements. While most of the disputes have not reached courtrooms, nearly all of them have required the social worker to engage legal representation and develop defenses. This in itself is a costly and inconvenient process which every worker wants to avoid. The balance of this chapter discusses some of these types of claims and offers some suggestions for avoiding similar fates or minimizing the consequences when they are not avoided.

Malpractice Suits for Incorrect Treatment

The professional conduct that results in the highest number of malpractice claims is providing the wrong type of treatment for the client. "Wrong treatment" cases are most likely to occur when the worker's therapy causes damage by keeping the client from receiving more appropriate treatment. The following case is an example.

A thirty-four-year-old man is referred to a social worker by a friend who had previously been successfully treated by the worker.

For six months, the man had been taking three five-milligram tablets of Valium daily because of anxiety. He tells the worker that the tension seems to have begun in the past year and is increasing. It becomes so severe, he says, that his heart pounds and he sweats profusely. He attributes his symptoms to the growing pressures of his job and to some unresolved conflicts about the death of his mother two years ago. He assures the worker that his last physical examination was normal and that he had no health problems.

After treatment begins, catharsis seems to help. The client has a marked diminution of the anxiety symptoms. But after three months, the symptoms return and seem to get worse. The worker recommends increasing the number of visits to twice weekly. Again a reduction of symptoms occurs for awhile, but then they return with even more intensity. One day at work the man becomes so upset he is taken to a nearby hospital. Tests follow. The consulting physicians discover that the symptoms are not caused by functional neuroses, as was assumed by the worker. The diagnosis was "mitral valve prolapse syndrome."

Such diseases result in many of the same symptoms as seen in people with severe anxiety disorders, yet the treatment for each is far different. It is not possible to know by merely talking with a client if behaviors that seem like anxiety are due to inner conflict or to medical disorders. Therefore, the appropriate standard of care and defensive practice is as follows: *Before commencing therapy, require the client to get a physical examination to rule out medical causes of presenting symptoms.*

Malpractice for Sexual Misconduct

The second most common conduct resulting in malpractice claims occurs when social workers engage in sexual relationships with their clients. It seems probable that there are many more common forms of professional misconduct than sexual intercourse with clients, but those forms of misconduct are more difficult to substantiate or to recognize as misconduct. There is less room for mistaking client-worker sexual contact as acceptable practice, so litigation is more likely to occur whenever it happens.

Even so, many therapists try to justify their action as something other than inappropriate conduct. Many defendants claim they ended the formal therapy sessions before actually engaging in such liaisons. At one time a common defense was to claim that such behavior was therapeutic and not harmful to the client, and that it was not that much a deviation from the standards established by well-known leaders in the psychotherapy fields. This argument has waned in recent years as every reputable professional indicates (and will in courtroom testimony) that there are no valid justifications for sexual relationships. Some leaders in the field say it should be treated legally as the crime of rape, and in fact some states do consider it a felony (Alexander, 1997b).

All mental health professions' codes of ethical conduct now include specific prohibitions against sexual relations with clients. The NASW Code of Ethics (1996), for example, clearly states: "Social workers should under no circumstances engage in sexual activities or sexual contact with current clients, whether such contact is consensual or forced." But what constitutes a client? Is there a point in time after which the person is no longer a client and thus eligible for such a relationship? Hopefully, the benefits of therapy are lifelong; the influence of the therapist exists equally as long. Thus, one never leaves the status of "client." The Code spells this out in a later paragraph making it clear that it is never acceptable to have sex with a former client. Moreover, the Code states the social worker should not have sex with client's relatives or associates; and they should not provide clinical services to individuals with whom they have previously had sexual relations.

Other social work Codes of Ethics stress the same admonition in their own words: The Code of Ethics of the Clinical Social Work Federation (CSWF Code, 1997) states "Clinical social workers do not, under any circumstances, engage in romantic or sexual contact with either current or former clients." The CSWF goes on to prohibit romantic or sexual contact with relatives or people who are in close association with the client. The American Board of Examiners in Clinical Social Work Code of Ethics is not so specific about the sexual prohibition, but strongly warns against any worker-client relationship that is exploitative or harmful to the client (ABE, 1999). The other major social work organizations, including the American Association of State Social Work Boards and the Council on Social Work Education do not have their own codes of ethics but make it clear in their mission statements that their members adhere to the established social work codes of ethics.

If a social worker violates this provision of the Code and engages in sexual contact with a client, the punishment is not limited to malpractice suits. Alexander (1997b) indicates that the insurance companies, which cover for other malpractice injuries up to $300,000, limit payments to $25,000 for sexual contacts. If the worker is employed in a social agency when the sexual impropriety occurs, the supervisor and the agency may also be held liable under the *respondeat superior* doctrine. Furthermore, according to Alexander, many states consider this a felony; therapists may be incarcerated for the crime and are also subject to paying for the client's subsequent mental health care. In these states, the therapist cannot use as a defense that the sexual relationship was consensual—it does not matter.

Therefore, the defensive practice against malpractice claims for sexual misconduct is this: *Once therapy has begun, a sexual relationship between the therapist and client is permanently inappropriate.*

Misuse of Influence

The third conduct that has led to malpractice lawsuits occurs when workers induce clients to do things that serve the professional's interests rather than those of the client. For example, a worker persuades a client to sell him his home at a low price, or convinces him to name the worker in his will. Social workers have encouraged clients to give them gifts, business deals, "insider" information for investments, or access to the client's finances. A story in a recent issue of *NASW News* (1998a) described a social worker who induced her client to grant the worker power of attorney and to name the worker in her life insurance policy. The worker also introduced the client to a friend of the workers, who then included the client in a business partnership, and they embezzled money from the client's savings.

Lawyers and judges call this act of malpractice a misuse of influence. Social workers, on the other hand, refer to it as a "dual relationship." By whatever name, it is unethical and forbidden by professional associations, and increasingly, by state law. Violations of this element of the ethics code can lead to probation or expulsion from professional membership and revocation of the professional license. Malpractice judges, however, would probably need to see evidence of specific financial or emotional harm before a claim against a professional could be won.

Dual relationships occur whenever a professional relationship exists as well as a social or business relationship, and they can occur simultaneously or consecutively. Dual relationships also occur when a professional assumes two different roles with the client. For example, it would be unethical for a worker to act as a therapist for a client, and then as a forensic investigator who will present information about the client to legal authorities (Berger, 1998; Strasberger, Gutheil, and Brodsky, 1997).

The NASW Code of Ethics (1996) warns against dual relationships, where there is risk of harm to the client. The Code cautions about accidental or unavoidable relationships with clients and suggests ways to minimize these contacts and prevent their recurrence. The Code also clarifies the possible conflict of interest that might occur when treating more than one client, such as in a family. In this case the worker is asked to indicate which individuals will be considered the client. Workers who anticipate any conflicts of interest when working with couples or family members (as when later asked to testify in a divorce or child custody disputes) should take appropriate actions to clarify their roles and minimize any conflict of interest.

Social workers have no trouble recognizing the impropriety of dual relationships when clients are financially or sexually exploited. Many of them seem not so sure about other types of dual relationship. A representative attitude survey of the nation's social workers, psychiatrists, and psychologists revealed that, while most respondents (98.3 percent) recognized that sexual relationships with current clients were unethical, only 68.4 percent thought sex with a former client was unethical, and only 14.8 percent thought that becoming friends with a former client was unethical (Borys and Pope, 1989). Perhaps if this ten-year-old study is replicated, it will be shown that fewer professionals will find dual relationships acceptable.

There are good reasons to maintain clear boundaries between professional and client. Because the therapeutic relationship is based on "unequal power and unequal responsibility," the worker could exert undue influence over the vulnerable client (Kagle and Giebelhausen, 1994, p. 216), even unintentionally. Dual relationships undermine the therapeutic relationship. As such they should not be allowed to occur during the therapy sessions or ever after. One may assume that the influences which the worker developed with the client during the course of therapy will endure for life.

Thus, the precaution here is as follows: *Permanently avoid any social, financial, or any other relationship with the client that is not explicitly therapeutic.*

Breach of Confidentiality and Defamation

The appropriate standard of care is for the therapist to say nothing about the client to others without the client's permission; moreover, the therapist should not write anything about the client for others to see, without the client's written permission. The principle of confidentiality remains in high regard by the social work profession. However, upholding it is becoming an ideal rather than a routine professional action.

Careless disclosures to outsiders about information obtained in formal interviews remain uncommon. But the laws and court rulings of the past fifteen years requiring therapist disclosures have made the principle very equivocal. It is even difficult for social workers to keep their own case records private. Information in them, if in the wrong hands, can also lead to malpractice actions. The following case illustrates this.

Several months after Mr. Jones successfully concluded his treatment with the social worker, he went up for promotion in a highly sensitive government agency. His applications indicated his recent therapy. Mr. Jones signed release of information forms so that the employer could obtain additional information about the therapy. In the face-to-face meeting with the employer's agent, the worker gave little information and tried to emphasize only the positive aspects of the client.

However, the investigator became suspicious about the social worker's minimal responses. Later the agency asked Mr. Jones to sign another release to obtain the worker's entire case record. The records were relinquished and contained information that was not positive about Mr. Jones. He did not get the promotion. The therapy and its record were the only factors to account for denial of the promotion. In a malpractice suit, Mr. Jones alleged he was harmed because of the information given by the worker, information that would not have been revealed if the worker had been more circumspect in what he wrote in the case records.

Cases such as this have been disputed between mental health professionals and their clients for many decades (Grinfeld, 1998). One of the first and most famous of this type was the *Yoder vs. Smith* case, in which a doctor was asked by a patient to send information to the employer; the information showed that the patient was unable to perform some of his former duties on the job. While this case was ruled in favor of the plaintiff, most are not. This is because the argument the defendant makes is that the allegedly harmful statements were not lies and had been solicited by the plaintiff. However, many more cases of this type are settled before they reach courtrooms. In these instances the settlements more often favor the plaintiff, as the defendant agrees to make some payment to avoid the negative publicity, legal costs, and loss of time. This was what Mr. Jones' therapist did.

Because the worker can never be sure nowadays when the case records can be subpoenaed and made public, the record itself should be prepared defensively against charges of defamation or breach of confidentiality (Marine, 1998b). Nothing derogatory should be written about the client or client's associates unless the statement can be documented independently of the client's verbalizations (Grabois, 1997-1998). Many professionals also recommend that in preparing a case record, the client participate in its writing and receive copies of everything written. This means that the worker will usually be more careful about what is written. If anything is written that is distressing to clients, therapists and clients can discuss it in the therapy office rather in than the courtroom.

The relevant standard of care and preventive action is this: *Unless the law requires otherwise, do not write undocumented derogatory information about a client in the case record or elsewhere, and do not disclose any information about clients, without the client's authorization.*

Faulty Diagnosis or Assessment

Historically, medical doctors have been more at risk for faulty diagnosis than other professionals; their mistakes could result in death or highly visible damage. The diagnostic mistakes made by social workers have not usually been so obvious, and the consequences have not usually been so life threatening. Their greatest risk of malpractice for faulty diagnosis has come from providing inaccurate information to other professionals, information which was then used by the others to arrive at a faulty diagnosis.

For example, when social workers investigate conditions in which children, older people, disabled persons, and others are living, they usually report this information to legal or medical officials for appropriate action. When that information leads to the client being institutionalized inappropriately, and when the decision to do so was based on the worker's input, malpractice liability is possible. The doctor who held the ultimate responsibility for the diagnosis and treatment decision would, of course, be the primary target of the suit. In all likelihood, the worker who participated in this procedure would also be named.

One of the most expensive settlements made by a social worker to date was over this issue. The social worker evaluated a client and prepared a report for a psychiatrist to use in court. The report said the client was not dangerous. Soon thereafter the client shot several people, including himself. Both the psychiatrist and the social worker became involved in extensive and prolonged litigation. They eventually settled a large claim out of court to avoid further litigation.

One of the challenges that confronts social workers more than psychiatrists or psychologists is the social work orientation to the person-in-environment perspective. Other mental health professionals can comfortably focus on a "medical model" of individual psychopathology. The problems presented by the individual patient can be seen under clinical conditions in relative isolation. Psychiatric diseases are listed in the American Psychiatric Association (1994) *Diagnostic and Statistical Manual of Mental Disorders* (DSM-IV) along with the traits that the client might exhibit to warrant a specific diagnosis. For the most part, the clients' self-reported behaviors and ways of thinking are used to locate the right diagnostic category. It is a relatively clean, focused, and objective way to make diagnoses—even though the procedure is also described as oversimplified, inaccurate, and not encompassing of relevant environmental or cultural factors (Kutchins and Kirk, 1997).

On the other hand, social workers who do their jobs properly must take all these factors into account, but not confine their diagnoses to the DSM-IV formulations. Some use the PIE (person-in-environment) model (Karls and Wandrei, 1994) or the "systems approaches" (focusing on interrelationships between individuals, people in society, and their environment) advocated by Meyer (1993) and by Germain and Gitterman (1996). Most good social work diagnosticians use extensive discussions about the interplay between the various forces in the clients' social system. While this is undoubtedly more accurate and representative of the way the client's life is, it is far more difficult to obtain and record all the knowledge that is relevant to make this kind of diagnosis. In other words, social workers have more chances for making diagnostic error than do psychiatrists or psychologists.

Nevertheless, the standard of care and preventive defense here is, of course, to be as complete and accurate as possible in arriving at the proper diagnosis, or in providing the information to others for their diagnosis. Accuracy will be more likely if the worker obtains the needed information from a wide range of sources. Legally, it is usually insufficient to base diagnoses exclusively on the information provided verbally by the client.

Judgments about placing clients, especially, must be made with as much input as possible from colleagues, other professionals, the client, those in the client's environment, and those in the environment where the client may be sent. Physical and psychological tests, reports from other professionals, and interviews with others who know the client can be helpful additions to the record.

The defensive strategy is to obtain diagnostic information from various sources and maintain complete and accurate records about all these sources. This record should include information about how it was obtained and disclaimers about possible inaccuracies therein.

Death/Suicide of Client

The death of a client, either due to accidents, untreated health problems, or suicide, is the most serious and visible form of damage. So, while death of a social work client may not occur with frequency, when it does it is very likely that legal inquiries will ensue. The authorities and attorneys of the family will want to determine the degree, if any, to which the therapist might have precipitated the results.

When professionals are investigated for client deaths, the experience is more painful than merely being concerned about malpractice litigation. The therapist will feel saddened by the client's death, but due to the nature of the relationship cannot express grief as can family members. Lawyers may advise therapists not to tell family members anything about being sorry or regretful, supposedly to gain distance from acknowledgment of culpability. Nevertheless, the therapist may feel somewhat responsible, even if little connection exists between the therapy and the death. While the therapist copes with these emotions, it is important to prepare for a defense.

Workers are sometimes burdened with contradictory expectations. On the one hand, they may be expected to know, at all times, if their clients are suicidal or in jeopardy of self-injury. Yet, when workers suspect that clients are in danger, they are limited in the extent to which they can incarcerate or otherwise control the client. And if they could keep a client in confinement or under constant surveillance, thus preventing suicide, the client or client's family could later claim that the confinement was unjustified—after all, no suicide occurred. The worker is then at risk of malpractice by supposedly making a faulty assessment and violating the client's civil rights.

Most ethical social workers would not worry about this, and would be inclined to err on the side of overcaution. Even so, they are limited in the controls they can exercise. They can notify police, family members, or other professionals, but they realize that this "buck passing" does not really solve the problem. What can be done by those who are notified?

The best way to avoid malpractice suits because of a client's death is, of course, to do everything possible to prevent that death. If that is not always realistic, the precaution is to remain knowledgeable about the problem. It also helps to enlist as many other people as possible in helping to prevent the client's death. This means taking assertive steps toward educating the client, and the client's loved ones and associates, about the symptoms, warning signs, and best possible responses.

It seems cynical and callous to discuss a defensive strategy against malpractice suits when the client's death is involved, but one way to reduce the odds of this happening is to work in advance with the people who would eventually be most likely to sue. If the professional who fears a client suicide works with the client's family to protect the client, the family would be less inclined to sue. They would have been cooperating participants in the effort to save the client's life. This is good practice in these circumstances and only incidentally is also good defensive strategy.

In sum, the standard of care and defensive practice is this: *Know all the signs of suicide ideation, medical symptoms, and the likelihood of the client being unable to avoid accidents. When any of these signs are observed, close monitoring is crucial. When protective incarceration is unfeasible, then enlist the client's family and other associates in the monitoring process.*

Failure to Refer to Other Professionals

An important component of the ethical treatment of clients is to provide whatever services are needed and to refer to other appropriate professionals whenever the needs are outside the worker's expertise. The referral should be made to a reputable professional who is properly trained to provide the service needed. Malpractice litigation often occurs when a worker fails to see the need for referral, or if referrals turn out to be harmful to clients.

In the exercise of reasonable care, the professional standard is well established. Social workers must tell their clients whenever they know (or should have known) that their forms of treatment will not or might not be effective, and that more effective treatments are available than the workers are trained to offer. The referral procedures that are common in the community, or similar communities, weigh heavily in this standard. That is, if the client lives in a small rural area, a consultation with the local family physician may be acceptable, whereas in a large metropolitan area it would only be acceptable to refer to a highly trained specialist or special treatment facility.

For example, if a client suffers from anxiety or depression, the therapist must nowadays consider medication first. It may be recommended as the sole method of treatment for the anxiety, or in connection with psychotherapy. Only after it has proved unsatisfactory, then the longer, drawn-out form of insight therapy or behavioral modification techniques alone may be used. This means that physicians must be consulted for this condition, because they are the professionals responsible for prescribing medications.

From a legal perspective, the nonmedical psychotherapist working with a client who has emotional problems should consider psychiatric consultation—especially when a question arises about which type of treatment to use. If the treatment later proves inadequate and harmful to the client, the worker could be liable to malpractice claims; if however, the treatment plan has been affirmed by a medical expert, the legal action would usually not get as far.

If a social worker treats a client who requires medical care in collaboration with the therapy, the worker must be careful not to encroach on the physician's activity. One case illustrates how this is so. In 1990 a social worker was found criminally guilty for dispensing medicine (Valentine, 1990). The worker shared offices with a psychiatrist and helped with the psychiatrist's patients. Often after an initial visit by the physician, the worker would virtually take over the case, writing prescription renewals and ordering medical tests in the name of the physician. Both the worker and physician lost their licenses, were placed on probation, were professionally sanctioned, and had to pay heavy fines for their actions.

The relevant standard of care and defensive practice is well established: *Social workers should know and stay within their professional limitation. They should refer their clients appropriately for any needs that go beyond those limits.*

Premature Termination

Ending the treatment relationship is also a source of potential malpractice liability. If the worker requires the client to stop, even though the need for help continues, the worker may be responsible for subsequent harm to the client. Workers sometimes discharge clients who still need help because the clients' funds or insurance coverages have been exhausted. This is unethical and illegal in most jurisdictions. An orderly and professionally prescribed process must occur by which the client discontinues therapy. If need continues, and the client is adhering to the treatment plan, the worker must continue or at least facilitate a suitable referral.

The professional standard of care indicates that treatment must continue until one of three conditions exist: both therapist and client agree to end it; the client explicitly and unilaterally decides to conclude; or the therapist decides to conclude because the client no longer needs service. Therapy ends only when one of these conditions is met, but some documentation must demonstrate that such is the case. When written contracts have been utilized at the beginning of the therapeutic relationship, termination processes may be expedited. In any termination it is wise to put the decision in writing, with a summary letter or a termination of treatment notice.

Sometimes the client forms a transference-based attachment to the therapist, or the therapist feels attached to the client through countertransference. These feelings may cause the treatment to extend beyond the point at which treatment is still productive. If the client wants to continue because of the attachment, but is not in need, the worker must use care to terminate without making the client feel rejected or personally abandoned. Sometimes if the treatment seems no longer productive, the worker should acknowledge the fact and refer the client to another professional for treatment or a "second opinion" consultation.

Some workers recognize that their clients do not need continued therapy but continue seeing them to collect fees. Some therapists collect reimbursement fees from insurance companies for services supposedly rendered after the client has stopped the sessions. Of course these are also unethical and illegal practices and violators have been jailed as well as banished from their professions.

The standard of care and defensive strategy regarding termination are the same: *Discontinue treatment only after needs have been met or the client has been appropriately referred.*

Treatment Without Informed Consent

Almost from its beginning, social work has embraced one of its major guiding principles, that of client self-determination. The principle means that it is the client who is the boss in the therapeutic relationship, the one who specifies what the goals are and what will be the means used to reach them. Even when the service is mandated or involuntary the client is entitled to refuse the service or obtain it from someone else (Regehr and Antle, 1997).

If a worker adheres to the principle of client self-determination, there is little risk of malpractice over the consent issue. By voluntarily entering therapy, one is consenting. By participating involuntarily, in order to receive specified benefits such as early parole or permission to resume driving privileges, one is consenting too. If the client is a minor or judged legally incompetent because of mental illness or other incapacity, consent is given by the parent or guardian.

Potential malpractice difficulty does not usually come from the "consent" part of the principle, but from the "informed" part. The client must possess enough knowledge about the relationship in order to agree to undertake it. In some circumstances it might be reasonable to assume that it is the client's responsibility to learn this information before entering therapy, but malpractice juries might well think differently. The prudent worker does not just assume that the client has the knowledge needed for informed consent; the worker provides it.

Some of the more common failures to obtain informed consent that are related to malpractice damages, occur in the following circumstances:

- The client is harmed in the treatment process, after not being properly informed about the methods to be used.
- The worker had not told the client of all the possible risks or dangers that might occur in the treatment.
- The worker did not warn the client about the limits of confidentiality and is then compelled by law to disclose some information to authorities that was revealed in the interviews.
- The client entered the therapeutic relationship without being told of the available alternatives.
- The client entered therapy expecting that positive results would be certain to occur in a very short time at a minimum of cost.
- The client entered therapy but was not literate enough or could not understand the worker's language enough to consent.

- The worker did not disclose his or her own profession, educational background, experience, or credentials.
- The client assumes that the social worker has certain expertise that the worker does not actually possess.

Most workers, most of the time, want to give their clients all the information necessary to make the relationship productive. But sometimes this essential step is ignored, taken for granted, or simply forgotten. Professionals often assume that their clients are more informed than is actually the case. This is particularly true for social workers, whose image remains somewhat murky, and whose methods are not always well known, even to the most informed and intelligent people. A notable recent example of this is seen in the remarks made by Supreme Court Justice Antonin Scalia in his dissenting opinion in the *Jaffee vs. Redmond* case. In attacking social work's claim to being able to provide psychotherapy services, Scalia (1996, p. 5) wrote "It is not clear that the degree in social work requires *any* training in psychotherapy." He went on to state, "I am not even sure there is a nationally accepted definition of 'social worker' as there is of psychiatrist or psychologist."

The social worker is obliged and cautioned to provide ample information to the client before and during the therapy process. It is advisable to put in writing, perhaps in the form of a written contract or letter of agreement, the facts that clients need to know. There should be proof that the client was told of the risks, the alternatives, and the background of the worker. There should also be proof that no assurances, guarantees, or claims about the treatment outcome was expressed or implied.

Failure to advise clients of the risks or dangers that might occur in their treatment is the most serious malpractice issue in informed consent. There are some risks in any treatment and, of course, the client has the right to know this. If adverse effects subsequently occur, and if the client had not been warned of the possibility, a court could rule against the therapist. So the standard in this instance is as follows: *Before therapy begins, provide the client (or the client's legal guardians) with adequate written information about the course of treatment proposed, possible alternatives, and risks or dangers each treatment may pose.*

Failure to Warn

Social workers and all other mental health professionals face a dilemma. Generally, they are required to respect client confidentiality. But the law also requires them to protect the public if the client constitutes a danger. Malpractice claims are increasingly made against social workers who have failed to warn either the public or intended victims when their clients have indicated their dangerousness. The decision made by the Supreme Court of California in the *Tarasoff vs. Regents of the University of California* (1976) case presents one horn of this dilemma. The effect of this decision is to require therapists to warn those who are threatened by their clients. However, the duty of confidentiality and the solid justification for it forms the other horn of the dilemma.

Malpractice claims have been upheld against social workers who failed to warn intended victims. But so too have claims succeeded when social workers have issued such warnings and the client has not subsequently harmed anyone. Charges of defamation as well as breach of confidentiality are then made. The fundamental conflict between two contradictory ideals, and a resolution of that conflict is the focus of the next chapter.

Chapter 6

When Laws and Ethics Collide

A Chinese proverb says, "Whether a stone hits a jar, or a jar hits a stone, it is the jar that is broken." So, too, when the law and a professional's ethics are in conflict—it is the ethical position that inevitably succumbs.

For the most part, such collisions should not occur. In an ideal world professional ethics should not be contrary to the laws of the jurisdiction in which the profession is practiced. Law exists for the maintenance of society and protection of its citizens. As such, law has precedence over the rules, codes, or statutes of self-regulating groups within that society. When considered as an abstract generality, this view seems unquestionable. And, in fact, most ethical principles held by a profession are consistent with the relevant laws. The most glaring exception, however, is that of the principle of confidentiality.

The legal versus professional debate about confidentiality has raged on for decades, especially as it pertains to social workers. Every attempt to find a clear and satisfactory resolution has failed. These efforts have included changes in professional codes of ethics, establishing and revising state licensing statutes, and successful lawsuits against social workers both for revealing confidences and for not revealing confidences.

Even the U.S. Supreme Court has debated about social work confidentiality. In the 1996 *Jaffee vs. Redmond* case, the Supreme Court ruled that there were confidentiality privileges between social workers and their psychotherapy clients; however, their ruling included many qualifications, exceptions, and unanswered questions. Many laws remained that required social workers to reveal confidences in certain situations. Many laws remained contradictory. Most social workers knew they still could not assure clients that the law protected their clients' confidentiality. Thus, even though social work's confidentiality principle has become a broken jar, the legal rock with which it keeps colliding seems to be developing a few cracks.

THE LIMITS OF CONFIDENTIALITY

From the days of its creation until the 1970s, social work held that its principle of confidentiality was the cornerstone of the therapeutic relationship. In one of social work's first textbooks, Mary Richmond wrote, "In the whole range of professional contacts there is no more confidential relation than that which exists between the social worker and the person or family receiving treatment" (Richmond, 1922, p. 29).

Professional practice wisdom taught that effective therapy could never occur if the client feared disclosure. It was considered unethical for social workers to reveal what a client said in the therapeutic interview. Violators of this principle were sanctioned by the profession and subject to legal action as well. Clients were reassured that they could say anything without fear of adverse consequences.

However, changes in the law in the past twenty years have dramatically altered the principle of confidentiality. Some professions, more than others, have been affected. While clergy and lawyers could still assure their clients that they would not (and could not be required to) reveal their confidential communications, professionals in mental health had to become more equivocal. Laws were written to compel social workers and other professionals to report suspected child abuse, neglect, and threats by clients to harm others.

Accordingly, the Codes of Ethics of social work and the other helping professions had to be revised frequently, to remain consistent with the new laws. For example, the first NASW Code of Ethics, adopted in 1960, stressed that worker-client confidentiality was paramount. In the next revision in 1979, a short list of exceptions to the principle of confidentiality was included. Ten years later, the Codes were again revised, with a longer list of exceptions, and it deleted a declaration that confidences were to be maintained. This new version stated, "The social worker should share with others confidences revealed by clients, without their consent, only for compelling professional reasons" (NASW Code of Ethics, 1989).

The most recent revision of the NASW Code of Ethics presents an even longer list of exceptions, including this statement: "In all instances, social workers should disclose the least amount of confidential information necessary to achieve the desired purpose; only information that is relevant to the purpose for which the disclosure is made should be revealed" (NASW Code of Ethics, 1996).

The absolute confidentiality principle had to go. Its demise was brought about by many factors, but the two most critical ones were the new child abuse laws and the *Tarasoff* decision.

CHILD ABUSE AND NEGLECT LAWS

By the 1960s Americans were starting to realize that its society faced a hidden epidemic. Millions of adults were revealing that they had been abused and neglected as children and that nothing had been done to protect them. It was clear that similar or worse circumstances faced contemporary children, and that the people who should know about it were not doing enough to help or prevent the problem. The public demanded a change.

As a result, a series of state and federal laws were enacted in the 1960s and 1970s, culminating in the federal Children's Justice and Assistance Act, effective October 1, 1986 (Saltzman, 1986). These laws, which are still on the books, generally require social workers, teachers, physicians, and other professionals to report suspected cases of child abuse or neglect to designated authorities. Criminal and civil liability could be imposed on those failing to comply.

Workers who observe or infer from indirect signs that the child is being abused or neglected are required to notify law enforcement authorities promptly. The grounds for reporting suspected child abuse or neglect, as summarized by Besharov (1998), are as follows: Direct evidence, such as (a) eyewitness observations of a caregiver's abuse or neglect, (b) finding the child in physically dangerous circumstances, (c) the child or caregiver's own descriptions of such behavior, (d) demonstrated inability by the parent to care for a newborn, and (e) disabilities by guardians that are so severe that they are not likely to be able to provide needed care.

Indirect or circumstantial evidence, according to Besharov, includes such concerns as (1) suspicious injuries suggesting abuse, (2) supposedly accidental injuries that show gross inattention to the child's safety needs, (3) injuries or medical findings suggesting sexual abuse, (4) signs of severe physical deprivation, (5) extremely dirty and unkempt home, (6) untreated injuries, illnesses, or impairments, (7) unexplained absences from school, (8) apparent caregiver indifference to the child's severe emotional or developmental problems, suggesting emotional maltreatment, (9) indifference or approval by the caregiver of the child's misbehavior, and (10) abandoned children.

To help bring professional standards into compliance with child abuse legislation, the National Association of Social Workers issued its standards for social work practice in child protection in 1981. Standard 38 states: "The Social Worker Shall Comply with Child Abuse and Neglect Reporting Laws and Procedures: It is the responsibility of every social worker to obtain knowledge of the state's child abuse and neglect laws and procedures, and to share this knowledge with employers and colleagues. In addition, whenever it is necessary to report a case of suspected child abuse or neglect, the social worker shall collaborate with the local office of Child Protective Services as appropriate, shall explain the report and the CPS process to family members" (NASW, 1981, p. 2).

The laws and professional guidelines probably saved many children from abuse and neglect. Many abusive or neglectful family members were apprehended and punished or treated. Many people who would have been neglectful or abusive refrained because of the knowledge that their children's teachers and doctors and social workers were watching and were required to turn in any offenders.

But, while the laws were good for many children, they were problematic for many professionals. Some examples:

- A teacher found severe bruises on a child's neck and throat and, not believing the child's story that he had been playing a literal version of "hangman" with a friend, notified the authorities. The parents were arrested before the friend came forth to admit his complicity. The parents successfully sued the teacher and the school.

- A doctor treated a ten-year-old girl who had a venereal disease. She claimed she had been with neighborhood boys and begged the doctor not to tell her mother. He successfully completed the treatment and complied with her request. But later the mother found about the girl's disease, treatment, and the fact that it had been caused by the girl's stepfather.

Many legal and professional conflicts followed the institution of child abuse-neglect laws and professional guidelines. Workers who have reported their suspicions that subsequently could not be legally substantiated have been fired, demoted, sued, and tried in criminal courts (Besharov, 1998). So, too, have been workers who failed to report abusive situations even though they may have had no way of knowing that actual abuse had taken place.

"DUTY TO WARN" LAWS

The law also requires social workers to disclose confidences when their clients reveal intent to harm others physically. Court decisions or statutes in many states compel mental health professionals to report such findings to authorities and/or intended victims. Professionals claim there is too little provision in the law to protect workers if they report such information and no harm actually ensues. Professionals have been successfully sued and fired for making such assertions.

In recent years the conflict has become even more confusing for mental health practitioners. Increasingly, courts are ruling that when clients disclose to their therapists any motivations to harm others, even when the others are not specific individuals, the notifications must be made. For example, in one recent case, a client revealed to the therapist that he had urges to sexually assault young boys. Eventually, he assaulted a boy (whose identity was never discussed . or even known during the sessions). The boy's family sued the therapist and received a large sum in settlement.

If juries are going to make such decisions in the future, therapists will be in an impossible dilemma. If their clients reveal thoughts of harming people in general, or certain kinds of people, who do the therapists warn? They would have to guarantee that their clients are not a threat to society or to the specific group; if they could not make such a guarantee, they would be expected to confine the clients until a guarantee could be made (Grinfeld, 1998).

A fundamental premise of psychotherapy is that the client verbalizes thoughts and emotions to understand them better. By doing so the client gains control over impulses that might otherwise be overwhelming. So the client comes to feel trust in the therapist and feels free to disclose all thoughts, no matter how strange or socially unacceptable they might seem.

By no means is it unusual for clients to fantasize about wanting to harm others, or cathartically to dissipate anger by describing feelings rather than acting upon them. However, when social workers are forced by law to reveal such verbalizations, such thoughts are far less likely to be expressed. If the feelings are felt, but not expressed and worked through, or if the client avoids therapy because of the fear of disclosure, the problem remains. Clients, both potential and actual, as well as therapists and society, may be at greater risk since "duty to warn" laws have been instituted.

THE TARASOFF CASE

Understanding how such laws came to be made requires a review of the case that started the "duty to warn" laws. The now famous *Tarasoff* decision was authored by the Supreme Court of California in July 1976. A University of California student named Tatiana Tarasoff decided to stop seeing another student she had been dating. The young man was so disturbed about her decision he entered therapy at the University Counseling Center. In the next few weeks, he told his therapist of his anger about Tatiana's rejection and of his growing urge to get even. Eventually, he told the therapist he planned to kill her.

Many questions ran through the therapist's mind. How serious was the threat? Most clients make angry statements in therapy at some time or other. If this was a serious threat, what could be done with the young man? Commitment or imprisonment were unlikely solutions. The young man was not psychotic, and no crime had yet been committed. Police usually tell people who are threatened that they really cannot do anything until an actual crime has occurred.

Even if arrested, the young man could not be held indefinitely. And after being released, would he ever want to see a therapist for help again? Should Tatiana and her family be warned? If nothing could be done anyway, it might be needlessly upsetting to them. If they are warned and nothing happens, would the therapist be liable for defamation?

After discussing the situation with the supervisor, the therapist decided that confidentiality was less important than a person's potential safety. The campus police were notified and they picked up the young man. They interrogated him about his relationship with Tatiana and of his stated plans for murder.

The young man minimized his threats. Yes, he said, he had been upset in the clinic. Sure, he told his therapist he was angry enough to kill Tatiana, but he was just letting off steam as the therapist told him to do. He was convincing and the police released him. A short time later, he carried out his threat and murdered Tatiana.

The parents brought legal actions against those involved in the case, including the therapist and the supervisor, their employer, and the University of California. They wanted to know why the police had been warned, but not the family. They believed that if they had known of the danger, they could have taken preventive measures and their daughter would still be alive. After many trials and reversed decisions, the case reached the state Supreme Court.

Ultimately, the judges decided that the therapist's actions were improper. It was not enough, they concluded, that the therapist had notified the supervisor and authorities and even attempted to have the student incarcerated. Because he and other university officials had reason to believe the client was at large and dangerous, the "failure to warn Tatiana or others likely to apprise her of the danger constituted a breach of the therapist's duty to exercise reasonable care to protect Tatiana" (*Tarasoff vs. Regents,* 1976, p. 2d).

Implications of the **Tarasoff** *Rulings*

Social workers and other mental health professionals across the nation were confused about the decision and its obvious consequences (Slovenko, 1995). It meant that henceforth therapists had to notify others, usually including people they had never met, that a client seemed likely to do them harm.

This became the law in California and eventually in most other states. The ruling was authored by the highly respected Judge Roger Traynor. Judge Traynor's influence with other judges and lawmakers was so great that his opinions tended to be adopted by his colleagues. Judges throughout the nation have used the *Tarasoff* decision as precedent in reaching similar conclusions.

These rulings have been applied to everyone who provides direct counseling or psychotherapy in all settings, whether institutional or private. This includes psychiatrists, psychologists, social workers, pastoral counselors, marital therapists, probation officers, and many others, and their supervisors as well. It also includes physicians, nurses, and other helping professionals who are not necessarily providing psychotherapy (Cooper, 1995). Supervisors who advise against such disclosures may share the liability even though supervisor liability does not absolve the direct practitioner from responsibility.

The *Tarasoff* decision is now a major influence in the way counseling and psychotherapy takes place in the United States. Obviously, when clients are told that what they say may be reported to authorities, they are going to be cautious about their words, but not necessarily their deeds. Yet therapists must tell every client at the beginning of therapy of the limits of confidentiality.

If therapy is undertaken and the therapist does not make the client aware of these limits, the therapist has failed to procure informed consent to treatment. And, as discussed earlier, failure to procure informed consent is a common and serious form of malpractice.

Confusion and Contradictions

Even when clients are informed about these issues, many uncertainties face the worker. The requirements and criteria for reporting are unclear and often inconsistent (Kopels and Kagle, 1993). Their purpose is ultimately to protect society and some of its more vulnerable members. However, unless the criteria for reporting are clear, protection is not certain and may even be impeded.

The confusion results in many questions: How should the intended victim be warned in such a way that it is not so alarming that the resulting upset itself constitutes a danger? How does the worker fulfill the ethical obligation to help the client through to termination after such disclosures have been made? What does the worker do if the client continues in therapy after disclosures and makes threats against other people too? If the disclosure results in incarceration for the client, what are the criteria for the client's eventual release? How long after the incarceration period will the client be considered dangerous? What are the criteria of dangerousness? Why should physical harm be the only threat that should result in disclosure? What protection does the law provide for workers against defamation actions when such disclosures have been made and proven to be unfounded? What should supervisors do when their workers report these concerns? If clients later deny they made threats in the worker's office, how far should the worker go to pursue the issue thereafter? Are Constitutional prohibitions against self-incrimination relevant? Can a client be confined indefinitely after making such assertions, when no crime has been committed?

RATIONALE OF JUDGES AND LEGAL OFFICIALS

Even though the requirements to disclose are troublesome and confusing for workers, judges and legal authorities have arrived at their decisions for good reasons (Gothard, 1989a). Judges always make their decisions after the fact, after someone has been harmed. Moreover, they assume the worker is competent enough to know when a person actually is dangerous to others. And they see the professional's responsibility as including helping to maintain the social order.

Judges and lawyers assume that specific harm could have been prevented if the therapist's knowledge had been shared. After someone has been victimized by a therapist's client, it seems just to reasonable and socially compassionate people that the victim should have been protected. Failure to do everything possible to protect the vulnerable person naturally seems irresponsible to social workers; to judges, and to victim's families; it also seems to constitute fault. Unfortunately for the worker, however, there is no certainty that a dangerous situation exists before the crime has actually been committed. The worker does not necessarily have knowledge that harm will take place, but only that the client has expressed such thoughts (Slovenko, 1995).

When judges rule that social workers should have warned intended victims when danger seems imminent, judges are assuming that workers can make such predictions accurately (Otto, 1994). Perhaps judges and others ascribe such prescient powers to therapists because of the effective public relations campaigns that therapists have conducted in the past decades to certify their worth. However, many studies show that therapists have no particular abilities to predict client behavior. Some studies have even indicated that therapists' predictions about dangerousness are more often wrong than right (Otto, 1994).

The major collision of law and professional ethics occurs when judges view therapists as having a social control function (Gambrill and Pruger, 1997). Representing society and the justice system, judges must be attuned to the rights of all citizens to be protected from individuals who intend to do them harm. Social workers and other therapists, on the other hand, tend to be oriented to helping the individual client to overcome current problems. Therapists see their primary purpose as helping their clients so they will not want to harm others. Perhaps too readily social workers want to achieve this with the client independently of the controls legal and social systems impose. Whatever they may want, therapists must recognize that the social control function is an important and inescapable part of their responsibilities.

GUIDELINES FOR COPING

In conferences about the collision between legal and ethical responsibilities, social workers invariably ask for specific and practical guidelines for resolving these issues. They are usually unhappy to learn that the decision about how to respond to such problems is left to them. Every case is unique; it must be dealt with on an ad hoc basis. What a professional person is supposed to do with a possibly dangerous client before a crime occurs is different from what a professional should have done after the crime occurs. A professional person must make professional judgments rather than follow clearly detailed sets of prescriptions.

Nevertheless, the professional can take some precautions and actions. First is that workers must inform all their clients about the limits of confidentiality in order to remain free of "informed consent" liabilities. The client should be told at the outset that in cases of suspected child abuse or danger to others it will be necessary to inform authorities. This is best done in writing.

If then, during the interviews the client strongly indicates an intent physically to harm someone, the worker must warn the client of the consequences. Inasmuch as there will be far more times that a client makes a threat than actually carries one out, the worker cannot immediately issue warnings. But if the client persists in such remarks, the worker should try to get the client to communicate the threat to the intended victim. Letters or phone calls made in the presence of the worker can help fulfill this responsibility.

If the worker believes that the client is not actually dangerous, but wants to minimize the probabilities of any problems without issuing warnings, considerable caution is in order. For example, the advice might be for the client to look at the grievances more objectively, and to get away from the other person for a cooling off period. Getting rid of any lethal weapons is imperative. Sometimes procuring the client's consent to attend a meeting with the other party in the therapist's office is a possibility. Any other therapeutic actions that can help the client look at the other person in a less threatening manner should also be taken.

IMPLEMENTING THE ACTUAL WARNING

If, however, such therapeutic activity does not have the desired effect, and if the worker is convinced that the client continues to be serious about the intent to harm someone, some systematic procedures for issuing the warning must be taken. Ideally, the disclosure should be made generally with as much input from the client as possible. If the client cannot or will not inform the other party about such feelings, then the therapist must do so. It must be done fairly promptly too, because some judgments have found professionals liable for not making the notification early enough.

To whom should the therapist make the disclosure? This varies from one jurisdiction to another. Social workers should first notify any of their own supervisors or employers. Then, in most cases, the appropriate division within the local police department and the office of the relevant county prosecuting attorney should be called. If the case involves suspected child abuse or neglect, the professional should also contact the local office of Children's Protective Services (or equivalent name in some jurisdictions).

To these authorities the worker simply says something like, "I'm a licensed social worker in your jurisdiction. I'm working with a client who has said (s)he intends to harm someone. The law in this state says I must report this to you and I told the client a few minutes ago that I am going to do this." The authorities receiving such a call will ask questions at this point, all of which should be answered completely and truthfully. The worker should then be available to the authorities at a moment's notice.

Whether or not the notification was tape recorded, the worker should immediately write notes describing what was said to whom. The names of those authorities receiving the call should also be listed. If the authorities misplace this notification, the case could be treated as though notification was never made. After writing these notes the worker should contact the local professional association and/or office of professional licensing.

Unless the worker has reason to fear physical harm from the client, maintaining continued therapeutic contact can be worthwhile. Continued contact enables the therapy to continue; hopefully, this can eliminate the impulse that led to the threats or otherwise resolve the problem. If the client is held by the authorities for questioning and arrested, the worker can do whatever is possible to see the client and maintain some therapeutic alliance.

Eventually, through this unpleasant ordeal, the intended victims will be apprised of the situation. It is better when the warning comes from the legal authorities than the worker. However, the people warned are then likely to contact the workers for further information. The client may also seek contact with the worker. The worker should not try to avoid the client or the other party; nor should the worker avoid the questions that will naturally be asked. However, these questions should be courteously referred to the authorities. The worker should be sympathetic with the intended victim but should not attempt to provide therapy.

If the social worker ascertains that the intended victim is in need of therapy, the worker may make a referral to another qualified professional. If the worker became the intended victim's therapist, the original client could feel even more betrayed and angry than ever. The client could feel there is collusion between the worker and the other party and could then easily transfer the feelings and intention to do harm to the worker. Workers in such situations have been endangered and harmed.

JAFFEE VS. REDMOND

On June 27, 1991, police officer Mary Lu Redmond responded to a call for police assistance about a fight in progress. As she arrived on the scene she saw several men running. One of these men, she claimed, was chasing another with a butcher knife. When he ignored her order to stop and drop the weapon, she shot him dead. Some witnesses disputed her version, claiming the man was unarmed and that Officer Redmond had drawn her gun before leaving her car. However, everyone agreed that before police backup arrived, a large group had formed and a threatening confrontation ensued between her and the crowd.

After the confrontation, Officer Redmond began therapy sessions with Karen Beyer, a licensed clinical social worker employed by the community. Meanwhile, the administrator for the dead man's estate, Carrie Jaffee, filed suit and sought damages, alleging that Officer Redmond had violated the man's rights, used excessive force, and caused his wrongful death. During the discovery process the petitioners learned that Officer Redmond and the social worker had had over fifty counseling sessions. The petitioners demanded the worker's therapy notes for use in their cross-examination. On the grounds of psychotherapist privilege, Beyer and Redmond refused to release the notes, even after being ordered to do so by the judge.

At the end of the trial, the judge told the jury that the social worker had no legal justification for concealing the notes; the jury could thereby conclude that this record would have been unfavorable to Redmond's case. The jury ruled in favor of Jaffee and a large award was granted to the estate.

The outcome was reversed on appeal. The appeals court concluded that the trial court had erred by refusing to protect the confidential communications between the social worker and her client.

The court pointed out that the state law extended the privilege of confidentiality to social workers; federal decisions that had rejected the confidentiality privilege for social workers were outdated. The appeals court also added that the confidentiality privilege would not apply if the need for evidence in the interests of justice outweighed the patient's privacy interests.

The United States Supreme Court heard the case and in a 7-2 decision issued on June 13, 1996, upheld the appeals court ruling. Justice Stevens, writing for the majority, stated that the federal privilege of confidentiality for licensed psychiatrists and psychologists "should also extend to licensed social workers in the course of psychotherapy." He added that because social workers provide a significant amount of mental health treatment, especially to the poor and those of modest means, there is no discernible purpose to having different confidentiality rules for them than for the more expensive psychiatrists and psychologists. The Supreme Court ruling also overruled the appeals court finding limiting the confidentiality privilege if the patient's privacy interests were outweighed by the need for evidence (Supreme Court of the United States, 1996).

Implications of Jaffee vs. Redmond

Social workers and members of many other disciplines were elated over the finding. It was the first reversal of a twenty-year-long trend in courtrooms that gradually eroded rights to privacy in therapeutic relationships. It came about as a result of a brave act by a conscientious social worker. Karen Beyer could have obeyed the court and disclosed the information in her memory and her records, and the matter would probably have been forgotten. If she disobeyed the judge she could have been incarcerated, had her license revoked, and lost her career. But for her to comply with the judge's order she would have had to harm her client and violate her own professional code of ethics and personal integrity. Because she thought the judge was wrong, she placed the good of her client over her own professional and personal well-being. It was, in effect, an act of civil disobedience (Brody, 1999).

Unfortunately, it did not resolve all the issues relevant to client-therapist confidentiality. Explicitly stated in Justice Steven's majority opinion were several qualifications which clearly limit the degree and quality of confidentiality. For example, the "duty to warn" laws remain in effect. If a client tells the worker of an intention to harm another person, the therapist is still required to notify the appropriate authorities. The ruling also excludes confidentiality when the client reveals to the therapist acts or inclinations toward child neglect or abuse. (These kinds of limitations on confidentiality no longer constitute a conflict with the social worker's code of ethics; however, as the latest Codes of NASW, CSWE, and ABE all state, the worker must fulfill this duty regardless of wishes to maintain confidentiality.)

Another unresolved issue is whether all communications with social workers are privileged, or only those which occur in therapy relationships. As Justice Stevens pointed out, many social workers are engaged in activities other than clinical counseling. The intent of this ruling is not to grant such privileges for all social work activities, but only for those in the clinical setting. The ruling was also intended to apply only to licensed professionals. Because some state laws regulating professional counselors are no more than mere registration, those who practice in those states may not have the confidentiality privilege, should the issue come up in that state.

Because some confidentiality issues remain unclear or unresolved in the *Jaffee vs. Redmond* decision, it seems a certainty that further arguments will be heard in the appeals courts and possibly the Supreme Court (Silver, 1998). Supreme Court Justice Scalia pointed out some of these issues in his dissenting opinion in the *Jaffee* ruling. The current ruling, he declared, confers the confidentiality privilege, not only to licensed clinical social workers, but to all social workers, to nurses, and indeed to "any other person not prohibited by law from providing mental health or developmental disabilities services or from holding himself out as a therapist if the recipient reasonably believes that such person is permitted to do so" (Scalia, 1996, p. 8). Another problem, he said, was that the majority ruling used state social work licensing laws as the arbiter of the extent of confidentiality. Inasmuch as there is wide variation in state licensing laws as to any restrictions on the confidentiality privilege, the Supreme Court's decision is meaningless.

This Scalia dissent may have influenced social work licensing boards of several states. Those states which have had confusing or weak provisions in the confidentiality provisions for workers have been in the process of strengthening them. It is anticipated that there will be much greater consistency in the state licensing laws for social workers, partly as a result of this opinion.

Whether the *Jaffee* decision signals a new trend toward extending social work confidentiality privileges, or merely signals more confusion for the profession, remains to be seen. What is certain is that there will continue to be conflicting political and social pressures on social workers and others who provide psychotherapy services and that all practitioners will do well to keep knowledgeable and cautious in their practices.

CONCLUSION

Social workers and other mental health professionals, without benefit of hindsight or powers of prediction, frequently must make judgments about potentially and actually dangerous clients. No single response can be best for all circumstances of these types. Social workers will always have to make decisions using their best professional judgment for each unique circumstance.

So many variables in clients' personalities and circumstances exist, and differing legal interpretations compound the problem so as to preclude hard and fast prescriptions for dealing with these situations. Until the courts clarify and make their interpretations more consistent, social workers and other therapists will remain uncertain about their legal and ethical obligations.

Chapter 7

Preparing for Litigation

Because litigation is increasingly probable for social workers, as it is for all members of modern American society, some advanced preparation and defensive strategies need to be taken (Lifson and Simon, 1998). As the odds increase that the worker will be named in a malpractice suit, or called to court to testify against or in behalf of clients and colleagues, the prudent social worker will know how to minimize the consequences, if not avoid them altogether.

Everyone wants to avoid litigation, knowing that trials and legal conflicts will be time consuming, professionally risky, and probably costly. Even winning a malpractice case will probably result in the loss of money, prestige, time, and emotional security. And the idea of losing is so horrendous it can hardly be contemplated. But the incessant risk of litigation requires thoughtful social workers to address the possibility and develop plans to deal with it effectively. Chapters 5 and 6 discussed what the risks are; this chapter will discuss the steps that could be taken to enable the social worker to survive and grow.

RECOGNIZING A POTENTIAL LEGAL HAZARD

The first step, of course, to be taken by a prudent social worker is to be alert to those situations that carry some risk of legal dispute. This in itself is often more difficult than it might seem. Professionals have almost always become involved in their legal situations before they are aware of the seriousness of their circumstances. The case of Mrs. W. illustrates.

Mrs. W., a twenty-seven-year-old social worker with four years professional experience in a family service agency, was asked to testify before a grand jury. She had recently concluded treatment with the

C. family because of their failure to keep appointments. The worker had noted that Mr. C. had a violent temper and was abusive to his wife and their eight-year-old child. On numerous occasions he had "spanked" the child so severely that medical care was needed.

On three occasions, the mother fled with the child to an emergency shelter. However, the family kept returning to their home. As the worker's notes indicated, the mother had symptoms of "learned helplessness," "masochistic tendencies," and "codependency" with her husband and his problems; the worker wrote that the mother's emotional problems led her to return repeatedly to her husband despite his behavior. The worker's diagnosis of Mr. C. was "explosive personality" and "paranoid personality disorder."

Two months after the worker's last session with the C.s, their child died. It happened in a hospital, but was the result of internal bleeding and organ damage. In the investigation the parents both agreed he had fallen out of a tree and that they had taken him to the hospital immediately. The autopsy showed that the death was not caused by a fall but by various blows that had occurred a few days before the hospital admission.

The grand jury tried to determine if the father and mother should be tried for the death. Mrs. W. was one of their witnesses. Under oath, the social worker said she believed the father had been dangerous to the mother and child and that she was trying to treat him for the condition; she indicated that the mother seemed to condone his behavior. The worker was then asked what she herself had done to notify the authorities about the danger. She said she discussed the matter with the physician who had treated the child for prior injuries; the physician said he had called Child Protective Services so there was no need for her to do likewise. There was no record of anyone having called CPS or any other authorities.

Before long, the worker found herself answering more questions about her own conduct in the case than she was answering about the C. family. Had she told her supervisors at the agency about how dangerous the client was? Had she told the doctor about what she had learned about both parents? Had she called any authorities? Had she followed up with the doctor to see if CPS was pursuing the case? Why did she not call CPS herself? Had she told Mrs. C. or the child where they could go or what they could do to avoid further risk? Had she terminated their treatment when they still needed help? Did she tell the doctor or any authorities that she had terminated with them?

The questions continued until it dawned on Mrs. W. that she, too, had now become a subject of the investigation. She had answered many questions, on record under oath, without legal counsel before she realized she would be charged with a crime—that of failing to protect the child in grave peril as prescribed by law. Later, her attorney said her statements before the grand jury made her defense much more difficult. Eventually she was convicted. The father, who later admitted abusing the child, was found not guilty by reason of insanity.

Had Mrs. W. known more about how to recognize her legal jeopardy early on, she might have experienced a happier outcome. Her situation illustrates how easy it is to become enmeshed in law actions even though apparently acting ethically and lawfully; she did not recognize in time that she was in a legal minefield.

As discussed earlier, some situations are more likely to be legally risky than others, including child custody issues, warning intended victims, involuntary commitment, and child abuse cases. Some clients are also more likely to be legally risky than others; professional therapists call them "litigious clients." They are the people who have a proclivity for bringing actions to court. Clients most likely to fit this group are those who have initiated lawsuits in the past, especially against other professionals. People who have indicated a history of financial and personal disputes with others, especially professionals, may also be in this category. People who have been diagnosed as "paranoid" or "personality disordered" also tend toward litigiousness. It must be said that litigious clients are just as much in need of professional assistance as any other, and the conscientious worker will accept them for treatment, as any other. However, work with them could be done with extra care to use the right procedures and document that such has been done.

THE EMOTIONAL RISKS OF LITIGATION

One of the risks of legal problems that receives too little attention is the stress and mental toll it exerts on workers. Testifying on behalf of plaintiffs usually leads to some emotional conflict and the stress can be intense—for the worker as well as the client (Melton et al., 1997). For social workers who are defendants in criminal or malpractice cases, the tension can be enormous. The procedure usually takes months or years from the time of initial inquiries to ultimate resolution through court decisions or settlements. Prolonged stress is never healthy.

Nevertheless, there is only so much one can do to prepare for the emotional stress of litigation. It includes gaining as much knowledge as possible, developing and maintaining a strong support system, being prepared financially to the extent possible, and procuring the best available legal counsel possible. It starts by maintaining one's physical health. A visit to one's physician and discussion of the anticipated stress is in order. This may result in a physical examination, stress-reducing medication, proper diet, and an exercise program.

Knowing about legal procedures, consequences, and possible outcomes will help reduce some stress (Anderson, 1996). The fear of ultimate disaster can be mitigated by knowing more about what the actual consequences might be (best and worst case scenarios). Understanding routine courtroom procedures and discussing the situation with others who had experienced similar situations can also help. Merely sitting in on ongoing courtroom trials can remove some of the anxiety.

Many social workers who face malpractice or other legal problems are deprived of one of the things they need most, a strong support system. They fear disclosure will result in loss of respect from colleagues, clients, and even family. So they tend to conceal their plight and even avoid others. The opposite action is healthier and more effective. Unless their lawyers advise against it, they should openly discuss the case and their rationale in it with their colleagues, friends, and family. Doing so will help them understand their own actions better and will usually help them articulate their defenses better. A group of supporters who are loyal and respectful no matter what happens will help most workers endure the most difficult of circumstances.

WHEN TO SEEK LEGAL HELP

Knowing when to consult an attorney should be thought out in advance. No social worker could hire an attorney every time a potential practice-related legal problem occurs, but one's case could be seriously weakened by waiting too long. Clearly, a lawyer should always be consulted when the worker is charged with a crime, named in a lawsuit, or contacted by a client's lawyer about the possibility of legal action. Also, it is usually advisable to seek legal representation before giving information to grand juries, prosecutors, or other law officials about any case in which the worker or worker's employing agency could become named as a defendant.

In most cases it will not be necessary to consult a lawyer whenever a client first threatens legal action (Houston-Vega, Nuehring, and Daguio, 1996). Experienced social workers recognize that threats of lawsuit are frequently made hastily and withdrawn when the intended intimidation is not forthcoming. Nor is it necessary when a worker is testifying in court as an expert witness or in court on behalf of most clients. Social workers are generally not vulnerable to legal problems as a result of their own testimony if their words are truthful and their opinions are requested in court and based on established expertise. However, if the direction of the testimony moves toward alleged wrongdoing by the worker, it is time to resist further self-disclosure and seek an attorney's advice at the first opportunity.

If the issue is professional review, rather than criminal or civil disputes in courtrooms, the need for lawyers is not so clear. The peer review process by professional associations, such as NASW and CSWF, explicitly states that lawyers may not accompany the worker into the hearing (NASW Procedures for the Adjudication of Grievances, 1994). Many state licensing boards also forbid lawyers in their hearings about the conduct of social workers. However, inasmuch as the worker may risk expulsion from professional practice, the matter may be serious enough to warrant obtaining some legal advice.

Nothing in the board procedures suggests that workers should not seek legal advice for these matters. Indeed, if the hearing could result in expulsion or probation, or if it is the result of an aggrieved client who might be considering a malpractice suit, legal counsel is a necessity. The lawyer can advise on how the worker could best present the case and show whatever mitigating factors should be considered to justify the conduct under review. The lawyer might also help the worker's argument so that it cannot lead to a malpractice action later.

There are always going to be gray areas and exceptions to whatever criteria are set out in advance. If in doubt, it is better to err on the side of caution and seek the attorney's assistance than to ignore potential problems and hope for the best. Many experienced social workers, especially those who work in highly sensitive areas such as child protection services, maintain professional relationships with lawyers so that they can have ready access whenever faced with gray-area situations. Also, most social agencies have ongoing relationships with attorneys who are consulted whenever potential legal problems occur. However, the individual worker's interest may not always be synonymous with that of the agency; seeking additional legal representation in such cases may be worth considering.

At what point in the case progression is the lawyer called upon? The goal is to get legal representation before potential risk begins to escalate, but to avoid premature haste and panic (Marine, 1998a). If there is some risk, the attorney should be called whenever the worker is asked for information that could be used in a law case. Disclosing such information should never occur without the attorney's concurrence. This point may vary according to the seriousness of the problem for the worker. The general rule is: the higher the degree of legal risk, the sooner the right lawyer should be consulted.

COSTS OF LITIGATION

Preparing for litigation also includes being ready for the economic costs that will accompany the situation. The process will be expensive for the worker, even one who is well covered by insurance. Attorney fees and costs to provide a defense are only the beginning. Less obvious costs include the inevitable losses of revenue that might be anticipated if the legal problem had not occurred. The worker usually must take considerable time away from clients or agency service which results in reduced income. It may also affect chances for advancement and pay raises, no matter what the outcome of the case.

If the worker has full insurance coverage against malpractice judgments, the costs are still painful. Premium fees for malpractice insurance may be raised. The worker is more likely to be dropped from future coverage and might have to seek coverage by independent insurance companies at far higher rates. Many policies do not include all the costs of the litigation. Policies might pay only for judgments made against the defendant-worker and not for the lawyer's fees, or vice versa. Some workers discover they are not covered if they have also been found to have engaged in sexual relations with the client or otherwise broken the law. Many insurance companies are not required to pay if they find any misrepresentation by the worker on the application. A professional would be extremely unwise to make a false statement on such an insurance form, no matter how unimportant it might seem at first.

The insurance companies that provide professional liability insurance (PLI) for social workers are competitive with other companies for the same types of coverage to different professions. Most coverages now go up to $2 million maximum per claim, and $4 million aggregate claims. Annual premiums for this coverage approach $250. It is advisable to get maximum coverage if financially feasible. Also, an important feature of some policies is the extended reporting period, or "tail" option. This option extends coverage beyond the end of the policy, for a finite time or forever. People who were the worker's clients during the time of insurance coverage continue to be reimbursable in malpractice actions. If the worker discontinues the policy, perhaps because of retirement, job change, or death, actions by former clients are still covered. Some policies limit the "tail" coverage to a few years, while others extend it for an unlimited time. It is important to obtain unlimited tail coverage, because sometimes years can elapse between the time the incident occurred and when the case goes to court.

No matter how much insurance the worker has, the costs of litigation will be onerous. Legal counsel expenses are usually quite significant (Cross, 1998). However, the seriousness of the situation is such that a worker can ill afford to do without a good lawyer or to settle for a cheap one. Retaining a good lawyer does not necessarily mean finding the most expensive one. Ultimately, the most expensive lawyer will be one who does not provide good service. The most economical lawyer will be the one who has enough knowledge, energy, time, skill, and interest in the case to pursue it efficiently. The right lawyer depends on one's realistic goals in the case (Coleman, 1997).

GOALS IN HIRING A LAWYER

Obtaining effective legal representation—the right lawyer for this particular case—is the most important single action the worker can take in such circumstances. As every case and social worker's situation is unique, so too are the experience, expertise, and resources of every attorney. The challenge for the social worker is to make the right match.

A serious self-examination about goals and expectations is an often neglected preliminary step toward employing legal assistance. Everyone facing a legal struggle has a myriad of different goals simultaneously. There are so many different possible goals, and each one might take very different techniques and attorney skills to achieve. Social workers in law cases have had goals as disparate as these: to help find the other opponent guilty of a crime; to be acquitted of a crime; to call public attention to the misbehavior of the opponent; to make the other side suffer some way; to avoid going to court at all; to get as much publicity as possible; to get as little publicity as possible; to spend as little as possible on the litigation expenses, and so on.

For example, a worker in one malpractice suit simply wants to get it settled and over with, with the smallest amount of publicity possible, and is willing to pay to achieve the goal. A worker in another malpractice suit might want vindication and possibly retribution for the humiliation of the experience, and is willing to fight long and expensively. Both are valid goals, but the attorney skills that might be best suited to achieving each goal are not the same.

Some lawyers work very effectively in low-keyed friendly encounters with their opposites and succeed at negotiating settlements that the litigants can be fairly happy with. Other lawyers simply need to be more confrontational, and these may be the ones to employ if the goal is to win at all costs.

Finding the Right Lawyer

Finding the best lawyer for the particular case should require careful planning and effort. The first step is to determine whether to employ a specialist or a generalist. A specialist will usually be more effective than a generalist who is not well versed in the relevant aspects of the issue to be adjudicated. A specialist in criminal law is essential if the worker is charged with a crime. Specialists in malpractice litigation should also be consulted for most types of potential malpractice suits.

Generally, it is better to employ a lawyer who practices in the area where the case is going to be heard rather than to retain an outsider. A lawyer who is part of a large law firm may be more expensive, but with the firm's research and other resources, the case might be handled more efficiently. However, if the lawyer in the larger firm cannot devote the attention needed to the case, or delegates much of the work to others, it might be advantageous to employ the services of a lawyer in a smaller firm. Many legal scholars advise that well-qualified but hungrier and more energetic younger lawyers may be able to do more for the worker in a malpractice suit than would the so-called "biggest and best" lawyers or firms in the area.

Once one has an idea of the type of lawyer needed, locating that person can be more focused. A list of possible lawyers should be compiled. This is done by consulting colleagues who have encountered similar situations, and by asking other lawyers who are not candidates for the job. These lawyers can be those previously known to the worker, attorneys who have provided personal legal services for the worker or the worker's clients, or lawyers with whom the worker has served in civic activities (Mierzwa, 1994).

Other names can be added to the list after checking the local bar association, lawyer referral services, the telephone yellow pages, or advertisements in the media. Lawyer advertising was once considered by well-established lawyers and law firms to be somewhat disreputable; only desperate lawyers and desperately undesirable clients would get together through such means, it was assumed. The situation has changed considerably in recent years. Now most lawyers who are willing to take on new cases advertise, in the yellow pages at least (Foonberg, 1995).

In most larger communities they are listed in the yellow pages by practice area specialty, although there is no uniform system from one community to another as to how these specialties are listed. Moreover, wide discrepancy exists among lawyers themselves as to how they define and describe their practice specialty. And, most problematic for the consumer, there is no way to know by reviewing advertisements how experienced, skilled, or ethical the lawyer is.

Somewhat more informative are the legal directories, such as the Martindale-Hubbell Law Directory, the Attorney's Register, the Directory of the Legal Profession, and local directories. The largest of these, Martindale-Hubbell lists over 800,000 lawyers and law firms throughout the world. Its full size is over twenty thick volumes, but it lists lawyers geographically by state, county, and city.

Every lawyer who wants to be included is listed alphabetically by geographic region, including the lawyer's name, date of birth, year of admission to practice, undergraduate degree, law school, and rating. Many of these same lawyers are also listed in the biographical listings section, which are paid for by the lawyer or firm. In these listings is information about the lawyer including the address of the current law firm or other place of employment and specific area of practice (of more than 600 specialties).

Martindale-Hubbell also has a rating system for each lawyer. The ratings are based on the rankings made by the other lawyers in the same community. Lawyers may also get a "V" rating in each category if they are considered very high to preeminent. These directories are available in most larger community libraries and in every law school library.

Another way to locate the right lawyer is through a lawyer referral service. Some of these are sponsored by private, profit-making firms, or organizations of lawyers. Better, for the most part, are the nonprofit bar association referral services. (They usually charge a nominal fee, under $50 or so, to help clients locate the most suitable attorney, but the money goes to worthy causes such as the bar association's legal aid system. The lawyer also pays the referral service a fee if the client retains the lawyer.)

The service helps the client make contact with the most suitable attorney, and the client is able to meet with the lawyer for an initial consultation. The lawyer is obligated to give the client at least twenty to thirty minutes and usually much more, to help determine what legal service needs, if any, exist. The attorney referral services are usually listed in the telephone yellow pages at the beginning of the "Attorneys at Law" listings; if not, a call to the local bar association will suffice.

Locating the right lawyer through the Internet is becoming a most convenient and informative procedure. Most of the law directories such as Martindale-Hubbell have all the information from their hard copies also available electronically, either directly or through the LEXIS/NEXIS system. The American Bar Association is now listing every one of its members (nearly 50 percent of all lawyers in the United States) on the Internet. Anyone who wants a lawyer through the ABA will be able to specify the kind of lawyer needed, in terms of location and practice specialty, and receive the names of those who fit the specifications.

Retaining the Lawyer

By the time the lawyer is hired, the social worker should have established that the lawyer is qualified to manage the case, is available at the time needed, has experience in similar cases, and has no potential conflicts of interest. To reach this understanding, of course, one must first present the problem. This means only the whole truth. Although it might be tempting to hide some information that might seem unflattering or unfavorable to the case, withholding any such detail is ill-advised. Unless the information presented indicates the client intends to commit a crime, the lawyer is obligated to keep everything confidential. And unlike the contradictory and confusing rulings about confidentiality that social workers have to face, no such equivocation exists in lawyer-client privilege about confidentiality. The lawyer is obliged to honor this pledge even if the worker decides to hire someone else.

During this initial presentation of the problem, it is time to discuss one's goals. Before the lawyer can discuss or even consider strategy, it is important to be clear about the goals, even if they are ignoble. It is appropriate for the lawyer to help modify or reframe these goals, or even to attempt to dissuade the client because of the impracticality of that goal. However, it is not appropriate for the lawyer to assume the role of therapist and analyze what the underlying emotional reasons are for having such motives. The social worker will have colleagues who can help with that in a much more capable way. If the lawyer disapproves of the goal, or thinks it cannot be reached, or does not wish to help achieve it for whatever reason, this is the time to make that clear and find a different lawyer.

Once the social worker and lawyer agree on the goal, the discussion about how the lawyer would attempt to handle the case is appropriate. At this point the worker can also determine how long the case will take before resolution, and how much of the work would be done by the lawyer and how much by associates. The social worker might also request references from the lawyer and ask some of those people if they were satisfied with the lawyer's handling of their cases.

If this is satisfactory, the social worker also needs to know in advance about the financial arrangement, especially whether the requirement is based on an hourly fee, a flat payment for specified services, or on some contingency fee arrangement. If the fee arrangement is "on the meter," or the hourly rate for the amount of time expended on the case, the lawyer should agree to regular (monthly or quarterly) billing that is detailed, rather than an overall summary. If the lawyer really has experience in cases similar to this one, it should be possible to get a rough estimate of the total costs. If the case is not too complicated, the estimate will be fairly close to the ultimate costs; however in malpractice cases, which can sometimes take years to resolve, the estimate may be highly conjectural. But at the very least the client can receive periodic updates about the anticipated costs as the case progresses.

The worker should only employ a lawyer who agrees to provide the following: satisfactory references, clear and acceptable fee arrangements and billing procedures, information about how the lawyer will keep the client informed as the case develops, and assurances about devoting enough time to the case to be effective.

When the agreement is made to employ the lawyer, the terms should be delineated in an engagement letter. This is accompanied by a nonreturnable retainer fee that may be paid in advance. This fee is to cover costs up to a certain point in the case before regular billing begins. Of course, the lawyer should also agree to refund any part of the retainer that is not used.

Costs can be minimized if the worker assists the lawyer in an effective way and avoids such inefficiencies as needlessly telephoning the lawyer for information about minutia or to gain more reassurance. Most lawyers who charge an hourly rate use a "minimal billing unit," most commonly one-quarter or one-tenth of an hour.

For example, if the lawyer's fee per hour is $200 and charges for a minimum one-tenth of an hour, the client would be charged $20 for a one-minute call. Law firms often bill at much higher rates for simple office services such as photocopying than is available outside, so the client can reduce costs by providing many copies of every needed document. Other efficiencies include doing most of the communicating by telephone instead of making office visits, and providing all the information requested by the lawyer in an organized fashion.

When the lawyer and social worker begin their efforts together on the case, the most effective approach is teamwork, with the lawyer serving as team leader. The social worker serves on that team with an attitude of trust, candor, and cooperativeness. This improves the likelihood that legal problems for the worker will be minimized.

TRIAL OR SETTLEMENT?

If the worker is being sued for malpractice, the preparations for courtroom action will be exhaustive and exhausting. The wait before actually going to court will seem interminable. In many cases, it will take over a year or two before getting close to a court date. The question that will loom larger with each passing month is whether or not to settle the case. Settlements are agreements between the plaintiff and defendant to make a cash payment before the case goes to trial, in exchange for dropping the suit. More cases, by far, are settled than tried, often because the risk of losing is a possibility and the cost of pursuing or defending the case becomes burdensome. Nevertheless, most professionals do not want to settle at first, unless they recognize they have done something so clearly unethical, incompetent, or criminal that settlement becomes their best option. Otherwise, most professionals will tell themselves the accusation is so unjust they will want a court decision to achieve vindication.

However, they know, or their lawyers will tell them, that their chances of achieving total vindication in court are uncertain. Even in the best case scenarios the accused professional may never be completely absolved. In the eyes of too many peers, other clients, and associates, doubt remains. Probably some people will continue to question the professional's competence and ethics, even if the court decision is favorable. The financial costs, even with a victory, will be significant, both in terms of payments to lawyers and in loss of income while proceeding in the case. If they lose the case, the consequences are much worse. The financial losses will be severe, even if the insurance company covers all the costs of the defense and the damages. The professional will still have lost income from the time away from work to deal with the case. Insurance premiums will increase; referrals probably will not.

At some point during the long wait for the trial, the idea of a settlement seems to have some merit. But then the idea is discarded. It would seem like an admission of wrongdoing and that would be an intolerable injustice! It would preclude one's chances to be publicly vindicated. And the most aggravating notion is that it would reward someone for making an unjust accusation and encourage others to do likewise.

And yet, on reflection the idea seems more appealing. Settlement would end the conflict and probably cost less, no matter what the outcome. Fewer clients, colleagues, and friends would have to know about it. It would mean not having to ask colleagues to appear in court; they would not have to defend the professional or certify that the treatment plan was not that bad. A settlement would mean there would be no painful trial and no cross-examination to face—no contemptuous lawyer poring over all one's records and asking impertinent cross-examination questions to show all the mistakes that a more capable professional would not have made.

There is, of course, no single best answer about whether to settle or go all the way. The lawyer's advice must be accorded the most consideration. The insurance company will probably also want to have some input. However, it is important to realize that the company's interests and those of the professional may not be identical. Insurance companies often prefer that the professional settles out of court; it will probably cost the insurance company less if it is over with sooner. After the case is resolved through settlement, and the payment is made, the insurance company has no further problem. The professional carries the hurt and angry feelings and damaged reputation for years more. Ultimately, whatever the lawyer or insurance company says, the decision to settle or go to court remains with the professional. At this point the challenge is to retain objectivity and calmness so that rational thinking and planning can be carried out.

Little empirical evidence exists to reveal how social workers feel about their decisions to settle their malpractice cases. Obviously, since a major reason for settling the case is to avoid being publicly identified as a malpractice defendant, researchers cannot identify them for systematic study. After the issue is settled, understandably, most professionals do not want to talk about it. Those who do may not be representative of all professionals who settle. But in talking with the few professionals who were willing to describe their feelings about the experience confidentially, and after reviewing the anecdotal accounts in the literature (e.g., Vidmar, 1996; Crawford, 1994), we are left with a strong impression, and it is this: Most professionals accused of malpractice do not regret their decision to go to trial; most professionals who have settled before going to court have regretted their decision at one time or another.

On Trial for Malpractice

When professionals go to trial as defendants in malpractice suits, they often report that the experience was not as bad as the preparation and the long wait. The trial, being an adversarial proceeding, has some of the drama and ebb and flow of any contest. While the professional is a focus of the trial, it is the defense lawyer who exerts more of the effort in the courtroom. The professional's major job is to respond to the carefully prepared questions with answers that seem reasonable. The goal, almost always, is to show that the professional had good reasons for doing what led to the dispute. Colleagues, experts, and fact witnesses will be called upon to show why these reasons were or were not valid. The professional almost always will be called, examined, and cross-examined.

Being in the witness box as a defendant is a wholly different experience than being there as a fact witness or expert witness. Nevertheless, many of the same rules apply—the principal one being to show the court a countenance of competence, knowledgeability, and the dedication to good practice.

The opposing counsel, of course, will seek to convey the opposite. To achieve this the questions will be designed to find inconsistencies, contradictions, indicators of ignorance, and emotional instability. The degree to which each adversary is able to achieve their goals will affect the outcome of the case almost of much as the actual facts presented. The professional's case will be strengthened immeasurably if there is ample documentation, witness presentation, and explanation by the professional that shows that the conduct was done according to established professional standards. Professionals who keep themselves apprised of these standards and work hard to live up to them, and then carefully document that they have done so, will significantly improve their chances of favorable outcomes.

Chapter 8

Professional Review: Judgment by Colleagues

Malpractice suits, criminal cases, and licensure hearings are not always the most appropriate mechanisms for protecting clients and policing a profession against the misconduct of its members (Bullis, 1995). The following cases illustrate:

A social worker recently treated a couple for marital problems. The short-term treatment was successful. Both the husband and wife were pleased with the worker's efforts. Eventually the couple submitted a claim to their health insurance company, despite the company's explicit disclaimer indicating it does not reimburse for the treatment of marital problems. Knowing this, but recognizing that the couple could not afford the service without insurance reimbursement, the worker submitted an insurance claim nonetheless. With the clients' concurrence, the worker identified the wife as the patient and stated that all the therapy sessions were for her problem of "dysthymic disorder" (depression). The company did reimburse for treatment of this condition.

The worker rationalized that the wife actually was depressed because of her marriage, and that the best treatment for the depression was to resolve marital problems. Accordingly, the husband was seen alone during several sessions, as was the wife. When the insurance company learned that it was being charged for services rendered not to the identified client, but to the client's husband, it acted against the worker. The insurance company decided to exclude the social worker from all future reimbursements.

In another case, a private practice social worker decided to stop treating a client after six months. The client was diagnosed with anxiety problems and sexual dysfunction. As treatment progressed with good results, the client began falling behind on payments and seemed indifferent to the worker's insistence on catching up. Eventually the worker terminated sessions. The termination process included an appropriate referral to a community mental health center which would be affordable to the client. Nevertheless, the client reported the worker to the licensing board alleging the ethical violation of premature termination of services.

Publications such as *NASW News* and the newsletters of state social work boards now include stories in every issue describing the circumstances of members who were sanctioned for violating professional ethics. A recent issue of *NASW News* (1998a) described one woman who was found to have violated nine of the Code's standards. Among other violations she revealed client confidences to a third party and practiced social work without a license in her state. Another worker, in the same story, was found to have had sexual activity with a client, misrepresented facts on his application for professional liability insurance, and submitted false billings for reimbursement from an insurance organization.

Unfortunately, these stories are not aberrations. NASW reports that the trend is growing (NASW, 1993). Most of the state licensing boards for social workers publish the names and circumstances of every social worker who has been sanctioned. For example, the Massachusetts Board of Social Work Examiners (1997), which supervises the licensure of over 21,000 social workers, has described over fifty new complaints each year. The New York Office of Professions (1999) usually describes over ten disciplinary actions every month for social workers.

NEED FOR ALTERNATIVES TO LAW COURTS

In all these cases, and thousands of others, the most appropriate forum for adjudication may not be courts of law. In the first case described above, the insurance company could hardly charge malpractice, and would probably be loathe to initiate costly criminal charges of embezzlement. In the second case, alleging premature termination, the aggrieved client would have a difficult time retaining a lawyer to take such a case to the malpractice court. Moreover, the state licensing board would not likely force the worker to continue seeing the client. Where could the client or the worker get a fair hearing or the third party go to get a fair and forceful decision?

In the third case, the worker could well be the target of a malpractice suit by the victimized client, but such a case could take years before coming to court. Meanwhile, during the wait for the court hearing, the worker could continue her practice. In the fourth case, the worker did go to court and pled guilty to some misdeeds; but the court would not seek his expulsion from the professional organization for these crimes. He would be allowed to continue as a social worker without the mechanism of professional review.

An alternative forum for adjudicating differences and policing professional practice is in order, and in fact exists for nearly all professionals. Social workers have to face many authorities which can review their professional conduct. These include the worker's professional associations, the government professional review organization in the relevant jurisdiction, the peer review committees of third-party organizations, the worker's employer/agency, and the review committees of their state licensing boards.

Professional associations, employers, and third parties seek to control the professional's work ultimately for their own protection and self-interest. Each of these organizations has its own procedures to determine whether or not the worker has engaged in wrongdoing and for punishing those found guilty. If they did not have such mechanisms, it would be necessary for grievances to be adjudicated by the public legal system. This would be costly and highly time consuming for everyone.

If all grievances against professionals had to be adjudicated in the public courts of law or licensing boards, it would also diminish the profession's ability to maintain its own standards. No profession wants to air its "dirty linen" in public. Every profession requires its members to perform their duties within the bounds of explicit standards. The professions claim they do so to provide additional protection to society and their clientele from the possible wrongdoing of their members; but they also do so to maintain public credibility and esteem. Organizations that employ professionals, such as hospitals and social service agencies, have the same concerns. If a high percentage of an employer's workers or a profession's members were publicly exposed as incompetent or malevolent, there would be a precipitous decline in the organization's or profession's prestige.

Third parties or host organizations that employ professionals have a strong interest in ensuring that their employees are doing their jobs properly. Otherwise, they could be paying for services that are not needed or not provided; or they could be seen by the public as sponsoring activities that are harmful to clients. This could jeopardize the very existence of the operation. Thus, the third party or host organizations, usually in a contractual relationship with the professional, specifies the expectations that the professional must meet; and they can also impose punishments or sanctions according to contracted procedures.

For the most part the profession, the employer, and the third party's interests are protected by the worker's own sense of responsibility, personal ethical standards, and other internal controls—the "social worker as moral citizen" (Manning, 1997). These standards are mostly developed through the worker's formal education and professional socialization experiences. Clearly the internal controls are more important to workers' meeting professional standards than any coercion or external threats could ever be (Reamer, 1995a). However, many workers, for whatever reason, obviously do not live up to their own standards, much less those of the profession. Hundreds of cases every year are reported by professional associations and licensing boards, revealing social workers who get involved with their clients, submit false claims to insurance companies, engage in practices for which they are not qualified, and a myriad of other unethical activities. Recent studies show that a high percentage of social workers engage in activities that are considered inappropriate by the profession, and even acknowledged as such by themselves (Jayaratne, Croxton, and Mattison, 1997).

If, on the other hand, the professional person has a grievance against a client, there is no alternative but the legal justice system. Such grievances are rare and have mostly been in the realm of fee disputes and, to a lesser extent, to client physical abuse of the worker. So far, society and the legal system have not appeared to be very favorably disposed toward protecting or compensating workers who have been injured by clients.

PHILOSOPHIES OF REVIEWING ORGANIZATIONS

The professional associations that have peer review mechanisms for social workers are the National Association of Social Workers (NASW), the American Board of Examiners in Clinical Social Work (ABE), and the National Federation of Societies for Clinical Social Work (NFSCSW). Other professional associations that exist for specific social work populations, such as the National Association of Black Social Workers and the Association of Native American Social Workers, have been working toward developing peer review procedures. Peer review mechanisms are also sponsored by multidisciplinary professional associations, including the American Association for Marriage and Family Therapy (AAMFT), American Group Psychotherapy Association, American Association of Orthopsychiatry, and the American Association of Sex Educators, Counselors, and Therapists (AASECT).

Government organizations that sponsor professional review procedures include the congressionally mandated Peer Review Organizations (also known as Professional Standards Review Organizations, or PSROs, and as Professional Review Organizations). The federal government also sponsors third-party funding organizations such as the CHAMPUS health insurance program for military dependents and retired military personnel.

Each system has its own goals and philosophy of review, which results in procedures for adjudication. The professional associations focus on behaviors that deviate from their codes of ethics and result in harm to clients. State licensing committees are oriented to whether any laws have been broken by the professional who holds the state license. The government organizations and third-party insurance companies focus on cost containment issues and whether the professional is charging fees appropriately.

Generally, those who serve on review committees are professional colleagues. Often their expertise is in the same realm as the person whose work is being reviewed. Usually the committee members are volunteers who serve, not on a case by case basis, but for all the cases that come up during a specified term. Usually the members of such panels are experienced, well-established professionals in their own right whose goals are to help preserve the integrity of the profession and protect clients from those who might lack professional integrity. The professionals who serve recognize that the legal risks of participating in peer review are not as great as some might fear (Qualliotine, 1991).

TYPES OF SANCTIONS

Because professional associations or third parties have no legal authority over service providers and members of the profession, the punishments or sanctions imposed seem generally less severe. Unlike the legal system, which can incarcerate the professional or require payment of damages, the strongest punishment that these organizations can impose is expulsion and/or requirements for restitution.

Nevertheless, sanctions made by professional associations and third parties are highly undesirable. Not only do they involve loss of face and peer contact but they can include significant economic loss as well. The resulting diminished professional credibility can translate into economic losses that far exceed the losses faced by malpractice litigation (Bromberg, 1996).

A third-party (insurance company) organization's most severe sanction is to disqualify the worker's eligibility to receive further funds from the organization. In some communities and states, the third-party organization does so by removing the professional's name from its list of preferred providers. Other sanctions include financial penalties. A third party can require the professional or the professional's employer/agency to repay money that it considers was improperly received. Usually the third-party organization accomplishes return of fees, not by requiring direct repayments, but by deducting the amount from future payments.

Employers of social workers exercise their sanctions primarily through personnel actions. They can, of course, fire their workers, give them less desirable assignments, or withhold promotions and pay raises. They might also require the worker to undergo corrective training or therapy. Usually the worker is also subject to closer monitoring or supervision.

The most severe sanction imposed by a professional association is expulsion. Other punishments may include suspension of membership until certain requirements are met, continued membership on some probationary status, or continued membership while fulfilling requirements made by the association. Some professional associations publicize the wrongdoing of the member by specifying in their newsletters and journals the name of the member and the particular part of the ethics code that has been violated.

By itself, expulsion from the professional association may not seem to social workers to be a severe penalty; they might believe they can continue to practice without the professional association's blessing. Besides, a sanctioned social worker might think there are many social work professional associations, and if membership in one is no longer possible, others may be joined. Even though many social workers are happy not belonging to any professional associations, it is quite a different experience to choose not to belong than to be expelled. Not only do they lose credibility, clientele, and peer group association, but they are also more likely to lose the legal right to practice in the jurisdiction through loss of license. In such a case, the professional cannot depend on the association or its members to assist when the licensing authority challenges the person's continued right to practice.

Sanctioned social workers cannot easily move from one professional association to another. Despite their rivalry in some matters, the social work professional associations generally are mutually supportive on this issue. No group is enthusiastic about including in its ranks someone who has been found in violation of serious ethical issues. Whenever a member is sanctioned by the professional association, part of the penalty is reporting the findings to the relevant state board of licensing. Nearly every state social work licensing board is then obliged to conduct its own investigation. The misconduct that led to professional sanctions must be addressed by the licensing board. The outcome may well be suspension or revocation of the license in that state.

Not long ago, social workers who were sanctioned in this way could shrug it off; they could practice anyway without a license, or they could move to another state and become licensed there. Nowadays it is very difficult to practice without a license. Third-party insurance programs will not pay for the services of unlicensed professionals. Social agencies will not hire them. Colleagues will not refer to them. And moving to another state no longer spares these workers; they now must contend with the DARS system.

DISCIPLINARY ACTION REPORTING SYSTEM (DARS)

The American Association of State Social Work Boards established the DARS system to deal with this very problem. Whenever a licensed social worker has been disciplined in one jurisdiction, the board in that jurisdiction notifies the AASSWB, which then flags the worker's file.

Whenever a worker applies for licensure in any state, a routine procedure of the state board is to notify AASSWB of the application. AASSWB, through its Disciplinary Action Reporting System, promptly replies to the state board. It discloses that the applicant is currently in a disciplinary action in a specified state or jurisdiction. AASSWB then encourages the reviewers to obtain the details from the state board that imposed the sanction. Since AASSWB does not, itself, issue licenses or impose the criteria for making licensing decisions, its role is limited to providing needed information to the participating state boards.

The DARS information can then be used by the new board in determining a candidate's eligibility for licensure. Unless the ethical standards and enforcement procedures of the two states are at great variance, it is probable that the applicant will not get a license in the new state or any other state.

The DARS databank is also available to related social work organizations, third-party payers of social work services, and other interested entities. The information is available through annual subscription. AASSWB thus informs potential employers, insurance companies, and social work colleagues about the disciplined social worker. It has become very difficult for sanctioned workers to continue their work as though they had committed no wrongdoing.

THIRD-PARTY REVIEW PROCEDURES

The third-party review organizations and the federally mandated professional review organizations do not wait for complaints to be filed against professionals. They monitor the records of those cases they help to finance. The cases to be reviewed are often selected at random from the forms that are submitted for reimbursement, or from hospital or agency charts. The work of some professionals or service providing agencies is scrutinized more intensely if they have had previous problems.

The panel of reviewers, usually paid physicians and other professionals, determine if the work done is justified and appropriate for the stated diagnosis. For example, if a worker submits a claim for three years of intense psychotherapy for a client with agoraphobia, the panel would probably require further justification from the worker, because this disorder is usually treated successfully with short-term therapy approaches. When disparities between the diagnosis and the expected treatment are identified, the panel notifies the provider of the inquiry and asks for specific information.

The panel may accept the information provided and authorize payment. Or it may make an adjustment and authorize partial payment only. Or it may reject the claim outright, in which case the payment is withheld. Typically, the panel or the third-party organization does not demand a repayment from the service provider, but deducts sums from future claims. On those rare occasions when the panel suspects fraud or unethical conduct based on the available records, the panel may notify the legal and professional authorities.

The panelists who participate in these reviews are employed by the government or the third party. In the case of social workers being reviewed, the panelists have not always been colleagues (Csikai and Sales, 1998). Sometimes psychiatrists and other physicians have evaluated the professional practice of social workers. Rarely do social workers evaluate psychiatrists.

Government scrutiny of professional practice has been reduced significantly in the past decade. The government organizations that were established for this purpose came into being in 1972 and were known as Professional Standards Review Organizations (PSROs). At that time Congress enacted amendments to the Social Security Act (PL 92-603) to make sure that taxpayers' money was being well-spent on health care, especially Medicare and Medicaid. PSROs were revised and reduced considerably with 1982 amendments to the law.

NASW PEER REVIEW PROCEDURE

The NASW Procedures for the Adjudication of Grievances (1994) is the nation's oldest and most tested system for the professional review of social work conduct. It has become the model upon which most other social work professional or peer review processes are based. Even most state licensing boards have modeled their adjudication procedures after NASW. Thus, NASW procedures are a paradigm one might examine in order to understand any of the other professional review procedures to which one might be subjected.

The adjudication process applies to two broad categories of cases: allegations of ethical malfeasance by an individual social worker who belongs to NASW, and violations of personnel standards alleged against agencies that employ social workers (Osman and Shueman, 1988).

The primary mechanism for implementing the adjudication procedure is through the local NASW chapters' Committee on Inquiry (COI), and the NASW National Committee on Inquiry (NCOI). The administrative functions of the NCOI are maintained by NASW's Office of Professional Review (which until 1998 was known as the Office of Ethics and Adjudication). This office and the NCOI provide each local chapter COI with written guidelines, provide advice, and monitor the COI to assure compliance. The local NASW chapter appoints members to staff its COI. The COI members decide whether a given case meets the criteria for review, and if so decides whether it warrants further action. After a case has been reviewed, the COI reports its findings and recommendations to the chapter.

The adjudication guidelines specify that the case will not be considered for review unless the complaint is made within one year after the client or worker comes to believe that a wrong has been committed. However, because complainants often need more time to recover or summon the nerve to formally make the allegation, this time limit is often waived (Berliner, 1989).

Cases come to the attention of the COI when a client or worker calls the NASW chapter to describe the alleged wrongdoing. The office then provides information about how to file a formal declaration, called a "request for professional review." Until 1998 the dispute was considered a "complaint" when the organization first received the call. Now the chapter officers, staff, or Committee on Inquiry reviews the issue to determine if it meets the criteria for acceptance into the adjudication process. Unless it meets this criteria, it is not listed as an official complaint. This change is designed to protect workers and agencies from harm or discomfort by unfounded complaints regarding professional ethics.

To meet the criteria and have the case accepted for professional review the caller must allege exactly which principle of the Code of Ethics has been violated. Typically the caller describes the problem and the staff reviews the Code for the most applicable paragraphs. Throughout the process the chapter staff members help the caller obtain the appropriate information, identify proper jurisdiction, and frame the allegation in a reviewable way. Then staff and COI members review the written declaration to determine if it is properly and completely filled out. At this point the COI convenes to determine if the case should be accepted. If it is not, the person who initiated the call may appeal the decision to the national COI.

NASW has recently developed a new procedure that could be used in the professional review procedure. It is known as the alternative dispute resolution (ADR), which involves mediation instead of adjudication. Mediation has become widely recognized as an efficient, effective, and less costly way to resolve disputes (Severson and Bankston, 1995). Either party in the dispute could request the ADR; if both parties agree, their issues can be worked out through a mediation process at the local/chapter level. This is an effort to make dispute resolution less contentious (*NASW News,* 1998b).

If the COI determines that adjudication is the most appropriate avenue, it formally accepts the case and it is thenceforth considered a "complaint." The COI notifies both the complainant and respondent about the time, place, circumstances, and discloses information about who will serve on the review panel. Either party may challenge the participation of any member of the review panel "who they believe to be prejudiced with respect to the matter to be adjudicated. Such a challenge, stating reasons, shall be submitted in writing to the chairman of the inquiry committee who will inform the member who challenged and provide an opportunity for voluntary disqualification" (*NASW Chapter Guide,* 1989, p. 6).

At the hearing, either party may bring an NASW member for assistance in presenting the case. They have the right to be present when witnesses are called by the panel and to ask questions of those witnesses. While they are entitled to seek the assistance of counsel or others in the preparation of their cases, they may not bring lawyers to the hearing (Abbott, 1995). When either party insists on having lawyers present, they must have their case adjudicated by the civil authorities in public courts of law. Given that the case might take years to come before the public courts, will be costly and open to the public and the media, the merits of the "in-house" peer review procedures seem more attractive.

After the formal hearing, the panel has forty-five days in which to report its findings and recommendations. If the allegations are sustained, the statement must be very specific about which element of the NASW Code of Ethics has been violated. In that case the statement also recommends the type of punishment to be levied.

The recommendation made by the panel is then reviewed by the full chapter COI and the chapter board members. This review is only to make sure the procedures were completed in compliance with NASW adjudication rules. The chapter executive officers may not reverse COI decisions. However, they may modify (but not increase) the recommended punishments.

The final report is sent by certified mail to the NASW Office of Professional Review and the National Committee on Inquiry. Copies of the report are also sent to both parties in the dispute. Either party may appeal the decision to the NCOI within the following thirty days. When the appeal is accepted, the other party is notified and has the right to rebut the appeal within thirty days. The NCOI then reviews the written documents relative to the appeal, but does not permit the parties to make personal appearances in the review. The decision of the NCOI is then transmitted simultaneously to both parties by certified mail. If either party is then dissatisfied with the NCOI decision, a further appeal may be made to the NASW national board of directors. Few people who go through this process want the case to endure to that level, and the national board would be unenthusiastic about overturning an NCOI decision unless an egregious error or injustice has been identified.

Outcomes of NASW Reviews

When the complainant's allegations are sustained through this process, the punishments are imposed by the National Association of Social Workers. The most common sanctions are private censure or supervision of the worker's practice for a specified time. The more serious sanction of suspension or expulsion from membership can only be imposed by the National Committee on Inquiry. Usually the NASW National Board of Directors reviews this recommendation before it is imposed. The worker or agency may appeal to NCOI or to the NASW Board of Directors if such a sanction is imposed and considered unjustified by the findings in the case.

The types of cases that are heard by COIs vary. The most common complaints include: sexual misconduct; breach of confidentiality; fee splitting; soliciting the clients of other workers; overall professional misconduct; failing to adhere to ethical responsibilities to colleagues; and failing to fulfill ethical responsibilities to organizations, the social work profession, or society.

NASW's Office of Professional Review indicates, in personal contacts with the authors, that about 10 percent of the cases brought to COIs are withdrawn before any hearing commences. Individuals withdraw their complaints for reasons such as fear of being further traumatized, deciding to pursue legal action instead, or trying to resolve their differences with the worker independently of any formal adjudication process.

Another 10 percent of all complaints do not receive formal hearings because of decisions by the Committee on Inquiry not to look into the matter. COIs decide this for several reasons. Some complaints are made against workers who are not NASW members and therefore outside the COI jurisdiction. Other complaints do not involve violations of ethical standards so the issue to be adjudicated is outside the realm of the COI. Another reason is that the complaint has not been issued within the sixty-day "statute of limitations," which the NASW guidelines specify as necessary.

The cases that are fully adjudicated by the COI and NCOI usually take several months and sometimes years to resolve. The NASW Office of Professional Review reported that 33.3 percent took at least nine months and 20 percent took more than a year. Observance of careful procedures and multitiered review processes account for much of the delay. But COI and NCOI adjudication is not a screen behind which the profession hides. COIs have determined in 41 percent of the cases that some violation of ethical standards did indeed take place (NASW, 1993).

CRITIQUE OF NASW ADJUDICATION PROCEDURES

Some social workers, especially those who have been subjected to NASW adjudication, have found fault with the NASW review procedures. Many believe that the process takes too long, primarily because the volunteers who serve on COI panels are busy with their own employment and are not available to serve on such panels as speedily as might be desired. Berliner (1989) suggests that this problem could be minimized through the greater utilization of retired or semiretired colleagues to serve on such panels.

NASW has been criticized for its policy of excluding legal counsel at hearings. Lawyers are permitted, even required, at most civil and criminal court proceedings and are considered essential in protecting the rights of the relevant parties. NASW points out that the Supreme Court has ruled that participation of a lawyer is not an element of due process unless imprisonment may be a result. It contends that legal training is not universally required for the proper decision of professional questions. NASW further states that legal representation of one party at grievance and adjudication proceedings may be "counterproductive and would place the parties on an unequal footing" (*NASW Chapter Guide*, 1989, p. 6).

Zastrow, in an important critique of these procedures (1991), indicated concern about the lack of opportunity to interview members of the hearing panel in advance to determine whether bias exists. In the legal justice system, opposing lawyers have the chance to interview and challenge prospective jurors, and sometimes to even move for a change of judges. But the parties in reviews do not have the right to challenge panel members, even for cause.

Zastrow also examined four other potential procedural defects: (1) the opportunity for the parties involved to be present during appeals is lacking; (2) the worker may be subject to "double jeopardy" in that the grievance may be heard by the panel after other authorities (licensing boards, ethics boards of other professional associations, law courts) may have already heard the case and ruled in favor of the worker; (3) verbatim transcripts are not taken during hearings and thus are not available for internal review or for the appeal process; and (4) the hearing panels sometimes bend their own rules rather than adhere to rigid procedures as is the case in legal hearings.

OTHER PROFESSIONAL REVIEW PROCEDURES

Despite potential problems, the NASW adjudication procedure is more carefully delineated and implemented than most of the alternatives, including the government, Professional Review Organizations, third-party systems, and even many state licensing boards. Mechanisms for mediating disputes with managed care organizations and other third-party systems have been developed, but their focus is not on professional conduct but on financial issues and questions about appropriate diagnoses and treatment (Strom-Gottfried, 1998). Other organizations that offer mediation, such as some child welfare organizations, specify the conduct expected of licensed workers based on the standards found in the NASW Code of Ethics (Wilhelmus, 1998).

In a few of the states that have rigorous social work licensing laws, the system closely approximates the NASW model. When an individual alleges that a licensed worker has violated the standards of professional practice, these social work licensing boards may appoint panels of colleagues to review the matter. Often these boards seek the services of NASW or another relevant professional association in the jurisdiction; sometimes the panel for professional review and licensing review are synonymous. Licensing boards are more likely than NASW to permit the participation of lawyers and to require written transcripts of testimony if the case might lead to expulsion, probation, or publicity.

In the professional review systems of government or third-party organizations, such as PROs and PSROs, the disputes are often not between worker and client, but between worker/client and the third party. The review panel often audits the worker's records without the worker's knowledge to ascertain if the treatment was in accordance with the stated diagnosis, and if that treatment could have been done more efficiently.

Only after the review panel determines that some discrepancy exists is the worker then likely to invoke rights to a defense. Defense occurs first by written and oral responses to questions from the panel, usually requesting justifications for the procedures taken. The panel may, but rarely does, contact the client for verification of the stated treatments. The worker may dispute the decisions the review panel makes, but because the penalty is mostly about money received for past services rendered, most workers do not pursue the matter. However, they may retain counsel and initiate actions against the review panel. These contentions may then be heard by the panel itself or in a public court of law.

INEVITABILITY OF PEER REVIEW

In the modern era, a professional person cannot avoid being scrutinized and subjected to peer reviews of some sort. Peer review will certainly occur when professional misconduct is credibly alleged and will also occur in random audits and examinations of the professional's records. Thus, a professional who asks, "How can I avoid peer reviews?" is asking the wrong question. The right question is, "How can I avoid sanctions?"

Obviously, sanctions are less likely to be imposed on the worker who adheres to the ethics and standards of the profession and fulfills the obligations required by third parties. However, the worker must be well versed in what these ethics, standards, and obligations are. Studies have shown that many workers are woefully underinformed about professional standards (Berliner, 1989).

Even when the worker is knowledgeable about the standards and has an avowed intention to meet them, problems can arise. As discussed in previous chapters, the standards are sometimes contradictory, unclear, and impossible to meet. At times standards are perceived as being unfair to the worker. But professional review will be better for most workers than the public courts of law. As long as there are unethical or incompetent workers, and as long as competent and ethical workers can be challenged by a litigious public, there is need for professional "in-house" reviews.

Many workers seek to avoid sanctions by obstructing the work of the review panel. They attempt to do so by challenging the authority or jurisdiction of the review board, by threatening legal action against the board, and by refusing to cooperate. These actions do not aid the cause of the worker and usually lead to costly, embarrassing, and drawn-out cases. If a worker refuses to cooperate, the likelihood is that the allegations of the complainant will be sustained.

HOW TO AVOID OR MINIMIZE SANCTIONS

If a social worker is brought before a review panel, the goal is to prevent the authority from imposing punishment. If punishment cannot be avoided, the goal is to minimize its severity and duration. Social workers in this unenviable position can take some actions to minimize, if not completely avoid, the sanctions established by their licensing boards, peer review organizations, or the professional review authority.

The first, of course, is to become as aware as possible of the professional ethics codes, and the issues surrounding their development. Ethics codes are human created and evolve through time based on changing social mores, laws, and professional considerations. The more one is familiar with these philosophies and procedures the less likely one is to run afoul of them. The literature on this subject is rich; excellent publications on the subject have been presented by Gambrill and Pruger (1997); Loewenberg and Dolgoff (1996); Reamer (1995a); Reid and Popple (1992); and Bullis (1995) to name a few.

Many social workers do not review their codes of ethics periodically, and some probably have not done so since they left professional school and completed their licensing exam studies. Others have not done so for many years and may have forgotten many of the finer points. For that matter, with the frequent revisions of the NASW . Code it is very probable that they are not up to date. Ignorance of the code is no excuse for violating it. And going before a committee on inquiry is "learning ethics the hard way" (Johnson and Corser, 1998).

If the worker has been notified by a review organization of some allegations, it is important to learn exactly what specific violation of the code has been alleged. Then these charges must be carefully evaluated and compared with the explicit standards and relevant part of the code of ethics.

Because the process may be just beginning, the worker may want to become familiar with the possible procedures to come. This would include a review of the 1996 NASW Code of Ethics and possibly of the current codes by the Clinical Social Work Federation and the American Board of Examiners of Clinical Social Work. Other codes of ethics of multidisciplinary organizations to which one belongs might also be helpful. All the codes are fairly consistent about the issues that usually cause workers to become sanctioned for code violations. Therefore, it is probably futile to seek escape by claiming to be following one code instead of another.

At this point, the worker will want to discuss the matter with others who may be helpful. One or more professional colleague can provide some objective opinions about possible responses. A consultation with a lawyer might also be worthwhile, especially if the charges can result in expulsion or suspension. Of course, if the issue is also potentially relevant to malpractice litigation, it is essential to seek professional legal counsel. Even though the lawyer may not be admitted to the professional review panel hearing, the advice about conduct, procedures, legal recourse, and effective presentation of one's case can be invaluable.

Prior to appearing before the panel, the worker should have prepared a thoughtful, thorough, and truthful statement to explain and defend the actions which were alleged to be harmful to the complainant. The resolution will probably be more favorable and the sanctions less severe if the written statement does not offer a counter-attack or angry denunciation of the review process. If the worker believes there were circumstances that justified the conduct, it should be so presented; however, any justification that claims ignorance of the ethical code, or challenges the merit of the code, is unlikely to lead to a favorable outcome.

If the worker explains that the conduct occurred in connection with some impairment, the details and documentation of this impairment should also be included. If impairment is to be presented as partial justification, it is wise to take steps to get help for the problem before the hearing. Then it is important to show and document what steps have already been taken about the impairment.

After the investigation and review, the worker may agree with all or part of the allegations. To do so promptly and without rancor toward the investigators will contribute to a more favorable disposition. A prompt admission of allegations that have a substantial basis in fact, along with sincere contrition, is likely to result in less severe penalty.

WHEN MISCONDUCT IS ACKNOWLEDGED

If fault is admitted, the worker could then propose an appropriate sanction and agree to adhere to it. This may include financial restitution, written apology to the client, agreement to undertake therapy or supervision for a specified time, or agreement not to engage in social work practice for a defined time. Proposing one's own punishment is likely to result in a more appropriate sanction and less negative publicity. It is not likely, however, to prevent the panel from turning over the information to the state licensing authority and to the AASSWB Disciplinary Action Reporting System.

If the social worker disagrees with the allegations, the worker should nevertheless be cooperative with the review organization. Although the worker may be angry at the review panel, showing contempt or hostility will accomplish nothing positive and may be detrimental to one's ultimate defense. Appeals procedures are ample and they will be more favorably received if the worker has been previously cooperative.

After all the appeals have been exhausted leaving the allegations sustained, the worker would do well to accept the sanctions imposed. The alternatives are unpleasant. It is no longer very easy to resume professional practice in another location and in nearly all cases contesting the action in courts of law will probably be futile. Even if it is determined that some of the professional review procedures were improper, judges and juries are not likely to reverse the outcome. Courts have traditionally placed confidence in peer review systems. Attorneys and judges are themselves subject to very similar procedures. And it might be difficult to find an attorney to handle such a case.

Finally, the worker is probably better off simply completing the penalty cooperatively. The goal here is redemption and, hopefully, renewed professional credibility. If return to the profession at some future date is possible, the worker can become more effective and ethical, having learned from the difficult experience. If returning to the profession is not possible, the worker will have to seek career opportunities elsewhere and will probably find a more suitable livelihood outside social work.

Chapter 9

Case Recording
and Written Contracts

In this current age of litigiousness, the most effective way to prevent or resolve disputes between social workers and their clients is clear communication about their mutual obligations and expectations. Clients often enter therapy without knowing why they are unhappy but still expect dramatic, rapid, and extensive cures; they may well feel aggrieved when the anticipated results remain elusive.

Therapists often start a new therapy relationship assuming the client already understands therapeutic procedures, knows the obligations about candor and payment, and above all, possesses considerable patience. When the client cannot follow these unknown rules, therapists may well think of the client as experiencing "resistance" or "transference problems" or is otherwise a "poor candidate for deep-insight-oriented psychotherapy."

With so many relationships between helper and client based on unclear mutual expectations, the rate of malpractice and professional review is understandable (Gardner, 1996). The risk has become so great that conducting therapy this way is foolhardy—and needlessly so. It is not that difficult to begin the therapeutic relationship by spelling out mutual obligations and the consequences for not carrying them out. This can be done, in part, through the use of a written contract. It is not that difficult for the worker and client to maintain their clear understanding about the progress of treatment as they go through its various stages. This can be done, in part, by maintaining good records, which are accessible to the client at all times. Good case records are not only essential for protection against malpractice risk, they are also indispensable for the worker as a tool for focusing, self-educating, goal setting, and keeping the relationship on task (Ames, 1998).

REPORT WRITING
FOR THE LITIGIOUS SOCIETY

Legislation, third-party review, and judicial interpretations in recent years have made the professional person's case records virtually part of the public record. In grand juries, courts of law, and other discovery procedures, the worker's record could be subpoenaed (*subpoena duces tecum*) as well as the worker. Consequently, the prudent worker will need to prepare them with thoughtfulness and caution.

Every client has a file. Everyone who is accepted by a professional psychotherapist deserves a file that is thoughtfully prepared, secure from everyone but those who have the legal right to see it, and that accurately reveals the substance of the treatment goals and process (Woodward, 1997). Different social work scholars argue about what is the best format for recording. What is considered best seems to depend on the theoretical orientation of the worker; behaviorists and task-centered social workers would probably have different recording styles than analytic and humanistic recorders (Kagle, 1995). Whatever the orientation, the prudent worker considers record keeping an important part of the treatment process.

There are several components of the case record that are essential for the litigious society. The diagnosis, and the symptoms for arriving at it, should be clearly indicated. The treatment plan should be rational and based on what professionals recognize as appropriate for the diagnosis given. And most important, the record must be accurate, legible, and up to date.

Practitioners know how easy it is to postpone this job. They might want to make entries in the record later in the day or even later in the month. It happens when the schedule of clients gets backed up, or the worker has to deal with emergency calls or situations between appointments during the time set aside normally for record keeping. It happens all too frequently to workers who tend to be disorganized or who dread "paperwork." But significant legal risks accompany those who do not prepare their records promptly upon seeing the client. Errors creep in. Memories lapse. Writing in haste to catch up leads to indecipherability. And, if the latest sessions have not been recorded when the worker suddenly takes ill or dies, the replacement professional may find it difficult to provide appropriate services.

When writing about the client's diagnosis, it would be worthwhile to indicate what definition of the diagnosis is being used (e.g., the *Diagnostic and Statistical Manual of Mental Disorders* (DSM-IV) (American Psychiatric Association, 1994), *The Social Work Dictionary* (Barker, 1999), the *PIE* assessment tool (Karls and Wandrei, 1994), or whatever. Then it would be useful to indicate what symptoms or other information is presented that leads the record writer to that conclusion. If the diagnosis is preliminary and subject to later revision or reversal, it can be followed by a question. Later in the document, when additional information is presented to suggest a different diagnosis, that should be so indicated, again with the source of the definition and the criteria for it.

Any risks of legal problems are dramatically reduced when the worker has well-documented case records which truthfully indicate the rationale for whatever actions are taken. If the worker has a good reason for the professional action in the care and treatment of a client, and if that reason is noted carefully in the record, it would be more difficult to sustain a malpractice allegation against the worker, even if the treatment outcome was not desirable. Social workers usually have, or certainly should have, good reasons for the type of treatment they provide for their clients, but too often they fail to indicate what that reason is in the case record.

RECORD KEEPING
FOR COUPLES AND FAMILIES

A troublesome aspect of case recording for social workers is that much of their professional activity is devoted to two or more people at once. In working with families, groups, or communities, the question arises as to whether each individual needs a separate file. The case of the Y. family illustrates:

Mr. and Mrs. Y. sought marital therapy with a social worker to help them resolve their many personality conflicts and life-style disputes. Mr. Y. preferred to stay at home and watch TV with the children, while Mrs. Y wanted to leave them with baby-sitters and participate in evening civic activities. Arguments in the worker's office about such matters were frequent. Mrs. Y occasionally exclaimed in frustration that she wished she had not had children so she could pursue her other interests better. Mr. Y claimed to be happy as he was.

A year after their marital therapy sessions ended, the Ys filed for divorce. A fight over custody of the children ensued. Mr. Y's attorney subpoenaed the worker and his client's case records. The worker, who personally believed that Mrs. Y was probably the more suitable parent for the children's upbringing, reviewed the records. There were no individual records for Mr. Y and Mrs. Y but only one for "The Y Family." In it information about both parties was intertwined—nearly every sentence had materials about both.

How, the worker wondered, could Mr. Y's record be brought to court without also including Mrs. Y's record? If information that the worker had recorded about her was included in testimony, it would unfairly harm her case and violate the worker's confidentiality pledge to her. The worker also contemplated deleting that part of the record that pertained to Mrs. Y. However, this would make the record incomprehensible and would clearly reveal that it had been improperly altered.

The worker explained this to Mr. Y's attorney who, more than ever, wanted the records brought to court. The worker then explained the situation to Mrs. Y and her attorney who emphatically did not want the records brought. Despite their protests at court the record was entered as evidence. Whether or not it influenced the outcome of the case was unknown, but Mr. Y won custody, and Mrs. Y felt her worker had weakened her case.

From that time on, the worker has questioned the best way to keep case records; her specialty was working with couples, families, and groups, and her theoretical orientation relied on "systems concepts" (in which relationships and interactions are considered the unit of study, rather than the dynamics within the individual).

There are advantages and disadvantages to whichever choice this worker, or any worker, makes. The only virtue in having separate files—but it is a significant one—is in the event that members of the client-group have major disputes. When their disputes lead to legal action, one client or another may seek the worker's files. An individual may be able legally to have access to his or her own records, but what about when the information is intertwined with that of another person, especially another person who is now an opponent in a lawsuit? If the files are written separately, then every person can claim access only to their own files, and the worker's position is much less uncomfortable (Berg-Cross, 1997).

On the other hand, this is such a laborious and cumbersome process that it is rarely done. And not only it is laborious, but it is also less accurate. In family and couples therapy, especially, the essence of the therapeutic intervention is the dynamic interchange between the parties, rather than what goes on inside the individual. It does violence to the nature of the session to omit the interchange from the records. How would a worker maintain a separate file entry for a session that consisted mostly of a strong argument between a mutually hostile husband and wife who seemed about to divorce and engage in a nasty fight over custody of children and property? Individual records might indicate what the client said or felt, but would have to leave out reasons for the reaction.

Inasmuch as the vast majority of any worker's cases with families or groups won't end up in vituperative court battles, it is probable that only the most exceedingly cautious, compulsive, and possibly paranoid worker would maintain separate records for each client. So the next best precaution is to minimize any information that puts one or the other client in a severe legal disadvantage. Indications that one or the other client is in the wrong about any given issue are out of place.

THE PROBLEM-ORIENTED (SOAP) RECORD

Another caution about records is to try to keep subjective and objective information separate. To do this many workers have used the Problem-Oriented Record. The format requires the writer to list each of the client's presenting problems and then add new or newly discovered problems as treatment progresses. Describing the treatment process in this type of record is organized around a problem list.

The acronym "SOAP" refers to a modification of the format. The record breaks down the information into four sections: "S" is for the subjective information, or the information discussed by the client or members of the client's family. It is considered subjective because it is, from a legal perspective, hearsay information; the worker has not observed it so its veracity cannot be certain. The "O" section of the record is where the worker places all of his or her direct observations, quoted material, test results, and other documents. The "A" section is for the worker's assessment information, that is all the diagnostic labels and information that leads one to that finding. The "P" section is for the worker's plans. Kagle (1995, p. 2031) wrote that this may be a useful and streamlined format for record keeping, but it tends to "partialize and oversimplify assessment" and other relevant concerns.

Keeping records in this way may not be the worker's preference, but it should be considered, at least for clients who are more likely to become involved in legal or professional disputes. The clients most likely to meet this criteria include married couples who have violent relationships; families where child or spouse abuse is alleged but not, originally, reliable enough to notify authorities; clients with paranoid ideation problems; and clients who have past histories of litigiousness.

ACCESSIBILITY OF CASE RECORDS

The case record will be the crucial document for the worker in the unhappy event of disputes with the client. Some laws might provide protection against public exposure of the therapeutic relationship—if the client chooses to keep it concealed. But if the client wants to use the record in legal actions against the worker, the worker almost always will have to relinquish the file.

For many decades the worker's traditional assumption has been that no one but the worker would ever see these notes; therefore, it could contain anything. This assumption is no longer valid, although most records are still not likely to be seen by anyone other than the worker. Ironically, the only records that will be seen by others are those pertaining to the cases that have gone awry.

Because the worker cannot know in advance which cases will go smoothly and which ones will have contentious outcomes, the only choice is to prepare them all with the same high degree of care and thoughtfulness. They should be written as though they will be closely examined by others: by aggrieved former clients, by angry family members, by aggressive lawyers, by colleagues who will serve as expert witnesses for the opposition, and by unsympathetic juries.

Therefore, the record should be written with no comments that are embarrassing to the client or others. They should avoid any factual errors about the client, inaccurate preliminary diagnoses, unflattering comments about the client or client's loved ones, or misleading speculations. Every sentence can be taken out of context and held up in court as evidence of the worker's ignorance, poor judgment, callous disregard for others, or flippant attitude about the client or the therapy process. Any statement can be accentuated by opposing attorneys in courtrooms and used to the worker's disadvantage.

Such an unpleasant scenario would be minimized if the record were written from the beginning as a collaboration between the worker and the client (Gelman, 1992). The worker could write the entries as always during or after the session. At the beginning of the next session, if the client wants, the record could be reviewed. The client could question the notes or the reason for their entry and could make corrections or elaborations. If the record includes diagnoses or descriptions of client misbehavior, it would be useful to discuss that anyway. By keeping the record open to the client, communication is improved, errors are minimized, goals are reframed. Significantly, if disagreements or confusion arise about how something is being described or understood, it can be worked through in the course of therapy—a far more desirable outcome than to have it worked out in a law court.

FORENSICS REPORTS VERSUS CASE RECORDS

Forensics reports, of course, exist to serve a different purpose than the case record. The forensics report is only summary and does not describe an ongoing therapeutic relationship. Rather it is based on a concrete and focused set of observations, interviews, tests, and other assessment strategies, conducted within a brief time. Most likely it is comprised of a final summary statement, followed by process notes of the interviews and whatever supporting documents that were used in reaching the conclusion.

Even more than the case record, the forensics report should be jargon free, or at least minimized. It must be written skillfully; a poorly written report in the hands of a skilled cross-examiner in court can be used to discredit the expert and the opinion presented. Factual data should be kept separate from the inferential data (that is, all the information that the writer obtained in arriving at the ultimate conclusion).

The report should be complete but should avoid "information overload." Some workers might be tempted to include every item of information, no matter how tangential to the case, to demonstrate thoroughness and to completely justify one's thinking. Reports that contain an excessive amount of this peripheral material also tend to be filled with equivocations and qualifications, to the point that they become useless. Such records convey to the readers an impression, not that the worker is thorough, but that the worker is uncertain and doubtful about the conclusions reached.

Excessive information can also be counterproductive from a legal perspective. The more data that appears, the easier it is for opposing lawyers to find inconsistencies or errors. Concise forensics reports are more useful and accurate.

Under no circumstances should the worker ever discard or rewrite a forensics report or a case record, especially after it has been subpoenaed. This is a serious offense and the worker can be charged with tampering with evidence and obstructing justice. The temptation after receiving notice of the need to bring records to court is to review it carefully. The worker might find that some statements have subsequently been shown to be untrue or misleading, or reveal that the worker was inaccurate in initial assessments. It is acceptable—though not encouraged if it can be avoided—to write supplemental notes at the end of the record to clarify some earlier statement. Then when the attorney challenges the document for some obvious mistake, it is at least possible to show where the worker acknowledged that fact and rectified it at the soonest possible time.

Records need to be up to date at all times. If the worker dies or is suddenly called away, the client is entitled to have a competent replacement arranged for by the worker in advance (*NASW News,* 1999). The replacement cannot be considered competent, no matter what the credentials and experience are, if the records are inadequate or outdated. This would be a violation of professional ethics, and many workers have lost licenses over nothing more than failure to keep adequate records.

THE WRITTEN CONTRACT

Objectives of the Written Contract

Ideally, one of the first entries in every case record is a copy of the written contract agreed to and signed by both the worker and the client. A written contract is an explicit statement detailing the goals, procedures, obligations, and conditions for fulfillment that are agreed to by all the parties to the contract. In professional psychosocial therapy relationships, the agreement is entered into by the person(s) serving and the person(s) served. The therapeutic relationship begins when the parties sign this contract; it concludes when all the terms and obligations of the contract have been fulfilled. The contract can be used to keep the focus on goals, and to minimize misunderstanding. If properly drawn and implemented, the contract will be very useful in resolving lawsuits or professional reviews.

A written contract should be a simple and concise document that the client can understand without a lawyer's interpretation. It can be written in "nonlegalese" and referred to as a "letter of agreement" rather than a "contract," to make it more user friendly. Of course the client should be free to show it to a lawyer or anyone else if further clarification or discussion is sought.

The written contract should contain information about generally what to expect in the therapeutic relationship. It should explain the worker's obligations to the client and vice versa. It should reiterate the client's obligation to seek a physician's examination to rule out any physical causes of the presenting symptoms. It should clarify any issue about confidentiality, indicating when the worker might be required to divulge information and how this would be accomplished. It should acknowledge that the client can review the case record any time.

The written contract should tell the client what to do when the worker is unavailable. It should discuss how the sessions should terminate when the goals are reached. It should give the client some knowledge about the qualifications of the worker or the agency. It should explain the required methods of payment and something about how to facilitate reimbursement with third-party institutions.

Finally, the written contract should contain space for the goals of the intervention to be written by the worker and the client. And it should contain space for the signatures of the client and the worker, following a statement that the undersigned agree with the terms of the contract.

Appearance of Contracts

A worker could use several different types of written contracts, depending upon what kind of client-system is being served. A contract used for an individual adult will not be the same as one used for a couple in marital therapy, a member of a group psychotherapy program, a family, or a community. One prepared for children of various ages would look different from one prepared for adults. If a worker has a variegated practice with different client-systems, the worker should have several versions of a written contract for each purpose.

There are many versions of written contracts. They can be easily produced and modified, for every type of client, using computer and desktop publishing technology. A simple and effective one is a document printed or typed on both sides of one sheet of legal sized ($8\frac{1}{2}'' \times 14''$) white paper. The sentences are printed in eight columns, about three inches wide each. The sheet is then folded three times, each fold occurring in the middle of the spaces between each column. This produces a document that is $3\frac{1}{2}'' \times 8\frac{1}{2}''$.

The front page contains only the worker's name, degree, address, telephone number, and a line indicating who the client can contact in emergencies when the worker is unavailable. The last page is blank except for GOALS printed at the top. This permits the client and worker to spell out the objectives of the intervention. When the contract is folded, only the front and back pages show. Usually, the client tapes the folded contract with only the "goals" page showing, in a prominent place, such as the refrigerator door.

A Prototype Contract

The following is a copy of a written contract used for years by the social work author for individual clients. It begins with the second page. A discussion about how the contract is presented to the client will follow:

LETTER OF AGREEMENT

Hello. Welcome to my office.

I hope your time here is worthwhile. I'm giving you this letter now in order to answer some questions you may have. It will tell you what to expect in our meetings and how we should work together.

Please go over this carefully. Feel free to ask me anything about it whenever you have questions. You are welcome to show it to others in your family or other professionals you trust.

At the end of this letter there is a place for us to sign our names. Signing means we agree with all the points in this letter. There is also space for us to write down the goals we hope to accomplish together. We can review these goals as we go along. We can change them any time we want if together it seems like a good idea.

Now let's discuss what you and I should understand and do to make our meetings worthwhile.

SEE YOUR DOCTOR. Please get a physical examination from your personal physician as soon as possible. This is important to make sure that none of your problems are the result of physical health difficulties. Since I am not a physician, I cannot know if you might have physical health problems that might be related to our work.

Your family doctor should know you are going to be working with me. Please tell him or her as soon as possible. It is

---

also important that I am informed about any work he or she is doing with you. I especially need to know about any health problems you may have. Please ask your doctor to send me this information as soon as possible.

I think information about your work with me should be included in your doctor's medical record. Therefore unless you say otherwise, I will write to your doctor to describe your progress. These letters can be included in your medical chart if your doctor desires this. You will be given a copy of these letters before they are sent. That way any possible corrections or information you feel should be left out or added can be done before it is sent.

TIME OF APPOINTMENTS. Each of our appointments is scheduled to last fifty minutes. I am usually able to begin promptly at the scheduled time. It is very rare that I am late for an appointment. If it ever happens I will try to let you know in advance, even if the delay is just a few minutes. If we must begin late, we will still be together for the full fifty minutes. If you arrive late for an appointment, we still have to end the meeting fifty minutes after it was scheduled to begin. The charge to you for these shortened meetings will be for the full amount. You will not be charged for a session if you cannot keep it and let me know at least twenty-four hours in advance. You will be charged if you fail to keep a scheduled appointment or do not notify me twenty-four hours ahead of time.

EMERGENCY MEETINGS. I will try to be available to you as much as reasonably possible. The telephone numbers on the front of this letter are attached to twenty-four-hour answering machines and I monitor them closely. I will try to return your calls promptly. If I am away from town during vacations or professional meetings, I will let you know how to reach me by long distance telephone, or I will have a qualified professional in the area return your call. Your case record will be available to that professional, unless you indicate otherwise. If you feel the need for help and cannot reach me or the other professional, please contact your family doctor.

STOPPING OUR SESSIONS. We should agree together when it is time for our meetings to end and for therapy to stop.

We can do this in two ways. If you prefer, we can specify as we get started when our last session will be. Then, when the time comes, we will stop, unless we make a new agreement and set new goals. If we end this way our last meeting will include a final discussion and summing up about things to do in the future. Of course, we can resume sessions after that if you want. The second way we might stop is to decide as we go along. We might decide together to stop because we have reached our goals. Or we might decide we are not going to reach them. This is a possibility because I cannot guarantee that we will reach all of the goals we establish together.

It should be understood that you may, at any time, tell me you wish to stop, for whatever reason. I'd prefer it if you came in for one final session after that so we can have a summing up and discussion about the future. If you stop coming without letting me know in advance I cannot assume responsibility for your care and well-being after that.

COSTS. The charges for each of these fifty-minute meetings is $___. This amount is the same if you attend the meeting alone or with other members of your family. The charge to you is the same, if with your consent, I see other members of your family in your behalf. If we agree in advance to have meetings that are longer or shorter than fifty minutes, the charges will be based on the amount of time we are together. For example, if you have a twenty-five-minute session the charge will be half that of a fifty-minute session.

METHOD OF PAYMENT. You may pay by cash, credit or debit card, check, or money order. You may pay me or my secretary directly at the time of each visit. If this is not convenient, we can discuss other possibilities such as monthly billing. If your bill has not been paid before the end of the month, you will be sent a statement, itemizing the charges and showing the total balance due. This amount should be paid within ten days after the month begins.

If you are having any financial problems that keep you from paying in this way, let's discuss it. We can make special arrangements if necessary.

INSURANCE. Your health insurance may help to pay these charges. You should find out by contacting your insurance company or agent as soon as possible. If they will help you pay my fees, please obtain the proper forms from them and give them to me. I will complete my portion of the form and return it to you, not your insurance company. After that it is your responsibility to submit the forms to your company. Ask them to send the money to you and not to me.

Your payment to me should be made on time even if your insurance company delays in reimbursing you. You should know that health insurance companies generally don't reimburse expenses they consider to be unrelated to health. That means some companies do not pay for marriage counseling, some forms of therapy, and educational counseling. Some companies will only reimburse you when your physician has referred you to me and is involved in your treatment. It is important that you seek this information from your insurance company if you plan to be reimbursed.

CONFIDENTIALITY. My profession and my professional ethics require me to keep everything you discuss here in strict confidence. I have no intention of ever giving out any information about you to anyone unless you ask me to. I have no objection, however, to your revealing anything you want to anyone you want about our meetings. I will not audiotape or video-record any of our sessions unless I have your permission in writing. If you permit me to record a session, you may have a copy of the tape.

I do keep a written record of our contacts. These notes help me focus on our goals. It also helps us get started where we left off last time. These notes are confidential, but I believe they are your property as well as mine. You may read these notes whenever you want, and you may have a copy at the conclusion of our work together.

There is one possible exception to the principle of confidentiality. It applies to me and all other mental health professionals in this state. In some very rare circumstances, I could be called upon (subpoenaed) to testify about you in court. This could happen if there was reason to believe I knew of certain types of criminal wrongdoing. Also, if you indicate to me seriously that you intend to harm someone, I may be required to take action to prevent that harm from occurring, including alerting the authorities and/or warning the person who is being threatened. My colleagues and I are also required by law to report any suspected child abuse. In such situations my records about you could also be reviewed in court. If the law ever required me to do this, I would try to discuss with you beforehand any testimony I might be compelled to present. Again, the likelihood of any of this happening is extremely rare, but you deserve to be informed of the possibility.

MY BACKGROUND. You are also entitled to know about my qualifications to provide service to you. I have been in private practice in this office since____. Before that I worked at____ . I am also on the faculty of ____, where I teach courses in____ . My profession is social work and I specialize in ____. My academic degrees are from ____University in ____. I have been licensed in this state since____ and am a member of the following professional associations: _____
_____.

OUR AGREEMENT. You are the boss and I am working in your interests. You determine what your goals are and my role is to help you reach them. I may show you how to define your goals or show you what the consequences of reaching these goals might be, but you have the last word on this. On the back of this letter we will list the goals we hope to achieve in our work together. We both agree they can be changed any time. If we change goals, we agree to restate them on another letter similar to this one.

SIGNATURE. We the undersigned have read this statement, understand it, and agree with its terms. We will comply with all the points in this on our personal and professional honor. It is understood that our relationship may discontinue whenever these terms are not fulfilled by either of us.

_____
(signature and date)

Presenting the Contract to the Client

The most effective way to use the contract is to present it at the end of the first session. Others have recommended that the contract be presented during the first session, but doing so greatly diminishes the time available to concentrate on the client's problem. If used at the end of the session, the worker can incorporate it into a discussion about the goals.

Usually the worker will take some time at the end of the session to suggest thoughts for the week and some preliminary actions toward problem resolution. This is a good time to show the contract. The worker merely hands the copy to the client explaining that this is a letter spelling out what is to come if they decide to continue working together. The worker simply asks the client to read it carefully before the next session.

When that time comes, the worker begins the second session by asking if the client has read the contract. Whether or not the answer is yes, the worker spends a few minutes going over its most important points with the client. This is important to make sure every element is understood. "Informed consent" is one of the most important issues ever raised in worker-client disputes and one of the most frequent causes of malpractice litigation and professional review conflicts, and this discussion about the contract frames the issue in a way that is clear and documented. Once the worker is sure the client understands, the goals of the helping relationship are discussed. Together the worker and client spend part of the session deciding on these goals and in stating them in specific and doable terms. Then the worker and client can write these goals on the contract in the space provided.

The worker and client each have identical copies of the contract and the explicated goals, both of which are signed by both participants. The worker's copy is kept at the beginning of the case record. During the ongoing therapeutic work the goals can be periodically reviewed. So, too, can any other of the contract's elements. This helps define, focus, and minimize misunderstanding.

Enforceability of the Contract

Even though legalese is minimized to the extent possible in the written contract, it may be advisable for the worker to show the various versions to a lawyer before using them. Various state laws and interpretations might necessitate some changes in the worker's prototype contract. The lawyer can help to put the language in terms understood in courts of law.

The primary purpose of the contract is not to develop a document such as used in other business transactions, in which the authorities can take legal action for failure of compliance. The purpose is to achieve clarity about expectations. The worker is highly unlikely to use the contract as a way to enforce its elements. If a problem arises about payment, it will be discussed during the ongoing sessions rather than being dealt with through the help of lawyers or law enforcement officials. No lawyer or law enforcement official would be called upon to help enforce the other provisions of the agreement, such as attending all sessions on time, or adhering to agreed upon goals. In this sense the contract is not enforceable as a legally binding document, nor should it be.

However, it would definitely be looked at by judges, juries, and professional peer reviewers if there were disputes. And if the agreement complied with the ethical and legal standards of the profession, and if the worker adhered to that agreement, it would be beneficial to the worker's case. It would also be beneficial to the client's case if the worker did not comply with the agreement, or if the agreement violated professional ethics and state laws.

Why Written Contracts Are Rare

Most social workers and other mental health professionals still do not use written contracts with clients. They feel it introduces a suspicious or "distrustful" element into the helping relationship. Many other clinical social workers specialize in work with families or groups and feel written contracts are too complex to maintain for an entire group, even though for many purposes they are considered effective (Klier, Fein, and Genero, 1984). A few professionals, such as Miller (1990), argue strongly against the written contract, because it supposedly detracts from the so-called covenant between worker and client.

However, most social workers who do not use contracts have no theoretical reasons for their choice. It is more a matter of habit or familiarity. Some believe their agency-employer would require it of them if it was considered so worthwhile. Many do not want to be doing something they do not see most of their colleagues doing. They did not learn about contracting in their professional schools or field placements. For some it is because they know so little about it; there is little in the professional literature about contracts, and that which exists is mostly devoted to discussions about the value and growing need for contracts without specifically delineating their contents (Fatis et al., 1982).

Many workers avoid the written contract because they believe it will cause them more malpractice and peer review problems than it will solve. These workers reason that the legalistic nature of the contract will diminish the attitude of mutual respect and will exacerbate any tendencies to litigation. Statements in the contract will remind the client of the essentially businesslike nature of the helping process. Pointing out in the contract that there are conditions in which confidentiality can be breached is distasteful to contemplate.

Perhaps the most important reason why many workers do not use written contracts is that it seems to be alien to their basic treatment model and professional orientation. Most psychotherapy-providing social workers consider themselves to be of the "psychosocial/ systems" or "humanistic" orientation; they think of contracting as being part of the orientation they oppose—the behavioral or task-centered treatment model.

Is Contracting Antipsychosocial?

The humanistic and psychosocial orientations in social work interventions do not emphasize the establishment of goals at the outset of treatment. Inherent in these orientations is the view that the human psyche is infinitely complex and the sociocultural milieu in which one functions is even more so. The professional's therapy role is to guide the client through this complexity, gradually uncovering and sorting out this material. When this point is reached, as determined by the professional rather than the client, then the thera-peutic relationship can come to an end.

Establishing specific goals at the beginning of the therapeutic relationship is rarely done in this orientation. Workers believe it is impossible to predict what new issues or problems will emerge during the course of therapy or how long the intervention will take. In this view, the client is best served by relying, not on any explicit-ly written set of mutual obligations, but on the worker's honesty, objectivity, ethics, and knowledge.

Often, if a client were to question the professional in any of these aspects, many professionals would probably interpret "resistance" or a "negative transference" problem. Such interpretations would mean that more time and money had to be expended by the client to deal with these issues even if they had not been relevant before therapy began.

The orientations in social work that seem more amenable to con-tracting are those which are short-term, behavioral, task-centered, or problem-solving approaches. Most social workers of the psycho-social/humanistic model believe these orientations force a "minimal-ist" approach to therapy, in which the professional is obligated only to meet the contract's conditions rather than considering client needs that go beyond these written terms. For example, a professional might stop seeing a client when the terms of the contract are com-pleted, even though the client has revealed symptoms of new prob-lems during the course of the intervention.

This contention is disputed by advocates of the contract. They point out that there is nothing inherent in the written contract that requires a professional person to terminate with a client when the conditions of the contract have been met. If and when new prob-lems or symptoms emerge in the course of the intervention, it is a simple matter to revise the contract or prepare a new one. In fact, a properly drafted written contract indicates that the professional is obliged to adhere to the professional code of ethics, which pre-cludes premature termination of services.

Despite objections by some social workers toward the use of written contracts, there is growing, if resigned, acceptance of this concept. Some psychosocially oriented workers now use them, if not for theoretical reasons, then for practical ones. The trend may be the result of four influences—the consumer movement, third parties, malpractice considerations, and the movement toward professional accountability.

Influences Toward Contracting

Consumerism and the Written Contract

The first factor influencing the trend toward contracting comes from the consumer of psychotherapy services. Many social workers have been reluctant to ask clients to sign contracts at the beginning of therapy, fearing client resistance. However, most workers who use contracts find that clients are not offended but tend to be more relieved and confident about entrusting their problems to such a conscientious professional.

In a perfect world, where professionals actually would have all the answers and actually would hold their client's interests paramount, the idea of a contract to regulate the therapy transaction might be superfluous. However, such a world does not and has never existed. While professionals might think of themselves and their colleagues as being wholly beneficent and dedicated to their clients, the clients cannot be so sure.

Potential consumers often hear about how clients are sometimes ill served and often victimized by professionals. For them to enter a therapeutic relationship solely on the basis of trust and hope, with no clear goals or time frame, seems unwise. To do so is no more sensible than making payments on the purchase of a house for years with no deeds, mortgage papers, or documentation.

Third-Party Influences on Contracting

If the consumer movement has not led professionals toward explicating the terms of their relationships with clients, the third parties have. Insurance companies, managed health care programs, and government funding agencies have led mental health professionals to reconsider the value of written contracts. While third-party paying organizations do not require professionals to use written contracts, they do require many of the elements found in written contracts.

In order for third parties to reimburse the professional for services to their insuree, third-party payers require that professionals indicate their goals in treatment, the reasons for the procedures used, and the estimated time frame within which goals are expected to be achieved. They require the professional to make this assessment in the beginning of the treatment, or at least as early as the reimbursements are supposed to begin. They also require that the professional is licensed or certified in the relevant jurisdiction and adheres to ethical professional standards. When a professional meets all of these conditions with the third-party organizations, the professional has already fulfilled most of the essentials of a contract.

Unfortunately, many professionals give more of this information to the third party than to the client. They often withhold from the client information about the client's diagnosis, treatment plan or procedures, or even information about the professional's credentials and background. They justify this by saying that such information would get in the way of the needed transference, cause the client to lose confidence in the professional, or focus the client's attention on such a narrow range of issues that the whole problem cannot be addressed. This view remains influential among social workers even though there is no empirical evidence to support it and substantial evidence to the contrary.

Malpractice Influences on Contracting

The third influence toward contracting is the specter of malpractice litigation. Written contracts significantly reduce these risks. As seen earlier, the most likely causes of malpractice suits include lack of informed consent, improper or faulty treatment, breaches of confidentiality, and premature termination and abandonment problems. Each of these potential causes of litigation is minimized through the contract.

If malpractice litigation were threatened, a statement about the explicated goals, procedures, and explanations would be crucial. The written contract would show that the professional was adhering to procedures to which the client agreed. When a client agrees to the conditions, any possible claim about a lack of informed consent would be remote.

A particular malpractice vulnerability involves the worker treating a client whose symptoms are caused by some underlying health problem. As we have seen, if the physical health deteriorates and the client is made to think that the social worker's help is all that is necessary, a high-risk situation exists. However, if a written contract recommends that the client obtain a medical examination at the outset of treatment in order to rule out related physical health problems, an attorney may not be able to argue successfully that the treatment was faulty.

Confidentiality problems are also reduced through written contracts. The contract can include an explicit statement about the conditions under which confidentiality may have to be suspended in order to comply with the law in the relevant jurisdiction. If the client agreed to these conditions, it would be difficult to later make a claim of malpractice for breach of confidences.

The contract could also address the potential problem of premature termination or abandonment. Premature termination means ending the sessions even though the client's problems remain.. It also applies to instances in which the ongoing client faces an unanticipated problem and cannot reach the professional or get proper backup coverage. This could happen, for example, if the worker has taken a vacation and has not provided coverage for the client, or has not given the backup professional access to the case record. A contract could tell the client what to do in such cases or what backup professional is available to contact. With this information available, the client can rarely argue a case for abandonment.

Accountability and Contracting

When a professional social worker is called before a peer review committee on inquiry, the allegations usually involve violations of standards or ethics code. These committees want to know if the worker has made false claims engaged in practices beyond the recognized expertise, or besmirched the good name of the profession by some conduct. The written contract can be useful in answering such questions and assuaging the concerns of the investigating bodies. The contract explicates the worker's credentials, background, procedures, and goals so that everyone knows at the outset what claims are and are not being made. Few reputable workers would be willing to put in writing blatantly false claims about their experience or expertise. It would be easy for the committee on inquiry to apprehend and apply sanctions on those who do. So the client, the worker, and the profession are all protected.

WRITTEN VERSUS VERBAL CONTRACTS

Many of the social workers and social agencies that do not use written contracts suggest that they use verbal or implied contracts. Workers say they reach agreements with their clients in their first meetings. In these meetings they indicate the conditions of the interventions, discuss the goals, and specify when termination should occur. Many workers say the verbal understanding between worker and client permits a more open, humanistic relationship; it is a covenant of mutual trust (Miller, 1990).

However, verbal or implicit contracts have many shortcomings. The most significant is that the client is probably not in a position to understand what the terms of the contract are. Usually, clients come for help at the time when they are distressed; they want to talk about their problems and end their pain. They are ill prepared at the time of the first interview to divert their attention from their problem to examining all the elements that must be a part of the contract. If the first session is taken up with a discussion of the presenting problem, no time exists to discuss the terms of the contract. On the other hand, if all the elements that must be considered in the therapy transaction are reviewed in the first session, there is scant time to look at the problem.

Verbal contracts are subject to misunderstanding, misinterpretation, changing rules, and problems of proof. They require clients to remember what was said during the stressful initial interview about such things as confidentiality, the worker's credentials, how to secure insurance reimbursement, the goals, and the ways of reaching goals. And even if the client could remember in times of dispute, malpractice claims, or peer review issues, how can any of this be documented? Putting it in writing provides documentation (Marine, 1998b).

THE PRESERVATION OF CONTRACTS AND RECORDS

The social worker has an ethical obligation to secure and preserve the client's records, and to ensure that they are accessible to those who have the right to them. For security, records should be locked in a fireproof file cabinet in or near the worker's office, and should be stored properly to protect them against theft, fire, water damage, or misplacement.

The worker should have a plan for permitting access to the records. In case of death, sudden disability, or unexpected emergencies by the worker, the client is still entitled to competent ongoing care. This right cannot be assured if no other professional can get to the file in a timely and convenient fashion. Thus, the worker is obligated to inform colleagues, staff, or family members how to obtain access to the files. Usually this is done by keeping an envelope with instructions and a cabinet key in the care of the designated person. The worker should have discussed this procedure with those designated to take over; otherwise, some instructions should also be left in the envelope.

The attorney who probates the worker's will, and the state licensing board should also be able to answer what happened to the records. And the clients should be notified of where the records are stored if the worker is deceased. NASW Insurance Trust Manager Loretta Robinson (*NASW News,* 1999) pointed out that a suit may be filed against a social worker's estate as long as twenty years after treatment ends, and a suit may be filed against the worker's estate for compensatory damages from a successfully prosecuted malpractice case. She therefore recommends keeping the records indefinitely.

This may be impractical for many social workers. An alternative could be to keep all records a few years after work with the client is terminated, and then condense some files. Those that have some chance of being needed in the future by anyone could be saved, possibly by placing them on microfiche or electronic files. Some records may be discarded after several years, but some must be retained virtually forever. These include records about adoptions and child abuse cases. All records of children should be kept at least until they have long reached adulthood (*NASW News,* 1999).

CONCLUSION

The original purpose of case records and written contracts was to facilitate the worker's memory and document the goals and treatment progression. This may still be the primary purpose but not the exclusive one. These materials are now used for the purposes of professional accountability.

Obviously, written records and contracts are not panaceas to eliminate all the potential difficulties confronting social workers in direct practice. Even when they are prepared and preserved carefully they will not prevent malpractice suits and peer review investigations. Nevertheless, the likelihood of problems for the worker will be significantly reduced with properly prepared records and contracts. And most important of all, clients will be served more efficiently and effectively.

Chapter 10

Legal and Professional Credentials

A social worker was recently expelled from membership in her professional association and reported to her state's professional licensing bureau for unethical and unprofessional conduct. She was found to have engaged a client for intensive treatment, even though she had no specialized training or supervised experience for it. She also misrepresented her professional qualifications by beginning to see clients before she had obtained her state license for the practice of social work (*NASW News,* 1998b).

For these and other unprofessional actions, the worker was not only expelled, but her actions were highly publicized among her colleagues, those who would refer clients to her, and to third party insurance organizations. No doubt she will find it difficult ever again to practice successfully in the profession for which she was trained.

PRACTICING WITHOUT CREDENTIALS

Social workers hope that such examples are rare. And yet, in the past decade, according to reports in the social work news releases during this time, hundreds of people have been found guilty of practicing without the proper credentials and punished accordingly. Reports describing the varieties of professional misconduct continue to be reported in social work publications and other newspapers, as seen in the following examples:

Recently a new private social work practice was opened. The worker's announcement indicated that she was a fully trained and qualified member of the social work profession. She began seeing clients and sending bills to their insurance companies. However, as the insurance companies and clients soon learned, she had omitted a few facts from her resume. She was still a student, and had not even obtained her MSW degree, much less her professional license. When this was discovered, the clients left, the insurance companies refused to reimburse her, and the professional association punished her after a professional review board hearing. Her social work career was off to an inauspicious start.

*   *   *

Another social worker did have his MSW degree when he began working with individual psychotherapy clients, but he had been trained and experienced exclusively as a community organizer. His state licensing law required that, to practice clinical social work, one is required to have specialized clinical training and supervision, and to document this training and experience in the licensing application. To circumvent the requirement, he misrepresented his background on his application. Soon the deception was discovered and the state licensing authority revoked his license.

*   *   *

A social agency had just hired a new social worker. The personnel forms indicated that the worker had all the qualifications they required—training, experience, and license. The worker had recently completed formal education, had taken the licensing exam, and was eager to begin work. After seeing clients for some time, the agency noted a discrepancy. The licensing board had omitted the worker's name from its list of licensed professionals. Eventually, it was revealed that the worker had failed the licensing exam and was practicing without a license. Because the personnel forms had been completed with deceptive information, the agency had to fire the worker.

*   *   *

The *NASW News* reported several cases in which clinical social workers got in trouble for treating clients who had symptoms of physical dysfunctions and not getting the clients examined by physicians before commencing treatment. In some of these reports, the workers were accused of practicing medicine without licenses. A recurring pattern in these stories is that social workers sometimes advertise themselves as psychoanalysts, hypnotherapists, or as some other psychotherapy specialist, rather than as social workers, even though they possessed no special training for these other practices.

*   *   *

Another frequently recurring pattern involves people with degrees in such fields as "educational counseling," "pastoral therapy," and "marriage and family guidance," but who fill out insurance claims as social workers. They find their fields do not permit them easily to become reimbursed for their services by insurance companies. Finding that social work is often reimbursable, and assuming mistakenly that social work is a more inclusive field than it is, they identified themselves as social workers. This pattern is often justified by the fact that many public and private organizations call their service employees "social workers" even though they have no specialized training in the profession.

*   *   *

Finally, this year a social worker listed herself on business cards, letterheads, and in yellow page advertising as "PhD (ABD)." Several colleagues knew she had not completed her doctoral work, and eventually challenged her. Her defense was that she had been forthright—she had added (ABD) to her degree. It was a designation she claimed was widely known as "all but dissertation" (Arizona Board of Behavioral Health Examiners, 1999).

CONSEQUENCES OF MISREPRESENTATION

Misrepresenting one's own professional credentials is considered a very serious offense. The sanctions for it can be devastating to a career, a reputation, and to a bank balance. The punishments have included one or more of the following: termination of employment;

being legally compelled to pay fines or perform community service activities; being compelled to repay money collected for services to clients or third parties; cancellation of professional or malpractice insurance; malpractice lawsuits (often at one's own expense because of canceled malpractice insurance); expulsion from membership in professional associations; rejection by and isolation from the professional community for an extensive period of time or forever; forfeiture of license; and imprisonment.

Why do these situations occur? No doubt malevolence or opportunism exists with some perpetrators of these frauds. Other excuses are harder to categorize: "I just didn't know I was supposed to get that kind of training." "No one ever told me I had to be licensed to do that." "Well, I was going to be eligible pretty soon, and I already know how to do it, so I didn't think it would matter." "I was just trying to help out the client; she wouldn't have gotten insurance reimbursement if I told them I didn't have my license yet."

No matter how the social worker justifies such behavior, it is clearly illegal and professionally unethical to claim possession of credentials that have not been granted. The "right" to engage in professional social work practice is reserved for, and limited to, those who have been awarded the appropriate credentials, by those who have the legal and professional authority to grant them. Not knowing that these rules exist does not give the person any rights. Every practitioner is expected to understand clearly what constitutes a credential, who is authorized to grant it, what is required to obtain and maintain it, and what rights or limits are inherent in its possession.

WHAT ARE CREDENTIALS?

Credentials, which take many forms, are explicit, widely recognized, and verifiable statements that the holder has fulfilled and continues to meet specified standards. Credentials provide the public with a priori evidence that the standards have been met. When consumers seek providers of services, they are entitled to know what the provider's background and current capabilities are. Usually consumers have no other way of knowing whether the potential provider is competent or not. Obviously, consumers would find it inconvenient, costly, and emotionally distracting to go from one service provider to another in the hope of finding out. Of course, this information does not constitute proof that one is currently competent, but it does offer some assurance that the provider has fulfilled the criteria established by the credentialing authority.

Not all credentials, of course, command equal respect. They range from rigorous, legally enforced documents to form letters from "degree mills." While anyone can print a certificate claiming that some standard has been met, the document is meaningless if not backed by a recognized and credible authority. The most credible credentialing authorities are the publicly funded government organizations that operate at the federal, state, or local levels. When the credential is written into law, enforced by officials of the government, supported by taxpayer money, and monitored by law officers or public representatives, it is considered unassailable by all.

At the other extreme, the credentials with the least credibility are those offered by private groups or individuals. Typically, the major, if not only, requirement to obtain such a credential is a payment to the issuer, for which the recipient receives an official-looking diploma or certificate. These kinds of credentials have virtually no credibility with insurance organizations, government overseers, and professional associations, but to undiscerning consumers they can sometimes be considered worthwhile.

Somewhere between these extremes are credentials offered by professional associations and recognized accrediting bodies. Generally, professional associations provide credentials to individuals while accrediting bodies offer credentials to organizations. Accrediting bodies review most of the nation's hospitals, reputable educational institutions, social agencies, charitable societies, business alliances, and other organizations. They demonstrate to consumers and the public that the organization is in compliance with predetermined standards, by indicating whether it is or is not accredited. Accrediting bodies are usually created and supported by the organizations they regulate.

Credentials by Professional Associations

The credentials offered by some professional associations are very important, usually because of the prestige of the association, its political power and history, and the rigor with which it examines its applicants. When an individual has a credential from such an organization, there is usually no question about the right to engage in the professional activity. With newer, less rigorous groups, there often is some question. For example, physicians who are accepted for Certification in the Board of Psychiatry and Neurology are authorized unequivocally to practice psychotherapy. But to meet the requirements of this credential, the physicians have had to complete extensive formal training, pass rigorous written and oral examinations, and maintain currency with specific continuing education courses every year. On the other hand, counselors who are granted a certificate by one of the nation's proliferating counseling societies may have to work hard to convince people they are actually qualified to practice psychotherapy.

Less authoritative credentials come from organizations that require little of their candidates beyond membership in the group. These organizations often do not even enforce their claims that the member has fulfilled the requirements indicated. They have no entrance examinations, or the exams are perfunctory. Some of these organizations claim to have entrance "examinations" but they consist mostly of general interviews and recommendations from colleagues. They say their testing is based on "oral examinations." The public may not be sure that exams of this type are worthwhile, compared with written exams which can be more objective and consistent from one applicant to the next (Gerdeman, 1998).

Many professional associations also offer credentials to their qualified members which typically represent achievements beyond the requirements for membership. The members who possess these elite internal credentials are identified by such names as "diplomate" or "academy member" or "board certified member." The qualifications for the advanced credentials include higher levels of academic training than are accomplished by the regular members, advanced years of experience, passing specialized examinations, and fulfilling certain continuing education requirements over a defined period of time. Holders of these advanced internal credentials may feel they are more highly regarded than their peers, but there is little evidence that these credentials result in significantly higher degrees of approbation by colleagues or the public.

Most of the professional associations see their role in credentialing as protecting the public and protecting their "turf" (Imber, 1999). They want their credentials to show that the holder can perform tasks that require special knowledge and skills, and they would like to show that only their members should be permitted to perform these tasks. The organizations that have been most successful in achieving this aim have been those with rigorous entrance exams and training qualifications. Less successful associations devote their energies to increasing their memberships and awarding certificates that sound and look authoritative.

Credentials by Public Statute

Credentials that have the authority of law behind them include registration, certification, and licensure. Of the three forms of legal regulation, registration is the weakest and licensing is the strongest. In registration, the jurisdiction lists people who have banded together under a certain title, such as "piano tuner," "plumber," "hearing aid specialist," or "social worker." The holder of this credential has the exclusive right to be known as a "registered" plumber or social worker. Those who are not listed in the registry can claim to be plumbers or social workers, but not registered ones—at least not registered on this particular list. Those who misrepresent themselves as being on the registry run the risks of negative publicity from those in the registry, and of civil actions by aggrieved consumers who can truthfully claim they were victimized by misleading advertising.

Legal certification is somewhat stronger than registration in that the designation involves more than a claim to a title. It also indicates that the one legally certified has fulfilled explicit experience and training requirements and is thus qualified to perform specific tasks. Thus, a plumber or piano tuner who is certified is assuring the consumer that the job will probably be done according to the standards established by the certifying authority. However, the certificate does not guarantee to the consumer that the job will be performed satisfactorily; consumers who are not satisfied may have to take civil legal actions rather than appealing to the certification authority. The legal assurance is only that the provider has obtained the duly recognized qualifications for the task, and makes no assessments about how the task itself is performed.

Licensing is the strongest form of legal regulation because it spells out requirements of education, knowledge, and skill. Licensing also uses the state's regulatory powers to ensure that the provider's behavior complies with the required standards. The relevant licensing law says that the state protects the public by applying sanctions to any licensee who violates the standards. The consumer thereby has some assurance that the provider has the requisite ability to fulfill the task, and will do so.

State licensing laws have much stronger control mechanisms than professional association credentials. When infractions of the licensing requirements occur, a crime has been committed and police or prosecutors may be called upon to initiate corrective action. When violations occur with the most rigorous professional association credential, the matter is settled "in-house" whenever possible.

ORIGINS OF SOCIAL WORK CREDENTIALS

Social work has never been at the forefront of professional efforts to establish credentialing. Indeed, until the 1970s most social workers had few credentialing opportunities other than their educational degrees. Professional association certificates had little, if any, authority, and licensing laws with enforceability existed in only a few states. Social work lagged behind many other professions, even those much younger and less well established. The efforts of some individual social workers and social work groups to get licensing laws and professional certification were thwarted by their own professional association leaders as well as lawmakers and competing professional associations. More social workers seemed resistant to, or at least indifferent to, efforts to establish strong credentialing. This is partly the result of social work's unique history and value system.

When social work emerged as an identifiable occupation in the 1890s and as a profession in the 1920s, its primary practice was within social agencies. Nearly all workers were employees of government or private agencies. Clients sought services from the agency/employer rather than the worker. The agencies were accountable for any problems so they exercised great care in their hiring and supervising of social work employees. No matter how much training the worker possessed, the job was essentially bureaucratic. They did what their employers hired them to do, were monitored carefully by responsible supervisors, and were fired if their conduct was inappropriate.

The social work establishment believed the consumer was well protected by this system, perhaps better than any of the professions whose members worked autonomously and regulated their own practices. Social work's clients paid the agency for services, or their fees were subsidized by philanthropic donations and public fund raising efforts. There were few third-party financing organizations involved to compel individual social workers to develop their own credentials.

Because social agency employment was predominant, and still is the primary employer of social workers, most people saw little need for additional regulation through the 1950s. It was believed that the supervisors could do everything needed. It seemed to most social workers that licensing was something only for private social work practitioners, a small proportion of the membership. And most social workers thought private practice was anathema to the goals and values of the profession.

Almost from social work's beginning, however, some sought regulation outside social agencies. In 1917, social workers themselves developed an employment registry, indicating the qualifications of those who could be listed. This group eventually formed the American Association of Social Workers, which in 1955 merged with other groups to become the National Association of Social Workers. NASW and its state chapters made few attempts and had little success in getting states to pass social work licensing laws until the late 1960s.

The first jurisdiction to legally regulate the practice of social work was in Puerto Rico in 1934, but it was little more than a registry to indicate who had the right to be called a social worker. The first state law pertaining to social work practice was not passed until 1945, in California; however, it too was basically a registry of graduate school-trained social workers in the state. Only a handful of states had any social work laws before the late 1960s.

In lieu of this, NASW developed a certificate program in 1960 known as the Academy of Certified Social Workers. It was restricted to experienced professional social workers and required its members to keep current by taking qualified continuing education units. Membership was open to social workers of all orientations and practice specialties. Eventually, applicants had to pass multiple choice exams, although the vast majority of members were not required to take the test because of a grandfathering privilege.

Despite its longevity, the ACSW has had many critics and its value has remained debatable (Thyer and Vodde, 1994). Some social workers claimed the exam, in its earlier incarnations at least, could be passed by almost any intelligent liberal arts graduate. ACSW administrators denied this, but would not disclose the exam's pass-failure rate. They also pointed out that, because the test was for all social workers of all specialties, it could not be too technical in the specialty areas. They claimed it would be unfair, for example, to ask community organizers difficult questions about clinical diagnoses, or to ask clinical social workers about complex social policy issues.

Nevertheless, with ACSW being the only opportunity for credentialing for most social workers, most experienced social work members of NASW sought and paid for annual membership. NASW made money for issuing the certificates but did little to ensure that it was at all meaningful.

By the 1970s, many social workers perceived NASW as being indifferent to the call for legal credentialing, or at least ineffective in helping to bring it about. Meanwhile associations representing competing professions became more active in establishing state licensing laws; soon every state licensed psychiatrists, psychologists, nurses, and many other specialties—but not social workers. The other professions even had their roles defined in the licensing statutes to include tasks that social workers had once considered their exclusive province. Many NASW members, especially those who provided clinical mental health services, began demanding that their association work harder to establish licensing. However, many more NASW members, especially educators and nonclinicians, objected to the licensing movement, claiming it was elitist and contrary to the values of the profession.

Two trends motivated NASW to begin seriously addressing the issue. First, many of its members began joining other professional social work associations which they perceived as being more sympathetic to their objective. In 1971 the Clinical Social Work Federation was established (originally as the National Federation of Societies for Clinical Social Work); one of its primary objectives was to establish licensing and public recognition for those social workers who provided professional services to individuals, families, and groups. Similar objectives were espoused by I-CAPP (the International Conference for the Advancement of Private Practice in Social Work), and later by ABE (the American Board of Examiners in Clinical Social Work).

The second trend that led to NASW's changed position and effort to establish social work licensure was stimulated by social work employers and insurance companies. Social workers without licenses were finding it increasingly difficult to get agency jobs and reimbursement from insurance companies for mental health care services.

NASW began working more enthusiastically and effectively for social work licensure. It prepared a Model Licensing Act and instructed social workers in every state on how to get their legislators to adopt the act into state law. They devoted money, staff, and educational resources to state social work organizations that were succeeding in getting laws passed. In the states where licensing laws had been passed, NASW helped their boards form a new association of state boards to facilitate communication and consistency from state to state. By 1979 the American Association of State Social Work Boards (AASSWB) was established. The combined efforts of these and other groups, as well as considerable competition and even litigation between the groups, led to social work licensure by all the states in the early 1990s.

The professional organizations themselves did not want to cede their credentialing authority to state licensing statutes. They continued and increased their own credentials. NASW maintained its ACSW certificate and has added several newer credentials. ABE has a diplomate credential and the Clinical Federation has developed two categories for its distinguished practitioners. Within a decade social work went from being a profession that was virtually uncredentialled to one that now has an abundance of them. Now social workers must contend with a confusing array of professional credentials to go with their licenses.

REQUIREMENTS
FOR PROFESSIONAL CREDENTIALS

Professional associations sponsor a variety of credentials for their social work members. The National Association of Social Workers currently controls the Academy of Certified Social Workers (ACSW) certification, the Qualified Clinical Social Worker (QCSW) certificate, the Diplomate in Clinical Social Work (DCSW) and the School Social Work Specialist (SSWS) credential. All require possession of a master's degree or higher from a school accredited by the Council on Social Work Education, and agreement to adhere to the NASW Code of Ethics. In other respects each certificate has unique requirements.

The ACSW

The credential for the Academy of Certified Social Workers is the oldest and most well-established social work credential still offered by a professional association. Over the years the requirements for ACSW membership have been modified and, according to some social workers, relaxed. At present, eligibility is limited to experienced NASW members (with master's degrees or above). They must have at least two years of full-time, paid, supervised professional experience and they must have passed the ACSW written examination (unless they are eligible for grandparenting). They are also required to submit two professional reference ratings (one from a colleague and the other from one's immediate supervisor). The examinations are offered twice a year throughout the nation and in some overseas locations. Once the worker has the ACSW certificate it may be renewed annually for a fee.

The QCSW

While the ACSW credential is for all eligible masters-degreed social workers, regardless of their specific expertise or focus of work, the Qualified Clinical Social Worker (QCSW) certification is more specialized. It was developed specifically for those social workers who focus on direct therapeutic intervention with individuals, couples, and families. QCSW eligibility is not limited to NASW members, as is the case with the ACSW, but it does require an earned master's degree or above from a Council on Social Work Education accredited school. It also requires the worker to be able to document more than 3,000 hours (two years) of postgraduate supervised clinical experience in an agency or organized setting. The QCSW must also pass a social work examination, which may be either the ACSW exam or one maintained by the relevant state's licensing board.

The SSWS

A third credential offered by the National Association of Social Workers is only for professionals who specialize in school social work. The SSWS credential may be awarded to experienced social workers with master's degrees or above from accredited schools, who provide social and mental health services in public or private schools and other educational facilities. Eligibility is for those workers who have had at least two years supervised employment in such settings, have provided letters of reference from a colleague and a supervisor, and agree to adhere to the NASW Code of Ethics and to the NASW Standards for School Social Work Services. To obtain SSWS certification the worker must also pass the School Social Worker Specialty Area test; this test is offered six times a year in many locations across the nation. The credential must be renewed periodically and the holder is required to successfully complete thirty clock hours of continuing professional education every three years.

The DCSW

NASW's highest clinical certification is the diplomate (DCSW), a professional association credential whose standards are higher than that of any other credential or state licensing requirements. In addition to meeting all the qualifications for the Qualified Clinical Social Work certificate, the diplomate also must be able to document two years of supervised clinical practice and then three additional years of advanced clinical practice, with at least two years of practice within the last ten years. The diplomate must also hold the highest level of social work license available in the home state and successfully complete the NASW Diplomate Clinical Assessment Examination. This exam is administered at different sites across the nation and overseas but is offered only once per year.

Other social work professional associations also offer credentials to qualified social workers, including the American Board of Examiners in Clinical Social Work (ABE), and the Clinical Social Work Federation (CSWF).

ABE's BCD

The major credential offered by ABE is its Board Certified Diplomate in Clinical Social Work (BCD). To become a diplomate the applicant must first have completed a master's degree in social work with specified clinical course content from a school accredited by the Council on Social Work Education. The applicant must also have achieved five years and 7,500 hours of direct clinical practice, including 3,000 hours under qualified supervision. The BCD must also have obtained the highest license or certificate in the jurisdiction where the practice takes place. To maintain the diplomate, the BCD must continue to meet the requirements for licensure and complete at least twenty hours of continuing education in clinical work; the BCD must also keep current with at least 3,000 hours of clinical practice during the past ten years.

In 1997, the American Board of Examiners in Clinical Social Work discontinued its requirement of ABE members to pass an objective written (multiple choice) exam. The current procedure is for the applicant to demonstrate competence primarily through personal interviews and by appropriate communications from colleagues and supervisors. It is arguable whether oral "exams" have the same weight and rigor (Biggerstaff, 1994) but ABE suggests that it is a more fair and accurate way to determine the worker's competence than by depending too much on multiple choice questionnaires. ABE is also developing an entry-level certification for social work students and for social work clinical practitioners with less experience.

The Clinical Social Work Federation established two specialization groups, the Family Therapy Practice Academy (FTPA) and the National Membership Committee on Psychoanalysis in Clinical Social Work (NMCOP).

The FTPA

Members of the Family Therapy Practice Academy, which promotes standards and professional participation for social workers in the field of family therapy, meet the qualifications of the Clinical Federation; no other special training or experience has been specified, but most Academy members are oriented in their professional practices to work with families rather than individuals.

The NMCOP

The other specialty group sponsored by the Clinical Federation is comprised of social workers who are also trained as psychoanalysts or who use psychoanalytic theory and treatment methods in their practices. NMCOP does not yet require that its members demonstrate special training or experience in psychoanalysis, but members are required to belong to the Clinical Federation.

NAP

Many distinguished social workers belong to the National Academy of Practice (NAP), an independent organization comprised of practitioners from the major professional practice disciplines in the United States. Established in 1981 and modeled in part on the National Academy of Sciences, NAP's membership includes leaders in major health disciplines including medicine, dentistry, nursing, psychology, optometry, and pharmacy, as well as social work. Each member belongs to NAP through one of its constituent entities such as the National Academy of Practice in Social Work. Because membership is by invitation only and limited only to professionals who have established distinguished professional careers, membership in NAP is considered by some to be one of the most prestigious credentials available.

Other Credentialing Organizations

Many other social work professional associations in the United States and other nations have been established in recent decades to enhance the level of expertise in different specialty areas within the field. While these organizations do not usually establish formal certification of expertise within their fields, members must meet the organization's qualifications to belong. Usually these qualifications include work experience and training in the field that is the group's focus, in addition to the usual graduate degrees from accredited social work schools. So, for example, a social worker employed in a hospital to assist with cancer patients and their families displays a plaque indicating membership in the Association of Oncology Social Workers. Or workers employed in maternity wards might belong to the National Association of Perinatal Social Workers.

Other social work groups, while not implying a special type of special social work expertise, do declare an orientation or focus on certain client groups that may be of significance to some consumers. These groups include the North American Conference of Christian Social Workers, the National Black Social Workers Association, the National Indian Social Workers Association, the Asian-American Social Workers Association, the International Conference for the Advancement of Private Practice in Social Work (I-CAPP), and the National Organization of Forensic Social Work. Many of these groups have established, or are in the process of developing, their own diplomate certificates for their members of special distinction.

Many social workers also belong to interdisciplinary professional practice organizations. Typically, the membership requirements of these organizations include degrees from the relevant accredited graduate professional schools as well as additional training and experience in the particular field or specialty. The major organizations of this type, to which social workers belong in significant numbers, include the American Association of Suicidology, the American Association of Sex Educators, Counselors, and Therapists (AASECT), the American Group Psychotherapy Association (AGPA), the American Association of Orthopsychiatry (Ortho), the American Music Therapy Association, and the National Association of Poetry Therapy.

Many of the interdisciplinary organizations also offer additional credentialing opportunities for their more distinguished members. Members who have been in the field for an extended period of time or who have achieved unique worthy accomplishments are acknowledged as "diplomates," or "academy members," or some other title to indicate special distinction.

SOCIAL WORK LICENSURE

Licensure for social workers in all jurisdictions has been a difficult journey which has yet to be completed. Even though social work licensing or legal certification of some sort now exists in all fifty of the United States, and the three territories of Puerto Rico, the District of Columbia, and the Virgin Islands, there are still widespread disparities in their relative strength, clarity, enforceability, and consistency with other jurisdictions. Each state or jurisdiction has spelled out its own requirements; only in recent years has there been an effective effort to make these laws more uniform from one jurisdiction to another.

The social work licensing laws are still, for the most part, unique in each state. That is, every state has its own version of what social workers do and what the penalties are for those who fail to perform their duties properly. The laws vary in their exact provisions for the management, financing, and regulation of the system. In many jurisdictions these laws also specify their own qualifications of the licensee, as well as continuing standards and procedures for enforcement; in other jurisdictions the law indicates that such elements will be determined by the board or its designees. The one consistency in all states is that the purpose of social work licensing statutes is not to protect the social worker or the social work profession but to protect the consumer from social workers.

Some states offer different licensing titles, usually referring to different levels of practice. These may include licenses for bachelor's degree level social workers, master's degree level workers with little or no experience, master's and doctoral degree level workers with several years of experience, and licenses specifically for workers engaged in clinical social work practice. The various titles for these licenses include Licensed Clinical Social Worker (LCSW), Associate

Clinical Social Worker (ASW), Licensed Independent Clinical Social Worker (LICSW), Licensed Independent Social Worker (LISW), and Licensed Clinical Social Work Associate (LSWA).

The licensing system is managed and maintained by a board of directors. Usually this board and its operations are financed by licensing fees paid by the social work applicants. Social workers pay initial application fees, annual renewal fees, and where applicable the fees to administer competency examinations and continuing education requirements.

The boards of social work examiners may or may not be exclusively social workers. Since the members are appointed by the governor or other executive, they may be political allies, bureaucrats, or members of related professions, as well as social workers. Usually the governor follows some or all of the appointment recommendations of the state social work associations, especially in the beginning. Those social workers who spearheaded the legislation that created the law have often been appointed to these boards. In most states the board members serve for a specified length of time, after which the governor replaces or reappoints them.

At the beginning of 1999, all but thirteen states had licensing boards exclusively for social work. Of the thirteen states, about half combined licensing boards for social workers with marriage and other counselor groups, while the other half had boards that included social work with other mental health professions (AASSWB, 1999). A list of all the licensing boards and their addresses that apply to social workers in the fifty states and three jurisdictions is found in the appendix of this book.

Functions of the Licensing Board

Members of the social work licensing board, with their staffs, enforce the statute and manage the system. If not already established in the statutes, the board develops the rules for granting and maintaining licensure, usually with proper input from professional associations, concerned individual social workers, client consumer groups, third-party organizations, and government and legal authorities. These ground rules indicate qualifications for licensure, such as level of education, experience, specialty, and proof of competence.

Proof of competence is supposedly established through systematic licensing examinations and documentation of continuing education requirements. In the jurisdictions where formal examinations are required, the board is responsible for developing the exams and procedures for taking them, or at least obtaining exams that have been provided to them by experts. Most states which require licensing exams use the ones developed by the American Association of State Social Work Boards (AASSWB).

Most state boards also maintain records of the status of each licensed social worker, inform licensees and consumers about the standards for licensure, and, where applicable, maintain records about continuing education. Some boards try to ensure that the licensee has kept current by taking the prescribed number of continuing education courses within a specified time period; many of them also try to make sure that the type of courses that are taken by the social worker are appropriate and meet their criteria for continuing education.

The boards maintain communications with other state licensing boards, primarily through their common membership in the AASSWB. This is important in developing greater uniformity between states, and especially in keeping track of social workers who move their residences and practices from one state to another. In many cases the social worker who moves to another state has licensing reciprocity granted fairly readily because of the AASSWB coordination. The license in the new state can be granted fairly readily, without examinations, if the worker is applying for the same kind of license in the new state and if the two states have comparable levels of licensure.

The board and the licensure procedure are usually financed entirely from the fees that licensed workers pay to be eligible for licensure. The fees are renewed annually, usually after the licensing board sends a bill to the worker. Generally, the billing statements also indicate the worker's current status as to continuing education. Of course, the fees for licensing exams and for help in preparing for these exams are extra.

Licensing Examinations

The licensing examinations are gradually becoming uniform in all the jurisdictions of the United States. Social work examinations have been developed for four categories by the American Association of State Social Work Boards. The categories are "basic" (for baccalaureate social workers upon graduation), "intermediate" (for master's degree social workers with no post-degree experience), "advanced" for MSWs or DSWs with more than two years supervised experience after graduation, and "clinical" (for MSW-DSW workers with two years of direct clinical social work experience).

Each exam consists of 170 multiple choice questions, of which 150 count toward the final score. The other twenty questions, which are interspersed throughout the exam, are pretest items, which the test creators are evaluating for possible inclusion in subsequent tests. The applicant is given four hours to complete the exam; applicants with special needs according to the Americans with Disabilities Act may be granted extra time if they arrange for it in advance. Scoring is done electronically and the applicant is informed of the outcome usually within a month in most states.

AASSWB provides applicants with valuable assistance in preparing to take the test. With a toll-free call (1-888-SSW-EXAM) to AASSWB headquarters in Arlington, Virginia, the applicant can learn more about what to expect in the exam, where and when to apply, and what the specific requirements will be. AASSWB has also developed an "examination candidate preapproval service," which can help licensing boards and applicants determine if they are ready to take the exam. In this system the applicant would submit the qualifications for review to see if everything is in order prior to entering the examination room. For example, the review would show that the applicant has obtained the right academic degrees and completed all the experience requirements for the particular license. AASSWB would maintain a database with this information which would "preapprove" the applicants eligibility to take the test. This is especially helpful to recent graduates who wish to establish themselves in states other than that of their university. It is also useful in sparing some applicants some embarrassment if they are not yet qualified to take the exam.

Content of Licensing Exams

Each of the four AASSWB exam levels or categories stress their own quality of content as well as the amount of weight that is given to each content area. AASSWB reveals to all applicants the proportional emphasis given to each content area in the exams. An abbreviated breakdown of their information for the basic social work licensing exam is as follows:

23%— Assessment (including indicators of abuse, neglect, danger to self or others, mental and behavioral disorders, client strengths and weaknesses, effects of environment on client, problem identification, use of assessment instruments, and social history and collateral data

23%— Practice with individuals, couples, families, groups, and communities (including intervention process and techniques)

15%— Human development and behavior (including theoretical approaches, human growth and development, human behavior in the social environment, impact of crises and changes, abnormal and addictive behaviors, and dynamics of abuse and neglect)

7%— Effects of diversity

7%— Interpersonal communication

7%— Professional values and ethics

4%— Social work relationship

3%— Each for content in supervision, research, and administration

The proportion of emphasis given in the ten content areas of the intermediate exam are as follows:

21%— Direct practice, including intervention theories and methods, the intervention process and techniques, consultation and interdisciplinary collaboration, and interventions with couples, families, groups, and communities

15%— Human development and behavior, including theories, human growth and development, application of knowledge, dynamics of abuse and neglect, and addictions

15%— Assessment, diagnosis and treatment planning

11%— Professional social worker/client relationship

10%— Professional values and ethics, including legal and confidentiality issues

10%— Communication principles and techniques
5%— Supervision and administration
5%— Service delivery
3%— Research, collection, analysis, and utilization

The advanced exam has twelve content areas in the following proportions:

23%— Assessment, diagnosis, and treatment planning, including social history and collateral data, use of assessment instruments, problem identification, effects of environment on client behavior, impact of change on systems, evaluation of client strengths and weaknesses, evaluation of mental and behavioral disorders, abuse and neglect, danger to self and others, general assessment issues and treatment planning

17%— Direct practice, including methods and processes, intervention techniques, interventions with couples, families, groups, and communities

10%— Human development and behavior including theories and models, human growth and development, and family functioning

8%— Professional values and ethics, including confidentiality and self-determination

7%— Relationship concepts

7%— Communication principles and techniques

7%— Social work interface with other systems

5%— Effects of culture, race, ethnicity, sexual orientation, gender, age, and disability

5%— Administration

5%— Service delivery

3%— Supervision

The clinical exam has eleven content areas in the following proportions:

19%— Psychotherapy and clinical practice, including intervention techniques with individuals, couples, families, and groups, and treatment planning

17%— Human development and behavior in the life cycle, including family functioning, impact of crises and changes, addictions, abuse, and neglect

12%— Diagnosis and assessment, including diagnostic classifications, information gathering, and indicators of danger to self and others

11%— Professional values and ethics, including confidentiality and legal issues

9%— Communication theories and techniques

9%— Service delivery

8%— Relationship theories and practice

5%— Diversity, including effects of culture, race, ethnicity, sexual orientation, gender, age, disability

5%— Clinical practice, including management in the organizational setting, advocacy, finance, and human resources

3%— Supervision

3%— Research

The differences in the four exams are greater than is apparent in this outline. While the subject areas are roughly the same for each level, although with different degrees of emphasis, the "degree of difficulty" increases with each advance in level of exam. With the less advanced exams there is greater emphasis on concrete and factual data, symptoms, and procedures, and with the more advanced exams there is greater emphasis on theory, interconnectedness of concepts, and the complexities and controversies encountered in the profession.

COMPARING CREDENTIALS WITH OTHER PROFESSIONS

Largely through the efforts of the American Association of State Social Work Boards, the profession has made enormous strides in the past few years in catching up with other professions in the development of its licensing process. It remains behind the other mental health providing professions—especially psychiatry, psychology, and nursing—in its licensing laws and professional credentialing, but no longer lags far behind such fields as optometry, audiology, speech pathology, physical therapy, and chiropractic.

Social work remained behind because, in many states, their licensing laws are not fully developed, and there was so much inconsistency in their professional association credentials. Until recently, many states did not require objective examinations to demonstrate social work competency—or the exams were so ill designed that they could be passed by people who had little or no social work training. One result was that in some of these states, people with no social work training whatsoever could practice as social workers. Another was that trained experienced social workers were excused from taking membership entrance exams through grandparent clauses.

The other professions were also ahead in the rigor with which they enforced continuing competency among their members. They have specific rules for periodic reevaluations, retesting, and especially continuing education requirements. Their members were required to take courses from preapproved educational resources and to provide to the state or professional authority documents proving that they had taken the required courses. Members who failed to meet the continuing education requirements would be notified and could be expelled if they remained out of compliance.

Social workers, for the most part, had far less external pressure to keep up to date. There were few mechanisms in professional associations or state licensing boards for keeping track of the worker's continuing education requirements. The "honor system" was implicitly used.

Partly because of this laxity, social workers might have had an easier time entering the profession and staying in it, but they suffered serious competitive disadvantages compared to members of other professions. Perhaps the quality of students who entered social work also declined. Many social work educators know of students who said they chose social work because it was the easiest, quickest, least demanding way they could become psychotherapists.

Agencies, institutions, and government organizations began hiring members of the other professions rather than social workers; they found that nurses, psychologists, educational counselors, and members of many other professions, were now performing many of the functions that were once the recognized province of social work—and they seemed to have more rigorous standards for entering their professions than did those in social work.

Only in the past decade has this disadvantage been reduced. However, it does remain and will continue to do so, at least until the remaining credentialing problems in social work are overcome.

UNRESOLVED CREDENTIALING PROBLEMS

There are still five major problems in credentialing that social work must overcome. These are (1) the confusing profusion of credentials; (2) the conflict between social work organizations about which kind of credentials to endorse; (3) the lack of standardization in qualifications for social work credentialing; (4) the grandparenting rules in credentialing; and (5) inadequate continuing education requirements and enforcement procedures.

The first difficulty is that there now exists so many potential credentials that their very number diminishes the worth of any one of them. Twelve different credentials have been described above and this does not count such additional important ones as the worker's degrees from accredited universities and graduate schools, and credentials from interdisciplinary organizations. Theoretically an experienced and well-trained social worker could list her name and credentialing initials as follows:

Ann Jones, MSW, PhD, LICSW, ACSW, ABE-BCD, NAP-SW, AFTA, DCSW, SSWS

After the first few initials the designations appear to become ridiculous, even though every one is considered important and would require considerable effort and expense to achieve. Whenever so many credentials exist, some workers might have to explain why they do not have any one of them. For example, if a worker were establishing her credentials as an expert witness in a court of law, the opposing attorney could ask, "Isn't it true, Dr. Jones, that one of the highest credentials in your field is the QCSW . . . a credential that you have not been granted?"

In view of this profusion, it might be time for the professional associations and licensing boards to turn their attentions to consolidation of credentials. However, this would be unlikely for some time to come because of the second credentialing difficulty, that of internal conflicts between social work organizations. When social workers become dissatisfied with existing credentialing bodies and the types of standards, they have tended to form new groups rather than seeking consolidation and compromise. They hope to remedy their grievance by developing new criteria and standards for licensure and then attracting workers to their new group and its credentialing authority. This leads to rivalry between social work groups and confusion for everyone else.

The antipathy and litigation that once existed between the American Board of Examiners in Clinical Social Work (ABE) and the National Association of Social Workers illustrates the problem. Both groups still compete to be the major professional credentialing authority for social workers by creating new certificate programs. For example, ABE claims that its BCD credential is "the gold standard in clinical social work—it has the most rigorous criteria, and is the most intensely promoted and widely recognized" (ABE, 1999, p. 2). Meanwhile, NASW makes almost identical claims for its Diplomate in Clinical Social Work. Unfortunately, both groups have devoted so much of their limited resources to competing with each other that less attention was devoted to seeking improved and consistent overall credentials.

The problem of competing professional groups has contributed to the third reason for credentialing problems, the wide disparity of standards for social work credentials. Each state and each professional association has unique criteria for social work credentials. For example, a social worker who seeks the Board Certified Diplomate in Clinical Social Work from the ABE organization must have five years or 7,500 hours of direct clinical practice, but no longer requires a written test of professional competence. A worker who seeks the Diplomate in Clinical Social Work from NASW must have the same amount of experience and must pass a written examination. Diplomates by other social work organizations specify less experience and may or may not require additional exams.

The Grandparent Rule

The fourth deficiency in social work credentialing is that of grandparenting. This refers to the practice of exempting experienced social workers from having to pass the qualifying examinations and other eligibility requirements that apply to newer workers. In many legal jurisdictions and professional credentialing bodies, some form of grandparent exclusion exists. The rationale is that veteran social workers are already so experienced that they should not have to prove merit through the examination or other evaluation.

The stated rationale is dubious. Experience does not guarantee that the worker has kept current. Furthermore, many older workers with experience in another social work specialty are granted this waiver even though they have little experience in the work for which they now want to be licensed. If the purpose of legal and professional regulation is to protect the consumer then grandparenting undercuts the purpose.

Experienced workers have argued other reasons for being grandparented. They claim that the exams are poorly administered, culturally biased, irrelevant to current social work practice, and generally not good indicators of competence. If this is so, then it is not any more appropriate to expect it of younger workers. Moreover, the examinations and procedures are improving significantly and these complaints are rarely heard anymore. Nevertheless, the demand for grandparenting continues.

Clearly the grandparenting waiver is not granted because of rationality or fairness. It is granted because the experienced social workers have the power and they do not want to run the risk of embarrassment in taking the tests. They want to share in the benefits of the credentials, that is, third-party recognition, increased prestige, and protection of the public, but they are less enthused about the effort to make credentialing work.

Continuing Education Requirements

Similar to the grandparenting problem is that of continuing education. Inadequate requirements and enforcement procedures prevail. Professional knowledge is not static and must be continually upgraded and developed for it to be valid. For social workers to remain competent, some form of continuing education is a necessity. If this competence is to be certified by a legal or professional body, some form of documentation or proof is in order.

Most professions document the continuing competence of their members by periodic reexamination and by requiring specified units of continuing education within accredited schools or professional meetings. For example, lawyers in most states are required to take fifteen hours of certified courses per year or forty-five hours over any given three-year period. Some physician specialties require members to earn fifty units per year. Other professions also require proof of continuing education. In some states, the licensed professional must file an annual affidavit with the board. In others, attendees must sign in for each continuing education session. The provider then certifies the names to the professional association. Some professional groups use both systems.

For the most part, social work has not yet achieved this standard. Many social work regulatory boards have vague or nonexistent requirements about continuing education. Others indicate that continuing education is needed but do not require proof of its acquisition. Theoretically, the worker keeps track of the number of educational hours logged and presents the number to any board that asks. Rarely do they ask.

Related to continuing education is the issue of periodic reexamination. Few jurisdictions or professional organizations presently require social workers to be examined in order to retain their licenses or certificates. Even if the worker accumulated continuing education credits, it is no assurance that the information has been relevant or retained. Nearly all the other professions, occupational groups, and even state drivers' license boards require this. But for now it seems highly unlikely that a profession that excuses its older workers from licensing examinations would require them to take periodic reexaminations. Clients can only hope that the experienced social workers they have dealt with are personally conscientious enough to remain up to date of their own volitions.

THE AASSWB MODEL
SOCIAL WORK PRACTICE ACT

Many of these problems could be corrected or at least minimized when all the states legislatures incorporate the AASSWB Model Social Work Practice Act into their respective states' laws. This proposed legislation was developed over a three-year period (1995-1997) by a task force established by the American Association of State Social

Work Boards. The task force members represented social workers in all geographic areas, professional specialties, levels of training, and philosophical orientations; they also solicited and received input from all the national social work organizations and, of course, from the state regulatory boards and legal consultants.

The mandate was to provide a resource to state social work boards that would provide them with standards of minimal social work competence, methods for properly addressing consumer complaints, and removing incompetent or unethical social workers from practice. The idea is to encourage all the states to establish a uniform social work regulatory bill. It would facilitate greater standardization of terminology, licensing levels, and interrelationships between the states.

The Model Act explicates a client bill of rights as well as a code of conduct which can be expected from social workers at all four levels of practice. It is not based on the Code of Ethics of the NASW or CSWF or any other professional group, though it encourages compliance with these codes. Rather, it covers ethical conduct in legally defensible ways rather than as presented in professional codes of ethics, which tend to help protect professionals as well as the public. The act was not designed to guard professional turf or secure specific job descriptions for social workers but rather to protect the public.

Anyone can examine the complete Model Act and an extensive commentary about its development, the issues in its creation, and a discussion of how it might be used by requesting a copy from the AASSWB. It is also found on the Internet at www.aasswb.org.

It will doubtless take many years for this act to be adopted by all the states and jurisdictions. The effort and controversy many social workers had to endure to get their current laws passed makes them hesitant about embarking on this new venture. However, inasmuch as the existing boards of social work examiners in nearly every state have already participated in the development of the act, along with the leadership of the major professional organizations, the task should be easier and faster than before. When the states adopt a uniform law about social work practice, the profession can redirect its major attention to its clients rather than its credentials.

CONCLUSION

The ostensible purpose of credentials is to protect the public in its dealings with professionals. And in light of all the misdeeds and mistakes described throughout this book, it is clear that the public needs the protection. However, social workers sometimes forget why credentials exist. For some social workers, the goal of acquiring them is not to assure the public of their capabilities and ethical conduct, but to enhance their own prestige, establish exclusive rights to some "turf," and to be eligible for insurance company reimbursement. To them, the purpose of credentials is more for their own protection than that of the consumer.

If it were otherwise, these social workers would be eager to eliminate grandparenting, upgrade and enforce continuing education requirements, and develop more rigorous licensing examinations. If it were otherwise, more social workers would be eager to support the efforts of organizations like the American Association of State Social Work Boards to upgrade and systematize standards. Yet many workers still do not support these initiatives; they complain that these standards are too elitist and restrictive to be consistent with the values of the profession.

Using credentials to achieve greater prestige and benefits rather than protection for the public is ultimately counterproductive. If credentials are not backed by high standards, the public eventually catches on and the credential is devalued. These credentials eventually meet the same fate as the currency of a poor nation that prints excessive money to pay its bills. And like that kind of money, the value of these credentials gradually becomes worthless, except to steer people away from it.

Whether social workers like it or not, the public can do without their credentials. As we have seen throughout this book, they can rely on other protections. They can sue professionals for malpractice. They know that the law and the legal system can protect them if the credential cannot. Accordingly, social workers must keep a wary eye on the legal system. Unfortunately, as the previous chapters of this book have illustrated, the legal system has its imperfections too. By now, many readers have become all too aware of that fact. The legal hazards into which they can fall, whether through misjudgment, misconduct, or bad luck can make even the most trusting social workers feel they have the symptoms of paranoid personality disorders. But as the old tag-line says, "You're not paranoid if they really are out to get you!"

The law is not out to get social workers who are honorable and competent. To the extent that it helps root out those who are dishonorable and incompetent, social workers should appreciate rather than fear or begrudge the law. No one denies that there are imperfections in the law. Some of its rulings have seemed unfair to social workers; some laws seem contradictory, or apparently require professionals to have powers that are beyond human capabilities. But over time these will be ironed out. Like social work, the law is a work in progress. Both professions and the institutions they represent will continue to change. They will change in ways that both would prefer if they work in harmony. This seems to be happening. More social workers have become involved in the legal aspects of professional practice. They are getting more training in the law and once again taking more jobs in law-related fields. Their use as expert witnesses is only beginning to develop and, if present trends continue, this should become an important social work specialty. As both professions learn more about each other, and work together in pursuit of common objectives, they will both become more effective in serving the cause of social justice.

State Boards of Social Work Licensure

Alabama

Alabama State Board of Social Work Examiners
Folsom Administration Building
64 N. Union St., Suite 129
Montgomery, AL 36130

Alaska

Board of Clinical Social Work Examiners
Division of Occupational Licensing
Department of Commerce and Economic Commerce
P.O. Box 11806
Juneau, AK 99811

Arizona

Board of Behavioral Health Examiners
1400 W. Washington St., #350
Phoenix, AZ 85007

Arkansas

Social Work Licensing Board
2020 W. Third St., Suite 503
P.O. Box 250381
Little Rock, AR 72225

This information is provided by: American Association of State Social Work Boards, 400 South Ridge Parkway, Suite B, Culpeper, VA 22701, 1-800-225-6880, e-mail: info@aaswb.org.

California

Board of Behavioral Science Examiners
Department of Consumer Affairs
400 R Street, Suite 3150
Sacramento, CA 95814-6240

Connecticut

Department of Health Services
Social Work Licensure
410 Capitol Ave., MS #12 APP
Hartford, CT 06106

Delaware

Board of Social Work Examiners
Cannon Building
P.O. Box 1401
Dover, DE 19901

District of Columbia

DC Board of Social Work
Department of Consumer and Regulatory Affairs
Occupational and Professional Licensing Administration
614 H St., NW, Room 904
Washington, DC 20001

Florida

Board of Clinical Social Work
Agency for Health Care Administration
1940 N. Monroe St.
Tallahassee, FL 32399

Georgia

Georgia Composite Board of Professional Counselors, Social
    Workers, and Marriage and Family Therapists
166 Pryor St. NW
Atlanta, GA 30303

Hawaii

Social Work Program
1010 Richards St.
Honolulu, HI 96813

Idaho

Bureau of Occupational Licensing
Board of Social Work Examiners
Owyhee Plaza
1109 Main St., Suite 220
Boise, ID 83702

Illinois

Social Workers Examining and Disciplinary Board
Department of Professional Regulation
320 W. Washington St., 3rd Floor
Springfield, IL 62786

Indiana

Health Professionals Bureau
IN Government Center
402 W. Washington St., Room 041
Indianapolis, IN 46204

Iowa

Board of Social Work Examiners
Bureau of Professional Licensing
Lucas State Office Building, E. 12th St.
Des Moines, IA 50319

Kansas

Behavioral Sciences Regulatory Board
712 S. Kansas Ave.
Topeka, KS 66612

Kentucky

State Board of Examiners of Social Work
Berry Hill Annex
P.O. Box 456, Louisville Rd.
Frankfort, KY 40602

Louisiana

Louisiana State Board of Certified Social Work Examiners
11930 Perkins Rd., Suite B
Baton Rouge, LA 70810

Maine

State Board of Social Work Licensure
Department of Business and Financial Regulation
35 State House Station
Augusta, ME 04333

Maryland

State Board of Social Work Examiners
4201 Patterson Ave.
Baltimore, MD 21215

Massachusetts

Board of Examiners of Social Work
100 Cambridge St., Room 1512
Boston, MA 02202

Michigan

Board of Examiners of Social Work
611 E. Ottawa St.
P.O. Box 30246
Lansing, MI 48909

Minnesota

Board of Social Work Examiners
2829 University Ave., SE
Suite 340
Minneapolis, MN 55414

Mississippi

Board of Examiners for Social Workers
  and Marriage & Family Therapists
P.O. Box 12948
Jackson, MS 39236

Missouri

Advisory Committee for Licensed Clinical Social Workers
Division of Professional Regulation
P.O. Box 1335
3605 Missouri Blvd.
Jefferson City, MO 65102-0085

Montana

Board of Social Work Examiners and Professional Counselors
111 N. Jackson, Arcade Bldg.
Helena, MT 59620

Nebraska

Board of Examiners in Social Work
Bureau of Examining Boards
301 Centennial Mall South
P.O. Box 94986
Lincoln, NE 68509-4986

Nevada

Board of Examiners of Social Workers
4600 Kietzke Lane, Suite A101
Reno, NV 89502

New Hampshire

Board of Examiners of Psychology and Mental Health Practice
Box 457
105 Pleasant Street
Concord, NH 03301

New Jersey

Board of Social Work Examiners
124 Halsey Street
P.O. Box 45033
Newark, NJ 07101

New Mexico

Board of Social Work Examiners
1599 St. Francis Dr.
P.O. Box 25101
Sante Fe, NM 87504

New York

State Board for Social Work
State Education Department
Cultural Education Center
Room 3041
Albany, NY 12230

North Carolina

Social Work Board
130 S. Church St.
P.O. Box 1043
Asheboro, NC 27204

North Dakota

Board of Social Work Examiners
P.O. Box 1043
Bismarck, ND 58502-0914

Ohio

Social Work Board
77 S. High Street, 16th Floor
Columbus, OH 43266

Oklahoma

State Board of Licensed Social Workers
3535 NW 58th, Suite 765
Oklahoma, OK 73112

Oregon

State Board of Licensed Social Workers
3218 Pringle Rd. SE, Suite 765
Salem, OR 93702-6310

Pennsylvania

State Board of Social Work Examiners
P.O. Box 2649
Harrisburg, PA 17105

Puerto Rico

Board of Examiners of Social Work
Ramon Ramos Casellas St.
Urb. Roosevelt
Hata Rey, PR 00918

Rhode Island

Division of Professional Regulation
Rhode Island Department of Health
3 Capitol Health, Room 104
Providence, RI 02908-5097

South Carolina

Board of Social Work Examiners
3600 Forest Dr., Suite 101
P.O. Box 11329
Columbia, SC 29211-1329

South Dakota

Department of Commerce and Consumer Affairs
Board of Social Work Examiners
P.O. Box 654
Spearfish, SD 57783-0654

Tennessee

Board of Social Worker Certification and Licensure
Department of Health
426 5th Ave. North
Nashville, TN 37247-1010

Texas

State Board of Social Work Examiners
Texas Department of Human Services
1100 W. 49th St.
Austin, TX 78756-3183

Utah

Social Work Licensing Board
Division of Occupational and Professional Licensing
1600 East 300 South
P.O. Box 146741
Salt Lake City, UT 84145-6741

Vermont

Office of the Secretary of State
Licensing and Registration Division
109 State St.
Montpelier, VT 05069-1106

Virgin Islands

Board of Social Work Licensure
Department of Licensing and Consumer Affairs
Property and Procurement Bldg.
1 Subbase, 2nd Floor, Room 205
St. Thomas, VI 00802

Virginia

Virginia Board of Social Work
Department of Health Professions
6606 W. Broad St., 4th Floor
Richmond, VA 23230

Washington

Mental Health Quality Assurance Council
Department of Health Counselors Section
1300 SE Quince St.
P.O. Box 47869
Olympia, WA 98504-7869

West Virginia

Board of Social Work Examiners
P.O. Box 5499
Charleston, WV 25361

Wisconsin

Board of Social Workers, MFTs, and Professional Counselors
Department of Regulation and Licensing
P.O. 8935
Madison, WI 53708-8395

Wyoming

Professional Counselors, MFTs,
   Social Workers and Chemical Dependency Licensing
2301 Central Ave.
Barrett Bldg., Room 347
Cheyenne, WY 82002

Glossary

Forensic social workers have a language all their own. The language derives from law terms as well as from the vocabulary of social workers. Language and nomenclature center around the words that social workers use in legal situations such as courtroom testimony, obtaining admissible evidence, public regulation, malpractice, professional review, and accountability. The following are definitions of some of the most important terms used in forensic social work, many of which are referred to in this book. Additional relevant terms for forensic social work may be found in Robert L. Barker (1999) *The Social Work Dictionary,* Fourth Edition, Washington, DC: NASW Press.

* * *

abandonment: Relinquishing one's rights, obligations, or possessions voluntarily, with no intention of subsequently reclaiming them. Abandonment of one's family may be used as grounds for divorce or loss of child custody in most states.

abduction: Transporting someone, often by force, coercion, or deception, against that person's will; or, if the person is a child or mentally incompetent, doing so without the consent of the parent or legal guardian.

abscond: An abrupt departure, usually to avoid some legal action.

adjudication: A court decision and the process of reaching that decision through a legal hearing or trial.

adoption: Taking a person, usually a child or infant, into one's home and treating him or her as though born into the family. The legal process involves changing court records to show the legal transfer from the birth parents to the adopting parents. Adoption gives the individual the same rights of inheritance as other children and the adoptive parents the same responsibilities and rights of control as other parents.

adversarial process: A procedure for reaching decisions by hearing and evaluating the presentation of opposing viewpoints. See also *ex parse* process.

alimony: See *maintenance.*

amnesty: An excuse granted to individuals or groups to free them from being tried or punished for criminal offenses.

appeal: A request of a higher court to review and reverse a lower court decision or grant a new trial. This higher court is called an appellate court. Its function is limited to determining if judgments made in lower courts were made in accordance with the law. Appellate courts review only written briefs and oral arguments about how the previous judgment came to be made and do not review new testimony or evidence.

arbitration: A method of settling disputes between two or more opposing factions by agreeing to appoint a neutral third party and abiding by that person's decision.

assault: An attempt or threat that creates in another the reasonable apprehension of imminent harmful or offensive bodily contact. Assault may be found even where no physical injury occurs if the victim has been subjected to a reasonable fear of harm or offensive contact. When such force through physical contact occurs, the term is called battery.

attachment: A court ordered lien against property, obtained before a final judgment is made. After the judgment is made, it is executed.

bail: A monetary or other form of security posted by or for someone accused of a crime. The purpose is to ensure that the accused will appear at subsequent legal proceedings, to enable the accused to avoid imprisonment while awaiting trial, and to relieve the authorities of the costs of incarcerating the accused during this period.

battery: Unlawful harmful or offensive bodily contact with another. The terms "battered child" and "battered spouse" refer to victims of this crime.

breach of contract: The failure of one of the parties to a contract to carry out what he or she previously agreed to do.

care and protection proceedings: The legal intervention on behalf of a dependent whose parents or guardians no longer seem willing or able to provide for the dependent's needs.

cease and desist order: A statement made by a court or judicial authority prohibiting an individual or organization from starting or continuing a particular activity. Similar terms are *injunction, temporary restraining order, preliminary injunction,* and *protective order.*

child abuse: Inflicting physical or emotional injury on a dependent minor through intentional beatings, uncontrolled corporal punishment, persistent ridicule and degradation, or sexual abuse, usually committed by parents or others in charge of the child's care.

child molestation: A form of child abuse involving forcing a child to participate in some sexual activity; i.e., behaviors that can include rape, incest, erotic fondling, or compelling the child to behave in a way that erotically stimulates the perpetrator.

child neglect: The failure of those responsible for the care of a minor to provide the resources needed for healthy physical, emotional, and social development. Examples of neglect include inadequate nutrition, improper supervision, deficient health care, and not providing for educational requirements.

Child Protective Services: Human services, often including social, medical, legal, residential, and custodial care, which are provided to children whose caregiver is not providing for their needs. Social workers who work in units of government agencies often help legal authorities with investigations to determine if children are in need of such services, help children obtain services when needed, and may provide such services themselves.

civil case: A noncriminal lawsuit. The outcome of such case usually are judgments declaring that the defendant must pay the plaintiff an amount of money; or the court issues an injunction compelling the defendant to perform, or abstain from performing, a specific action. See also *criminal case.*

class action suit: A civil legal action taken by or on behalf of a group, community, or members of a social entity against an alleged perpetrator of harm to that group or some of its members.

clemency: An official grant from the highest legal officer that forgives an individual from liability or punishment for specified criminal acts. Clemency differs from amnesty in that it applies to specific crimes and people rather than classes of people.

code of ethics: An explicit statement of the values, principles, and rules of a profession that regulate the conduct of its members.

commitment: Consigning an individual to a hospital or prison, usually after undergoing due process of law.

community property: Assets jointly owned by a husband and wife by the fact of their marriage. In states that have community property laws, both spouses are generally considered by law to equally share all property either has acquired during the marriage, but not before the marriage.

community service sentence: Punishment for a crime imposed by courts of law requiring a convicted person to perform some activity for the social good in lieu of imprisonment. Typically, the crimes are nonviolent and the duties often consist of working a specified number of hours in such settings as homeless shelters, social agencies, hospitals, and inner city recreation centers.

competence: The ability to fulfill the requirements of an obligation and the capacity to understand and act reasonably. For lawyers this term refers to the client's sanity, or the ability to comprehend sufficient to conduct legal obligations.

competent evidence: The convincing, reliable, valid, and relevant facts about a case that are admissible in courts of law, as distinguished from the opinions, guesses, or secondhand data.

confidentiality: The principle of ethics according to which the professional may not disclose information about a client without the client's consent. This information includes the identity of the client, content of overt verbalizations, professional opinions about the client, and material from records. In specific circumstances professionals may be compelled by law to reveal to designated authorities some information (such as threats of violence, commission of crimes, and suspected child abuse) that would be relevant to legal judgments.

conservator: A court appointed guardian or custodian of the assets belonging to someone who is incompetent to manage them properly.

contempt of court: Behavior that interferes with the administration of justice or shows disrespect for the dignity and authority of the court. Such behavior may occur within the courtroom during a trial (known as direct contempt) or outside (constructive contempt). Such behavior is punishable by fine or, to a limited extent, imprisonment.

contingent fees: Fees linked to the amount recovered; the lawyer may be paid only when there is a win.

contributing to the delinquency of a minor: The crime by parents, legal guardians, or others who have influence with a child of facilitating unlawful behavior in that child through neglect, coercion, example, or encouragement. These actions include permitting the youngster to avoid school, to stay out late at night, to consume alcohol and drugs, and to be exposed to unlawful activities by the parents.

corroboration: Independent evidence that tends to support or confirm other evidence. For example, a defendant's confession to shooting his boss is corroborated by witnesses who saw him do it.

costs: An allowance granted by the court to the winner of a suit as reimbursement for the expenses of conducting the suit.

criminal case: An action whose purpose is to identify and punish a defendant for an act of committing a crime; criminal acts are wrongs, not only against the victim, but against all society, and as such are prosecuted at public expense in the name of the people.

cross-examination: The courtroom procedure which follows the direct examination questioning done by the party who called for the testimony; an adversary's questioning of a witness after he or she has been questioned in direct examination by the party who called the witness. The purpose of cross-examination is to impeach the witness's credibility or bring out other aspects of the truth. Leading questions are permitted in cross-examination but not in direct examination.

custodial parent: The parent in whose home the child lives and who is responsible for the care and supervision of the child.

custody: A legal right and obligation of a person or group to possess, control, protect, or maintain guardianship over some designated property or over another person who is unable to function autonomously (for example, children and certain disabled adults).

custody of children: A legal determination in divorce cases specifying which parent or other guardian will be in charge of the child. The court awards custody to the mother or father who is deemed most likely to promote the best interests of the child. This parent is called the "custodial parent" and thereby has the ultimate responsibility for the care and control of the child. In some circumstances joint or shared custody is awarded so that both parents retain responsibility. Typically, in joint custody the child lives with each parent for a fixed period of time and both parents are equally responsible for all relevant decisions regarding the child's upbringing.

damages: The money recovered by court action for the plaintiff's loss or injury.

defamation: Written or spoken false statements about a person that cause harm. This term is now preferred over the terms libel (written statements causing harm) and slander (spoken statements causing harm).

default judgment: A decision made against a defendant who fails to appear for a court hearing after due notice has been given and the statutory periods of responses have elapsed.

defendant: One who is charged with a crime or sued in a civil action. See also *plaintiff.*

DeShaney **decision:** The 1988 U.S. Supreme Court ruling (*DeShaney vs. Winnebago County Department of Social Services*) that social workers and their agencies could not be held liable for damages for failure to protect an abused child. The decision to grant some immunity from malpractice lawsuits was applicable only in very limited circumstances.

Disciplinary Action Reporting System (DARS): A national database service developed by the American Association of State Social Work Boards (AASSWB) to prevent a social worker who has been sanctioned in one licensing jurisdiction to withhold that information from another licensing jurisdiction. Information about the disciplined social worker is reported to AASSWB by its member jurisdiction. Aggregate information on disciplined licensees is sent to all social work licensing boards bimonthly.

divorce: A legal declaration that a valid marriage has come to an end.

double jeopardy: Being subjected to prosecution and trial a second time for the same offense. Freedom from this is guaranteed by the Fifth Amendment of the U.S. Constitution.

dual relationships: The unethical practice of a social worker's assuming a second role with a client, in addition to that of professional helper. The other roles are friend, business associate, family member, or sex partner. Dual relationships tend to exploit clients or have long-term negative consequences for them. Workers who engage in these relationships are liable to legal as well as professional sanctions and probably should seek help.

due process: Adherence to all the rules, procedures, protections, opportunities, and considerations of fairness legally available when a person accused of a crime or offense is brought to trial or hearing involving possible deprivation of life, liberty, or property.

durable power of attorney: A document giving a person power to make health care and medical care decisions (often including life and death) for another who is unable to make those decisions.

Durham Rule: The 1954 court decision declaring that if a person's unlawful act was the product of mental disease then the accused is not criminally responsible.

duty to warn laws: Legislation and court judgments obliging professionals to disclose their clients' future intentions to do harm to a specific person, specified organization, or anyone who belongs to an identified group. Beginning with the 1976 *Tarasoff* ruling, various states have passed laws, and courts have issued decrees defining the conditions under which these warnings should be made.

emancipation: Freeing an individual or members of a social group from the control of another or others. For example, a minor child may become emancipated from parental control (and from the right to parental support or maintenance on getting married).

evidence: Proof of the allegations at issue; any written or verbal statement or object that is used to induce belief in the minds of jurors or the court.

***ex parte* process:** A legal proceeding in which, because of urgent concerns involving the welfare of a child or likelihood of irreparable damage to a person or property, a court grants relief after hearing only one side of the dispute. See also *adversarial process.*

expert witness: One who testifies before a court or lawmaking group based on special knowledge of the subject in question, which can result in a better assessment of the evidence or merits of the case. See also *fact witness.*

expunge: A legal procedure in which certain records about an individual are destroyed. In many jurisdictions some juveniles may have records pertaining to delinquent acts expunged upon reaching adulthood. Individuals who have been arrested unlawfully or not convicted may apply to have their arrest records expunged.

fact witness: One who is asked or required to testify in court or lawmaking group regarding what he or she has directly observed. Also called a "lay witness" this individual cannot render an opinion or reach a conclusion about what was seen or heard. See also *expert witness.*

false memory syndrome: The act of filling gaps in memory by fabricating and reporting thoughts about events that did not happen. Frequently, in cases involving child molestation, the defense is that the crime did not occur, that the "memory" of the event was "implanted" in the client's mind through the influence of the therapist.

family court: A court of law that hears cases pertaining to conflicts among family members, such as divorce, custody, adoption, or support matters. Often cases involving juvenile delinquency are also heard in such courts.

fiduciary relationship: A relationship based on trust and mutual confidence; a fiduciary is a trustee, a person who possesses rights and powers to be exercised for the benefit of another person.

forbearance: Refraining from doing something, or promising not to do something that the individual has a legal right to do.

fraud: The intentional deception of someone who is thereby injured.

garnishment: A legal process in which a debtor's money or other property (such as wages, salary, or savings) in the possession of another person is applied to a debt owed to another third party. Due process requires that the debtor be given notice and an opportunity to be heard by a court, which may order the employer, banker, or other holder of the property to remit such funds to an agent of the court or to the person to whom the money is owed until the obligation has been fulfilled.

Gault decision: The 1967 U.S. Supreme Court decision that affirmed the right of juveniles to the same legal protections as are given adults in criminal court proceedings, including advance notification of charges, right to counsel, freedom from self-incrimination, and the opportunity to have counsel confront witnesses.

Gideon vs. Wainright: The 1963 U.S. Supreme Court ruling that all indigent defendants in criminal cases involving imprisonment have the right to free legal counsel.

good faith: An honest intention not to take advantage of another.

grievance committee: A formal group established to evaluate whether an organization's policies and activities have resulted in harm to a complainant, to recommend changes in the policy/activity which has been deemed harmful, and to recommend ways to make amends for those harmed. Grievance committees are usually comprised of members of the organization.

guarantee: The assurance of the quality of a product or service; also a contract whereby one party agrees to be responsible for the debt of another.

guardian: One who has the legal responsibility for the care and management of a child or incompetent adult. Guardian ad litem refers to a temporary guardian, an officer of the court appointed by the court to manage the affairs of another for a specified time.

habeas corpus: The legal right of an individual who is held in a prison or other institution to appear before the judge so that there can be a determination whether that person is being held in violation of constitutional rights to due process.

hearsay evidence: Statements made by witnesses in courts of law based, not on their direct observation, but on what they heard others say; it is offered to prove the truth of the matter stated.

implanted memory: The unethical practice of influencing a client to "remember" events in the past that did not actually happen and to convince the client that the memory represents actual experience.

implied consent: An agreement to participate as expressed by gestures, signs, nonresisting silence, or inaction. This is often used as a defense in rape trials in which the defendant claims to have acted in the belief that the victim consented to his advances.

implied contract: A contract created by the acts of the parties rather than their oral or written agreements.

impound: To seize or attack funds, records, or property by an officer of the law or court, usually until some matter that involves those items can be legally adjudicated.

in loco parentis: A relationship involving the legally sanctioned assumption of parental responsibilities of a child or incompetent adult without a formal adoption. Such relationships most commonly exist when a child is in a residential institution, reformatory, or boarding school.

incapacitation: Lack of ability to provide sufficient care or judgment for oneself, due to diminished physical or mental functioning.

incarceration: Confinement in an institution, such as a prison or mental hospital.

incompetent: Without ability to fulfill obligations. In a legal sense this term refers to inability to consent legally to make or execute a contract; insufficient knowledge needed to carry out some legal obligation, unfitness to stand trial because of inability to assist in one's own defense; or inability to understand the nature of the charge or the consequences of conviction.

indictment: A sworn, written accusation presented by a grand jury to the court charging a person with a felony.

informed consent: The client's granting of permission to the professional and agency to use specific intervention procedures, including diagnosis, treatment, follow-up, and research. This permission must be based on full disclosure of the facts needed to make the decision intelligently. Informed consent must be based on knowledge of the risks and alternatives.

injunction: A court order issued by a judge ordering a person to do or not to do a specified act.

insanity: A legal term used to indicate the presence of a severe mental disorder, which negates the individual's responsibility for certain acts, including criminal conduct. The person declared legally insane is thought to lack substantial capacity either to appreciate the wrongfulness of a criminal act or to act in conformity with the requirements of the law.

insanity plea: See *McNaughten rule.*

interlocutory decree: In law courts, an interim decision that does not determine the final outcome of the case.

intestate: Having died without leaving a valid will.

Jaffee vs. Redmond: The 1996 U.S. Supreme Court decision that federal courts must recognize social worker's right to privileged communication; social workers could no longer be compelled to disclose confidential information in civil lawsuits filed in federal court. This ruling may not extend to certain actions in state courts (many of which do not provide absolute confidentiality for social workers or other mental health professionals).

joint liability: The mutual responsibility of a group of persons which requires all or any one of them to pay obligations or damages. In joint and several liability, an injured party has the choice of suing all the parties together or one or more of them separately.

"jump bail": A slang term referring to the actions of some defendants in failing to appear for their criminal trials after depositing significant funds with the court to ensure that they will appear for their trials or will remain in the jurisdiction. If they fail to appear, or leave the jurisdiction, they forfeit the deposit.

jurisprudence: The philosophy and science of law in terms of its origins, nature, and structure.

legal aid: The provision of free or reduced fee legal counsel to a litigant who cannot afford a private attorney.

legal malpractice: Professional negligence by the lawyer, usually for such things as conflicts of interest, abandonment, and missed deadlines. The claimant must prove that there was negligence and that the result of the case would have been different without the negligence.

legal regulation: The control of certain activities, such as professional conduct, by government rule and enforcement. In social work, legal regulation occurs through licensing, certification, or registration. In each of these, the public is assured by the relevant legal jurisdiction that the social worker possesses the knowledge or qualifications required by law to receive that designation.

libel: Written false statements about a person which cause harm. See also *defamation.*

license: Legally regulated permission to do or refrain from doing some act.

licensing board: An official organization that regulates a professional or technical practice in a specific jurisdiction. State licensing boards are usually comprised of a combination of professional and public members appointed by the governor. Social work licensing boards usually regulate social work practice by requiring formal licensing examinations, issuing licenses to practice, overseeing license renewals and disciplining social workers who have violated the law or its rules and regulations.

litigation: Disputes contested in courts of law. A litigant is one who is actively involved in a lawsuit either as a defendant or plaintiff. A litigious client is one who indicates a predisposition to initiate lawsuits.

litigious client: One who partakes of the services of a professional person and indicates a predisposition to initiate lawsuits toward that professional, the professional's employer, or other people or entities in society.

litigious society: The socio/cultural orientation marked by the tendency to resolve conflicts through an adversarial system in courts of law rather than by negotiation or compromise.

maintenance: Money paid to an ex-spouse by the other in accordance with legal requirements to provide for independent living expenses. Maintenance is the modern term for alimony and is distinct from the obligation of child support payments.

malpractice: Behavior by a professional person in the course of his or her job involving a failure of the person to bring to the matter at hand that amount of care, skill, and knowledge possessed by the ordinary, reasonable professional in that or similar communities, resulting in harm to the client.

McNaughten rule: A set of legal principles for the guidance of courts in helping to determine if a defendant may be declared not guilty by reason of insanity. Based on the 1843 British case of Daniel McNaughten, the court considers the accused not responsible for the crime he or she committed if a mental disease rendered the person unable to know the nature or quality of the act or that it was wrong to do. Many jurisdictions use different criteria. For example, the American Law Institute's formulation states that "a person is not responsible for criminal conduct if at the time of such conduct as a result of mental disease or defect, he lacks substantial capacity either to appreciate the wrongfulness of his conduct or to conform his conduct to the requirements of law."

mediation: Intervention in disputes between parties to help them reconcile differences, find compromises, or reach mutually satisfactory agreements.

Miranda rule: The 1966 U.S. Supreme Court ruling, in *Miranda vs. Arizona*, requiring police to inform suspects of their constitutional rights before questioning them.

mistrial: A trial that has been declared void because of errors arising during the development of the case, creating the need for a new trial before a different jury.

neglect: Failure to meet one's legal or moral obligations or duties, especially to dependent family members. When such conduct results in harm or potential harm to others, legal proceedings may be taken to compel the person to meet the relevant obligations or face punishment.

negligence: Failure to exercise reasonable care or caution, resulting in another person being subjected to harm or unwarranted risk of harm; also failure to fulfill responsibility that is necessary to protect or help another.

NGRI patient: The legal term for people tried but found "not guilty by reason of insanity." Such people are then committed for an indefinite time to mental hospitals.

obstruction of justice: The crime of preventing or attempting to prevent officers of the law and court from accomplishing their duties. Specific activities include attempting to bribe, intimidate, or influence jurors, witnesses, or officers of the court; interfering with police when they are in pursuit of a criminal suspect; and concealing or destroying evidence.

parens patriae: The legal doctrine that refers to the role of the state as the guardian of people who are unable to care for themselves. The concept is most often used in courts in deciding to intervene in family matters, such as custody of children, divorce disputes, and removal of children to foster homes.

parental liability: The obligation by parents to pay for the acts, damages incurred by, or debts of, their children.

paternity suit: A legal proceeding to determine whether or not a particular man is the father of a child.

perjury: A false statement made while testifying under oath in court, made willfully concerning some material point.

plagiarism: Appropriating the scientific or literary writings of another person and presenting it as one's own work.

plaintiff: One who brings an action in court against another person, i.e., one who sues another.

plea bargain: Negotiation between a prosecutor and a person accused of a crime, resulting in a disposition of the case. Typically, the accused agrees to plead guilty to a lesser charge and forgoes a jury trial. The advantage to the accused is that the case is resolved sooner and at less risk of serious penalty. The advantages to the public are that court dockets are less backlogged and cases can be resolved with less cost.

power of attorney: A written document that empowers one person to act for or represent another in specified matters.

prenuptial agreement: A contract entered into by two people who plan to marry, delineating the rights and obligations of each in the event of divorce, annulment, or death.

prima facie: Legally sufficient for proof unless successfully contradicted and refuted.

pro bono publico: "For the good of the public," the Latin phrase, often shortened to pro bono, refers to a professional person (usually a lawyer) providing services at no charge to a needy recipient, especially one whose case has broader social implications.

process server: A court official or other law officer who notifies the various parties in a lawsuit by handing them subpoenas.

protective custody: The placement of an individual by the legal authorities in a facility to prevent the person from danger of harm by others or from self-inflicted injury.

public defender: A state-supported attorney for persons who are accused of crimes but are unable to pay for their own counsel.

punitive damages: Money, in excess of actual damages incurred by the plaintiff, awarded by the court as punishment for the defendant's wrongful and intentional acts.

***Ramona* decision:** The 1994 judgment in a California court that psychotherapists may be held liable for damages by "indirect victims of the therapy." In the case a father claimed his career and marriage were destroyed because his daughter's therapist convinced her in a "false memory syndrome" that the father had sexually abused her.

rape: The criminal act of forcing a nonconsenting person to engage in some form of sexual contact. The force may take the form of violent assault or real or implied threat. In "statutory rape," the sexual relationship involves a person who consents but who is below the legal age of consent.

respondeat superior doctrine: Liability of employers or supervisors for the job-related actions of their employees.

restraining order: A temporary decree made by a judge or other legal authority without a prior hearing, prohibiting an individual or organization from performing some action pending an outcome of a later trial or hearing. An injunction differs in that it is made only after a formal hearing and has a permanent character to it.

right to refuse treatment: The legal principle, upheld in numerous court cases, that an individual may not be compelled to undergo any form of treatment, unless there is a life-threatening emergency or the person exhibits seriously destructive behavior.

right to treatment: The legal principle, established in the 1971 *Wyatt vs. Stickney* decision, that an individual who is confined to an institution has the right to receive the treatment necessary to offer a reasonable chance for improvement so that the person can function independently and gain release from that institution.

Roe vs. Wade: The 1973 Supreme Court decision that state laws forbidding abortion were unconstitutional under specified circumstances. The Court held that, in the first trimester, abortion must be left to medical judgment. In the second trimester, the state may, if it chooses, regulate abortion to protect maternal health but may not prohibit abortion. In the third trimester, the state may regulate or prohibit abortion except when necessary to preserve the mother's life.

sanction: Permission to carry out some plan granted by the established authority, or a penalty imposed on an individual who does not conform to the authority's rules.

search warrant: An order by a judge authorizing specified law officers to examine a subject's premises or possessions to bring them to the court. Search warrants can be issued only if there is probable cause to believe a crime has been committed and must particularly describe the place to be searched and the items or persons to be seized. The U.S. Constitution, Fourth Amendment, guarantees citizens freedom from unreasonable searches or seizures.

slander: Spoken false statements that damage the reputation of another person. See also *defamation.*

statute of limitations: A law that prevents the initiation of an action if it is not begun within a specified time.

subpoena: A legal order requiring the individual to appear in court at a specified time. A subpoena duces tecum is one that requires the witness to bring to the court or deposition any relevant documents or materials possessed.

***Tarasoff* decision:** The 1976 ruling by the Supreme Court of California stating that, under certain circumstances, psychotherapists whose clients tell them that they intend to harm someone are obliged to warn the intended victim. Subsequently, this decision has been adopted by courts and legislatures in many other states.

test case: A lawsuit to determine whether a law or legal practice is valid.

tort: A civil wrong that harms someone for which the injured party has the right to sue for damages in civil courts. Examples include malpractice, defamation, and negligence. Crimes and breaches of contract are not considered torts.

undue influence: Pressure or manipulation exerted, usually by one in a position of trust or power, over another.

victim compensation: Public payment to people who are judged to have been harmed as a result of another's negligence or criminal conduct. When the perpetrator of the crime pays the victim the term is "restitution."

white-collar crime: Nonviolent crimes by individuals or business organizations, usually committed in the course of the offender's occupation. The most frequent of these crimes include embezzlement, fraud, forgery, theft of property, fraudulent use of credit cards, stock manipulation, securities fraud, and other violations of trust.

Wyatt vs. Stickney: The 1971 legal ruling in Alabama declaring that patients with mental illness who are committed on civil grounds have the constitutional right to receive such individual treatment as will give them a realistic opportunity to be cured or to improve their mental condition.

Bibliography

AASSWB (1999). *Social Work Laws and Board Regulations: A State-by-State Comparisons Study.* Culpeper, VA: American Association of State Social Work Boards.

ABA Journal (1999). Experts on experts. *ABA Journal, 85,* 64-66.

Abbott, A.A. (1995). Professional conduct. In R.L. Edwards, J.G. Hopps, and others (Eds.), *Encyclopedia of Social Work,* Nineteenth Edition, (pp. 1916-1920). Washington, DC: NASW Press.

ABE (1999, January 22). Most frequently asked questions and answers. *American Board of Examiners in Clinical Social Work Online,* <http://www.abecsw.org>.

Addams, J. (1899). The subtle problems of charity. *Atlantic Monthly, 83,* 163-168.

Addams, J. (1902). *Democracy and Social Ethics.* New York: Macmillan.

Albert, R. (1986). *Law and Social Work Practice.* New York: Springer.

Alexander, R. (1989). The right to treatment in mental and correctional institutions. *Social Work, 34,* 109.

Alexander, R. (1993). The legal liability of social workers after *DeShaney. Social Work, 38,* 64-68.

Alexander, R. (1995). Social workers and immunity from civil lawsuits. *Social Work, 40,* 648-654.

Alexander, R. (1997a). Social workers and privileged communication in the federal legal system. *Social Work, 42,* 313-408.

Alexander, R. (1997b). Social workers and sexual abuse of clients: Recent legislation and court decisions. *Journal of Law and Social Work, 7,* 3-16.

American College of Forensic Examiners (1999). *ACFE Mission Statement.* Milwaukee, WI: Author.

American Medical Association (1996). *Principles of Medical Ethics.* Chicago: American Medical Association.

American Psychiatric Association (1994). *Diagnostic and Statistical Manual of Mental Disorders,* Fourth Edition. Washington, DC: American Psychiatric Association.

Ames, N.R. (1998). Recording in social work education. Doctoral dissertation, West Virginia University. *Dissertation Abstracts International, 59-08A.*

Anderson, B.S. (1996). *The Counselor and the Law,* Fourth Edition. Alexandria, VA: American Counseling Association.

Anderson, P. and Winfree, L. (1987). *Expert Witnesses.* Albany, NY: State University of New York Press.

Andrews, A.B. (1991). Social work expert testimony regarding mitigation in capital sentencing proceedings. *Social Work, 36,* 440-445.

Appelbaum, P.S. (1997). Ethics in evolution: The incompatibility of clinical and forensic functions. *American Journal of Psychiatry, 154,* 445-446.

Appelbaum, P.S. and Zoltek-Jick, R. (1996). Psychotherapists' duties to third parties: *Ramona* and beyond. *American Journal of Psychiatry, 153,* 457-465.

Arizona Board of Behavioral Health Examiners (1999). Disciplinary actions. *Newsletter of the Arizona Board of Behavioral Health Examiners,* Summer Edition. Phoenix, AZ: Author.

Axinn, J. and Levin, H. (1992). *Social Welfare: A History of the American Response to Need,* Third Edition. New York: Longman.

Ayres, B.D. (1994). Jury awards father accused of incest in memory therapy. *The New York Times,* May 14, A1-A4.

Bailey, F.L. (1994). *To Be a Trial Lawyer,* Second Edition. New York: John Wiley.

Barker, R.L. (1992). *Social Work in Private Practice,* Second Edition. Washington, DC: NASW Press.

Barker, R.L. (1999). *The Social Work Dictionary,* Fourth Edition. Washington, DC: NASW Press.

Bass, E. and Davis, L. (1994). *Courage to Heal: A Guide to Women Survivors of Child Sexual Abuse.* New York: Harper Perennial.

Bell, P.A. and O'Connell, J. (1997). *Accidental Justice: The Dilemmas of Tort Law.* New Haven, CT: Yale University Press.

Berg-Cross, L. (1997). *Couples Therapy.* Thousand Oaks, CA: Sage Publications.

Berger, S.H. (1997). *Principles and Practice of Forensic Psychiatry: A Practical Guide.* New York: W.W. Norton.

Berger, S.H. (1998, June). Ethics and dual agency in forensic psychiatry. *Psychiatric Times, XVI,* 1.

Berliner, A.K. (1989). Misconduct in social work practice. *Social Work, 34* 69-70.

Besharov, D.J. (1998). *Recognizing Child Abuse: A Trainer's Manual.* New York: The Free Press.

Biggerstaff, M.A. (1995). Licensing, regulation and certification. In R.L. Edwards, J.G. Hopps, and others (Eds.), *Encyclopedia of Social Work,* Nineteenth Edition, (pp. 1616-1624). Washington, DC: NASW Press.

Biggerstaff, M.A. (1994). Evaluating the reliability of oral examinations for licensure of clinical social workers. *Research in Social Work Practice, 2,* 184-197.

Birge, S.N. (1996). Ethical and legal issues for mental health counseling in higher education. Doctoral dissertation, University of Bridgeport, Bridgeport, CT.

Borys, D. and Pope, K. (1989). Dual relationships between therapist and client: A national study of psychologists, psychiatrists, and social workers. *Professional Psychology: Research and Practice, 20,* 283-293.

Branson, D.M. (1990). Derivative litigation. In *Basic Corporate Practice.* Seattle: University of Washington School of Law, 53-79.

Brieland, D. and J.A. Lemmon (1985). *Social Work and the Law.* St. Paul, MN: West Publishing Co.

Brody, P.M. (1999). *The Implications of the Supreme Court's Confidentiality Opinion.* Boston: American Board of Examiners in Clinical Social Work.

Bromberg, J.I. (1996). A retrospective analysis of psychologists' experience being disciplined by the American Psychological Association's Ethics Committee. Doctoral dissertation, Massachusetts School of Professional Psychology, Boston, MA.

Brown, D.P., Scheflin, A.W., and Hammond, D.C. (1998). *Memory, Trauma Treatment, and the Law.* New York: W.W. Norton.

Brown, J.A., Unsinger, P.A., and More, M.W. (1990). *Law Enforcement and Social Welfare: The Emergency Response.* Springfield, IL: Charles C Thomas Co.

Bryan, M.L.M., Slote, N., and Argury, M.D. (1996). *The Jane Addams Papers: A Comprehensive Guide.* Indianapolis: Indiana University Press.

Buder, L. (1979). Social worker ordered to prison for 25 years in murder of client. *The New York Times,* September 11, B3:5.

Bullis, R.K. (1990). Cold comfort from the Supreme Court: Limited liability protection for social workers. *Social Work, 35,* 364-365.

Bullis, R.K. (1995). *Clinical Social Worker Misconduct.* Chicago: Nelson-Hall.

Burke, C.A. (1995). Until death do us part: An exploration into confidentiality following the death of a client. *Professional Psychology, Research and Practice, 26,* 278-280.

Campbell, T.W. (1994). Challenging psychologists and psychiatrists as witnesses. *Michigan Bar Journal, 54* (January), 1161-1176.

Ceci, S.J. and Bruck, M. (1995). *Jeopardy in the Courtroom: A Scientific Analysis of Children's Testimony.* Washington, DC: American Psychological Association.

Ceci, S.J. and Hembrooke, H. (Eds.) (1998). *Expert Witnesses in Child Sexual Abuse Cases: What Can and Should Be Said in Court.* Washington, DC: American Psychological Association.

Chesler, P. (1998). Confessions of an expert witness. *Women's Rights Law Reporter, 19*(2), 161-166.

Clark, P.A. (1997). Applying respondeat superior to psychotherapist-patient sexual relationships. *American Journal of Trial Advocacy, 21,* 439-444.

Cole, B.S. and others (1995). Social work education and students with disabilities: Implications of Section 504 and the ADA. *Journal of Social Work Education, 31,* 261-268.

Coleman, R.D. (1997). *The American Bar Association Guide to Consumer Law.* New York: Times Books Random House, Inc.

Collins, G. (1997). Experts play major and highly paid roles in divorce litigation. *The New York Times,* April 4, B1:2.

Conroy, R.J. (1995). Access to medical records vs. patients' privacy interests. *New Jersey Lawyer, 173,* 24-28.

Cooper, S. (1995). Duty to warn vs. right to privacy: Victims vs. patients—a physician's dilemma. *Medical Trial Technique Quarterly, 42,* 93-105.

Costin, L., Karger, H., and Stoesz, D. (1996). *The Politics of Child Abuse in America.* New York: Oxford University Press.

Council on Social Work Education. (1994). *Statistics on Social Work Education in the United States, 1993.* Alexandria, VA: Author.

Crawford, R.L. (1994). *Avoiding Counselor Malpractice.* Alexandria, VA: American Counseling Association.

Cross, F.B. (1998). Lawyers, the economy, and society. *American Business Law Journal, 35*(4), 477-483.

Csikai, E.L. and Sales, E. (1998). The emerging social work role on hospital ethics committees: A comparison of social work and chair perspectives. *Social Work, 43,* 233-242.

CSWF Code (1997). *CSWF Code of Ethics.* Washington, DC: Clinical Social Work Federation, Inc.

Davidson, J.R. and Davidson, T. (1996). Confidentiality and managed care: Ethical and legal concerns. *Health and Social Work, 21,* 208-215.

DeAngeles, D. (1993). *State Comparison of Laws Regulating Social Work.* Washington, DC: National Association of Social Workers.

Dershowitz, A. (1994). *The Abuse Excuse.* Boston: Little, Brown.

DeShaney vs. Winnebago County Department of Social Services, 812, F.2d 298 (7th Cir.998 (1989).

Dickson, D.T. (1998). *Confidentiality and Privacy in Social Work.* New York: The Free Press.

Dorpat, T.L. (1996). *Gaslighting, the Double Whammy, Interrogation, and Other Methods of Covert Control in Psychotherapy and Analysis.* New York: Jason Aronson.

Dubin, S.S. (1981). Obsolescence or lifelong education: A choice for the professional. *American Psychologist, 81,* 486.

Duquette, D.N. (1990). *Advocating for the Child in Protection Proceedings.* Lexington, MA: Lexington Books.

Edwards, L.M. (1995). Florence Kelley (1859-1932) In R.L. Edwards, J.G. Hopps, and others (Eds.), *Encyclopedia of Social Work,* Nineteenth Edition, (p. 2594). Washington, DC: NASW Press.

Elliott, L.J. (1931). *Social Work Ethics.* New York: American Association of Social Workers.

Ezell, M. (1995). Juvenile and family courts. In R.L. Edwards, J.G. Hopps, and others (Eds.), *Encyclopedia of Social Work,* Nineteenth Edition, (p. 1556). Washington, DC: NASW Press.

Falk, P.J. (1995). Novel theories of criminal defense based on the toxicity of the social environment: Urban psychosis, television intoxication, and black rage. *North Carolina Law Review,* 39, March, 636-651.

Fatis, M. and others (1982). Written contracts as adjuncts in family therapy. *Social Work. 27,* 169.

Feder, H.A. (1993). *Succeeding As an Expert Witness: Increasing Your Impact and Income,* Revised Edition. New York: Tageh Publishers.

Flynn, J.P. (1987). Licensing and regulation of social work services. In R.L. Edwards, J.G. Hopps, and others (Eds.), *Encyclopedia of Social Work,* Eighteenth Edition, (pp. 43-47). Silver Spring, MD: NASW Press.

Fontana, V.J. and Besharov, D.J. (1995). *The Maltreated Child: The Maltreatment Syndrome in Children—A Medical, Legal, and Social Guide,* Fifth Edition. Springfield, IL: Charles C Thomas.

Foonberg, J.G. (1995). *Finding the Right Lawyer.* Chicago: American Bar Association.

Fraser, M.W. (Ed.) (1997). *Risk and Resilience in Childhood.* Washington, DC: NASW Press.

Gambrill, E. and Pruger, R. (Eds.) (1997). *Controversial Issues in Social Work: Ethics, Values and Obligations.* Needham Heights, MA: Allyn and Bacon.

Garb, H.N. (1998). *Studying the Clinician: Judgment Research and Psychological Assessment.* Washington, DC: American Psychological Association.

Gardner, K.T. (1996). Physician-patient communication and medical malpractice risk exposure. Doctoral dissertation, University of Denver.

Gazzola, R.A. (1998). Social workers: Unsung heroes. *Social Work, 43,* 474-375.

Gelman, S.R. (1992). Risk management through client access to case records. *Social Work, 37,* 73-79.

Gelman, S.R., Pollack, D., and Auerbach, C. (1998). Liability issues in social work education. *Journal of Social Work Education, 32,* 351-362.

Gendreau, P. (1996). The principles of effective intervention with offenders. In Harland, A. (Ed.), *Choosing Correctional Options That Work,* (pp. 117-120). Thousand Oaks, CA: Sage Publications.

Gerdeman, A.M. (1998). Understanding the oral examination process in professional certification examinations. Doctoral dissertation, University of Arizona, Tucson, AZ.

Germain, C.B. and Gitterman, A. (1996). *The Life Model of Social Work Practice: Advances in Theory and Practice,* Second Edition. New York: Columbia University Press.

Gibelman, M. (1995). *What Social Workers Do.* Washington, DC: NASW Press.

Gothard, S. (1989a). Power in the court: The social worker as an expert witness. *Social Work, 34,* 65.

Gothard, S. (1989b). Rules of testimony and evidence for social workers who appear as expert witnesses in courts of law. *Journal of Independent Social Work, 3,* 7-14.

Grabois, E.W. (1997-1998). The liability of psychotherapists for breach of confidentiality. *Journal of Law and Health, 12,* 39-84.

Grinfeld, M.J. (1998). Psychiatrists found guilty in two verdicts: Malpractice awards renew concerns over confidentiality issue. *Psychiatric Times, XV,* December, 8.

Grinfeld, M.J. (1999). Peering through the looking glass: Forensic examinations and privacy issues. *Psychiatric Times, XVI,* June, 1.

Hagen, M.A. (1997). *Whores of the Court: The Fraud of Psychiatric Testimony and the Rape of American Justice.* New York: Regan Books.

Hall, G.C.N. (1995). Sexual offender recidivism revisited: A meta-analysis of recent treatment studies. *Journal of Consulting and Clinical Psychology, 63,* 802-808.

Hanson, R.K. (1996). Witness immunity under attack: Disarming "hired guns." *Wake Forest Law Review, 31,* 497-511.

Haynes, K.S. (1998). The one-hundred-year debate: Social reform versus individual treatment. *Social Work, 43,* 501-511.

Haynes, K.S. and Mickelson, J.S. (1997). *Affecting Change: Social Workers in the Political Arena.* White Plains, NY: Addison Wesley Longman.

Hearn, T.J. (1999). Social regulation: The rule of law. *Vital Speeches of the Day, LXV,* 220-225.

Hepworth, D.H., Larsen, J., and Rooney, R. (1997). *Direct Social Work Practice: Theory and Skills,* Fifth Edition. Chicago: Dorsey Press.

Hess, A.K. (1998). Accepting forensic case referrals: Ethical and professional considerations. *Professional Psychology: Research and Practice, 29,* 134-139.

Houston-Vega, M.K., Nuehring, E.M., and Daguio, E.R. (1996). *Prudent Practice: A Guide for Managing Malpractice Risk.* Washington, DC: NASW Press.

Hughes, D.S. and O'Neal, B.A. (1983). A survey of current forensic social work. *Social Work, 28,* 393-394.

Hutchison, E.D. (1993). Mandatory reporting laws: Child protective case finding gone awry. *Social Work, 38,* 56-63.

Hyman, I.E. and Pentland, J. (1996). The role of mental imagery in the creation of false childhood memories. *Journal of Memory and Language, 35,* 101-117.

Imber, J.B. and Horowitz, I.L. (1999). Ferment in professional associations. *Society, 36,* 5-8.

Isenstadt, P.M. (1995). Adult Courts. In R.L. Edwards, J.G. Hopps, and others (Eds.), *Encyclopedia of Social Work,* Nineteenth Edition, (pp. 17-21). Washington, DC: NASW Press.

Jacobs, D. (Ed.) (1998). *The Harvard Medical Guide to Suicide Assessment and Intervention.* New York: Jossey-Bass.

Jaffee vs. Redmond (1996). *Supreme Court of the United States.* No. 95-266.

Jayaratne, S., Croxton, T., and Mattison, D. (1997). Social work professional standards: An exploratory study. *Social Work, 42,* 187-200.

Jenkins, L.A. (1995). Pre-trial diversion strategies for drug involved offenders: Focus on social work involvement. *Journal of Offender Rehabilitation, 22,* 129-140.

Johnson, P. and Cahn, K. (1995). Improving child welfare practice through improvements in attorney-social worker relationships. *Child Welfare, 74,* 383-394.

Johnson, W.B. and Corser, R. (1998). Learning ethics the hard way: Facing ethics committees. *Teaching of Psychology, 25,* 26-28.

Kagle, J.D. (1995). *Social Work Records,* Second Edition. Homewood, IL: Dorsey Press.

Kagle, J.D. and Giebelhausen, P.N. (1994). Dual relationships and professional boundaries. *Social Work, 39,* 213-220.

Karger, H.J. and Stoesz, D. (1995). Political correctness, social work, and the breakdown of the child abuse system. *Early Childhood Development and Care, 106,* 5-17.

Karls, J.M. and Wandrei, K.E. (1994). *Person in Environment System: The PIE Classification System for Social Function Problems.* Washington, DC: NASW Press.

Klein, A.J. (1994). Forensic issues in sexual abuse allegations in custody/visitation litigation. *Law and Psychology Review, 18,* Spring, 189.

Klier, J., Fein, E., and Genero, C. (1984). Are written or verbal contracts more effective in family therapy? *Social Work, 29,* 264.

Kopels, S. and Gustavsson, N. (1996). Infusing legal issues into the social work curriculum. *Journal of Social Work Education, 32,* 115-126.

Kopels, S. and Kagle, J.D. (1993). Do social workers have a duty to warn? *Social Service Review, 66*(1), 101-126.

Kruk, E. (1997). Mediation and conflict resolution in social work and the human services: Issues, debates and trends. In E. Kruk (Ed.), *Mediation and Conflict Resolution,* (pp. 1-19). Chicago: Nelson-Hall.

Kurzman, P.A. (1995). Professional liability and malpractice. In R.L. Edwards, J.G. Hopps, and others (Eds.), *Encyclopedia of Social Work,* Nineteenth Edition, (pp. 1921-1926). Washington, DC: NASW Press.

Kutchins, H. and Kirk, S.A. (1997). *Making Us Crazy: The Psychiatric Bible and the Creation of Mental Disorders.* New York: Free Press.

Ladds, B. (1997). The growing need for more services and more research. *International Journal of Mental Health, 25,* 3-10.

Laird, J. (Ed.) (1993). *Revisioning Social Work Education: A Social Constructionist Approach.* New York: The Haworth Press.

Landers, S. (1992). Social work now regulated across nation. *NASW News, 37,* June, 6.

Lawson, D.M. (1998, June 19). Impeachment of the expert witness: What the expert witness can do to protect himself/herself. Presentation at the National Expert Witness and Litigation Seminar, Hyannis, MA.

Lecroy, C.W. (1998). *Case Studies in Social Work Practice,* Second Edition. New York: Brooks/Cole Publishers.

Levy, C.S. (1993). *Social Work Ethics on the Line.* New York: Haworth Press.

Lifson, L.E. and Simon, R.I. (Eds.) (1998). *The Mental Health Practitioner and the Law: A Comprehensive Handbook.* Cambridge, MA: Harvard University Press.

Lindsay, D. (1994). Mandated reporting and child abuse fatalities: Requirements for a system to protect children. *Social Work Research, 18,* 41-54.

Linhorst, D.M. and Turner, M.A. (1999). Treatment of forensic patients: An expanding role for public psychiatric hospitals. *Health and Social Work, 24,* 18-26.

Linzer, N. (1998). *Resolving Ethical Dilemmas in Social Work Practice.* New York: Allyn and Bacon.

Litzelfelner, P. and Petr, C.G. (1997). Case advocacy in child welfare. *Social Work, 42,* 392-402.

Loewenberg, F. and Dolgoff, R. (1996). *Ethical decisions for social work practice,* Fifth Edition. Itasca, IL: F.E. Peacock.

Longres, J.F. (1995). Mary Ellen Richmond (1861-1928). In R.L. Edwards, J.G. Hopps, and others (Eds.), *Encyclopedia of Social Work,* Nineteenth Edition, (p. 2605). Washington, DC: NASW Press.

Lundblad, K.S. (1995). Jane Addams and social reform: A role model for the 1990s. *Social Work, 40,* 661-669.

Madden, R.G. and Parody, M. (1997). Between a legal rock and a practice hard place: Legal issues in "recovered memory" cases. *Clinical Social Work Journal, 25,* 223-247.

Mallen, R.E. (1997). Legal malpractice: A look at the trends. *Trial, 33,* 59-61.

Manfredi, C.P. (1998). *The Supreme Court and Juvenile Justice.* Lawrence, KS: University of Kansas Press.

Manning, S.S. (1997). The social worker as moral citizen: Ethics in action. *Social Work, 42,* 223-229.

Mares-Dixon, J. (1997). Mediating workplace harassment complaints. In E. Kruk (Ed.), *Mediation and Conflict Resolution,* (pp. 263-278). Chicago: Nelson-Hall.

Marine, E.C. (1998a). Facing professional liability litigation. *American Professional Agency,* 4 (August 11), 1-2.

Marine, E.C. (1998b). The importance of records in malpractice litigation. *American Professional Agency,* 5 (August 11), 1-2.

Mason, M.A. (1992). Social workers as expert witnesses in child sexual abuse cases. *Social Work, 37,* 30-34.

Massachusetts Board of Social Work Examiners (1997). *Disciplinary Actions.* Boston: Author.

McDowell, C.M. (1997). Authorizing the expert witness to assassinate character for profit: A reexamination of the testimonial immunity of the expert witness. *University of Memphis Law Review, 28,* 239-280.

McGough, L.S. (1994). *Child Witnesses: Fragile Voices in the American Legal System.* New Haven, CT: Yale University Press.

Melton, G.B., Petrila, J., Poythress, N.G., and Slobogin, C. (1997). *Psychological Evaluation for the Courts: A Handbook for Mental Health Professionals,* Second Edition. New York: Guilford Publications.

Mersky, H. (1996). Ethical issues in the search for repressed memories. *American Journal of Psychotherapy, 50,* 323-335.

Meyer, C.H. (1993). *Assessment in Social Work Practice.* New York: Columbia University Press.

Mierzwa, J.W. (1994). *The 21st Century Family Legal Guide.* Highlands Ranch, CO: ProSe Associates.

Miller, J.G. (1995). Criminal justice: Social work roles. In R.L. Edwards, J.G. Hopps, and others (Eds.), *Encyclopedia of Social Work,* Nineteenth Edition, (pp. 653-659). Washington, DC: NASW Press.

Miller, P. (1990). Covenant Model for Professional Relationships: An Alternative to the Contract Model. *Social Work, 35,* 121-125.

Millstein, K.H. (1994). The power of silence: Ethical dilemmas of informed consent in practice evaluation. *Clinical Social Work Journal, 22,* 317-329.

Minan, J.H. and Lawrence, W.H. (1997). The personal liability of an attorney for expert witness fees in California: Understanding contract principles and agency theory. *San Diego Law Review, 34,* 541-570.

Mullaney, J.W. and Timberlake, E.M. (1994). University tenure and the legal system: Procedures, conflicts and resolutions. *Journal of Social Work Education, 30,* 172-184.

NASW (1993). A study of the trends in adjudication of complaints concerning violations of NASW's Code of Ethics. Unpublished report of the National Center for Social Policy and Practice, National Association of Social Workers.

NASW Chapter Guide (1989). *NASW Chapter Guide for the Adjudication of Grievances* (Revised Edition). Silver Spring, MD: National Association of Social Workers.

NASW Child Protection Standards (1981). *National Association of Social Workers Standards for Social Work Practice in Child Protection.* Silver Spring, MD: National Association of Social Workers.

NASW Code of Ethics. (1960). *The National Association of Social Workers Code of Ethics.* New York: National Association of Social Workers.

NASW Code of Ethics. (1979). *The National Association of Social Workers Code of Ethics.* Silver Spring, MD: National Association of Social Workers.

NASW Code of Ethics (1989). *The National Association of Social Workers Code of Ethics.* Washington, DC: NASW Press.

NASW Code of Ethics (1996). *The National Association of Social Workers Code of Ethics.* Washington, DC: NASW Press.

NASW News (1998a, November). Two sanctions imposed. *NASW News, 43,* 4.

NASW News (1998b, November). Adjudication's first step is altered. *NASW News,* November 19.

NASW News (1999, February). "I bequeath my files to. . . . " *NASW News, 44,* 7.

NASW Procedures (1994). *Procedures for the Adjudication of Grievances,* Third Edition. Washington, DC: NASW Press.

National Victim Center (1994). *Sexual exploitation by psychotherapists and other treating professionals.* Arlington, VA: National Victim Center.

New York Office of Professions (1999). *Summaries of Regent's Actions on Professional Discipline.* Albany, NY: Author.

NOFSW (1999). *The National Organization of Forensic Social Work Mission Statement.* Ann Arbor, MI: Author.

Oates, R.K. (1993). Three do's and three don'ts for expert witnesses. *Child Abuse and Neglect: The International Journal, 17,* 111-172.

Oberlander, L.B. (1995). Psycholegal issues in child sexual abuse evaluations: A survey of forensic mental health professionals. *Child Abuse and Neglect: The International Journal, 19,* 475-490.

O'Hare, T. (1996). Court-ordered versus voluntary clients: Problem differences and readiness for change. *Social Work, 41,* 417-422.

Olson, W.K. (1991). *The Litigation Explosion.* New York: Dutton.

Osman, S. and Shueman, S.A. (1988). A guide to the peer review process for clinicians. *Social Work, 33,* 345-349.

Otto, R.L.K. (1994). On the ability of mental health professionals to predict dangerousness: A commentary on interpretations of the "dangerousness" literature. *Law and Psychology Review, 18,* 43.

Pflepsen, W.L. (1997). Is American society too litigious? Yes. *Update on Law-Related Education, 21,* 18-21.

Poertner, J. and Press, A. (1990). Who best represents the interests of the child in court? *Child Welfare, LXIX,* 194-199.

Pollack, D. (1997). *Social Work and the Courts.* Chicago: Garland Publishing Co.

Polowy, C.I. and Gorenberg, C. (1997). Legal issues: Recent developments in confidentiality and privilege. In R.L. Edwards, J.G. Hopps, and others (Eds), *Encyclopedia of Social Work,* Nineteenth Edition, *1997 Supplement.* (pp. 179-190). Washington, DC: NASW Press.

Priest, G.L. (1990). The new legal structure of risk control. *Daedalus, 119,* 207.

Prince, A.H. (1998). Patterns of continuing professional development (CPD) activities of social workers in local departments of social services or welfare in Virginia. Doctoral dissertation, Virginia Commonwealth University.

Prince, K. (1996). *Boring Records: Communication, Speech, and Writing in Social Work.* New York: Jessica Kingsley Publishers.

Qualliotine, R. (1991, January 21). The legal risks of doing peer review are overblown. *Medical Economics, 15.*

Quam, J.K. (1995a). Robert Weeks deForest (1848-1931) In R.L. Edwards, J.G. Hopps, and others (Eds.), *Encyclopedia of Social Work,* Nineteenth Edition, (p. 2580). Washington, DC: NASW Press.

Quam, J.K. (1995b). Sophonisba Preston Breckinridge (1866-1948). In R.L. Edwards, J.G. Hopps, and others (Eds.), *Encyclopedia of Social Work,* Nineteenth Edition, (pp. 2575- 2576). Washington, DC: NASW Press.

Reamer, F.G. (1994). *Social Work Malpractice and Liability: Strategies for Prevention.* New York: Columbia University Press.

Reamer, F.G. (1995a). *Social Work Values and Ethics.* New York: Columbia University Press.

Reamer, F.G. (1995b). Malpractice claims against social workers: First facts. *Social Work, 40,* 595-601.

Reamer, F.G. (1998a). *Ethical Standards in Social Work: A Critical Review of the NASW Code of Ethics.* Washington, DC: NASW Press.

Reamer, F.G. (1998b). The evolution of social work ethics. *Social Work, 43,* 6, 489-500.

Regehr, C. and Antle, B. (1997). Coercive influences: Informed consent in court-mandated social work practice. *Social Work, 42,* 300-306.

Reid, P.N. and Popple, P.R. (Eds.) (1992). *The Moral Purposes of Social Work.* Chicago: Nelson-Hall.

Richmond, D.R. (1993). The emerging theory of expert witness malpractice. *Capital University Law Review, 22,* 693-710.

Richmond, M.E. (1898). *Friendly Visiting Among the Poor.* New York: Russell Sage Foundation.

Richmond, M.E. (1917). *Social Diagnosis.* New York: Russell Sage Foundation.

Richmond, M.E. (1922). *What Is Social Case Work?* New York: Russell Sage Foundation.

Roberts, A.R. (1997). *Social Work in Juvenile and Criminal Justice Settings,* Second Edition. Springfield, IL: Charles C Thomas.

Roediger, H.L., Jacoby, J.D., and McDermott, K.B. (1996). Misinformation effects in recall: Creating false memories through repeated retrieval. *Journal of Memory and Language, 35,* 300-318.

Roser, R. (1994). *Principles and Practice of Forensic Psychiatry.* New York: Chapman and Hall.

Sagatun, I.J. and Edwards, L.P. (1995). *Child Abuse and the Legal System.* Chicago: Nelson-Hall.

Saltzburg, S.A. (1994). *Federal Rules of Evidence Manual: A Complete Guide to the Federal Rules of Evidence.* Sixth Edition. Charlottesville, VA: Michie.

Saltzman, A. (1986). Reporting child abusers and protecting substance abusers. *Social Work, 31,* 474-480.

Sattler, J.M. (1998). *Clinical and Forensic Interviewing of Children and Families.* La Mesa, CA: Jerome M. Sattler, Publisher, Inc.

Scalia, A. (1996). *Dissenting Opinion in Jaffee vs. Redmond.* Washington, DC: Supreme Court of the United States. No.95-266.

Scalise, D.G. and Farmer, K.P. (1998). Disclosure of a patient's medical information to third parties: How much is too much? *Law and Psychology Review, 22,* 199-218.

Schlichtmann, J.R. (1998, June 18). Use and abuse of expert witness testimony in high stakes litigation. Presentation at the National Expert Witness and Litigation Seminar. Hyannis, MA.

Schlosser, E. (1998). The prison-industrial complex. *Atlantic Monthly, 282,* 51-77.

Schroeder, L.O. (1995). *The Legal Environment of Social Work.* Washington, DC: NASW Press.

Schultz, L.G. (1991). Social Workers As Expert Witnesses: Guidelines for Courtroom Testimony. *Journal of Independent Social Work, 5,* 34-40.

Schutz, J.S. (1997). The expert witness and jury comprehension: An expert's perspective. *Cornell Journal of Law, 7,* 107-119.

Severson, M.M. and Bankston, T.V. (1995). Social work and the pursuit of justice through mediation. *Social Work, 40,* 683-691.

Shamroy, J.A. (1987). Interviewing the sexually abused child with anatomically correct dolls. *Social Work, 32,* 165.

Sifferman, K.A. (1994). *Adoption: A Legal Guide for Birth and Adoptive Parents.* Second Edition. Hawthorn, NJ: Career Press.

Silver, S.A. (1998). Beyond *Jaffee vs. Redmond* (116 S.Ct.1923 (1996): Should the federal courts recognize a right to physician-patient confidentiality? *Ohio State Law Journal, 58*(5), 180-186.

Singer, S.I. (1996). *Recriminalizing Delinquency: Violent Juvenile Crimes and Juvenile Justice Reform.* New York: Cambridge University Press.

Skidmore, S.L. (1990). Suggested standards for child abuse evaluations. *Psychotherapy in Private Practice, 8,* 25.

Sklar, K.K. (1995). *Florence Kelley and the Nation's Work: The Rise of Women's Political Culture, 1830-1900.* New Haven, CT: Yale University Press.

Sleek, S. (1998, February). Is psychology testimony going unheard? *APA Monitor, 29,* 1.

Sloane, H. (1967). Relationship of law and social work. *Social Work, 12,* 86-94.

Slovenko, R. (1995). The duty of therapists to third parties. *Journal of Psychiatry and the Law, 23,* 383-410.

Smith, M. (1997). Is American society too litigious? No. *Update on Law-Related Education, 21,* 18-21.

Smith, S. (1989). The changing politics of child welfare services: New roles for the government and the non-profit sectors. *Child Welfare, 68,* 289-299.

Sobin, C. and Sackeim, H.A. (1997). Psychomotor symptoms of depression. *American Journal of Psychiatry, 154,* 4-17.

Solomon, P. and Draine, J. (1995). Issues in serving the forensic client. *Social Work, 40,* 25-33.

Spakes, P. (1987). Social workers and the courts. *Journal of Social Work Education, 14,* 29.

Specht, H. and Courtney, M. (1995). *Unfaithful Angels: How Social Work Has Abandoned Its Mission.* New York: The Free Press.

Stein, T.J. (1998). *Child Welfare and the Law,* Second Edition. Washington, DC: Child Welfare League of America.

Stocks, J.T. (1998). Recovered memory therapy: A dubious practice technique. *Social Work. 43,* 423-436.

Strasburger, L.H., Gutheil, T.G., and Brodsky, A. (1997). On wearing two hats: Role conflict in serving as both psychotherapist and expert witness. *American Journal of Psychiatry, 154,* 448-456.

Strom-Gottfried, K. (1998). Applying a conflict resolution framework to disputes in managed care. *Social Work, 43,* 393-410.

Sundel, M. and Sundel, S. (1985). *Behavioral Modification in the Human Services,* Second Edition. Englewood Cliffs, NJ: Prentice-Hall.

Supreme Court of the United States (1996). *Carrie Jaffee v. Mary Lu Redmond, et al.* (95-266). June 13.

Swenson, C.R. (1998). Clinical social work's contribution to a social justice perspective. *Social Work, 43,* 527-538.

Szasz, T. (1998). *Cruel Compassion: Psychiatric Control of Society's Unwanted.* New York: John Wiley and Sons.

Tarasoff vs. Regents of the University of California (1976). 551, P.2d 334 (California, 1976).

Thyer, B.A. and Biggerstaff, M.A. (1989). *Professional Social Work Credentialing, and Legal Regulation.* Springfield, IL: Charles C Thomas.

Thyer, B.A. and Vodde, R.I. (1994). Is the ACSW examination valid? *Clinical Social Work Journal, 22,* 105-112.

Tice, K.W, (1998). *Tales of Wayward Girls and Immoral Women: Case Recording and the Professionalization of Social Work.* Chicago: University of Illinois Press.

Trattner, W.I. (1999). *From Poor Law to Welfare State,* Sixth Edition. New York: Free Press.

Treger, H. (1995). Police social work. In R.L. Edwards, J.G. Hopps, and others (Eds.), *Encyclopedia of Social Work,* Nineteenth Edition, (pp. 1843-1848). Washington, DC: NASW Press.

Valentine, P.W. (1990). College Park Psychiatrist, 2 Aides Sentenced in Prescription Case. *The Washington Post,* January 21, A-1.

Vandenberg, G.H. (1993). *Court Testimony in Mental Health: A Guide for Mental Health Professionals and Attorneys.* Springfield, IL: Charles C Thomas.

Vidmar, N. (1996). *Medical Malpractice and the American Jury.* Ann Arbor, MI: University of Michigan Press.

Vigilante, J. (1974). Between values and science: Education for the profession or is proof truth? *Journal of Education for Social Work, 10,* 107-115.

Weismiller, T. and Rome, S.H. (1995). Social workers in politics. In R.L. Edwards, J.G. Hopps, and others (Eds.), *Encyclopedia of Social Work,* Nineteenth Edition, (pp. 2305-2313).Washington, DC: NASW Press.

Wesley, S.C. (1997). Values and ethics in undergraduate social work education. Doctoral dissertation, Case Western University Cleveland, OH.

Whitesell, J.M. (1996). Ridicule or recourse: parents falsely accused of past sexual abuse fight back. *Journal of Law and Health, 11,* 303-331.

Whiting, L. (1995). Vendorships. In R.L. Edwards, J.G. Hopps, and others (Eds.), *Encyclopedia of Social Work,* Nineteenth Edition, (pp. 2427-2430). Washington, DC: NASW Press.

Wilhelmus, M. (1998). Mediation in kinship care: Another step in the provision of culturally relevant child welfare services. *Social Work, 43,* 117-126.

Wilk, R.J. (1994). Are the rights of people with mental illness still important? *Social Work, 39,* 167-175.

Witkin, S.L. (1998). Human rights and social work. *Social Work, 43,* 197-199.

Woodward, B. (1997). Medical record confidentiality and data collection: Current dilemmas. *Journal of Law, Medicine and Ethics, 25,* 88-97.

Yates, A. (1987). Should young children testify in cases of sexual abuse? *American Journal of Psychiatry, 144,* 1476.

Zakutansky, T.J. and Sirles, E.A. (1993). Ethical and legal issues in field education: Shared responsibility and risk. *Journal of Social Work Education, 29,* 338-347.

Zastrow, C. (1991). Safeguarding rights in NASW processes for adjudication of grievances. *Journal of Independent Social Work, 5,* 34-40.

Index

HAWORTH Social Work Practice in Action
Carlton E. Munson, PhD, Senior Editor

SOCIAL WORK: SEEKING RELEVANCY IN THE TWENTY-FIRST CENTURY by Roland Meinert, John T. Pardeck and Larry Kreuger. (2000). "Highly recommended. A thought-provoking work that asks the difficult questions and challenges the status quo. A great book for graduate students as well as experienced social workers and educators." *Francis K. O. Yuen, DSW, ACSE, Associate Professor, Division of Social Work, California State University, Sacramento*

SOCIAL WORK PRACTICE IN HOME HEALTH CARE by Ruth Ann Goode. (2000). "Dr. Goode presents both a lucid scenario and a formulated protocol to bring health care services into the home setting. . . . This is a must have volume that will be a reference to be consulted many times." *Marcia B. Steinhauer, PhD, Coordinator and Associate Professor, Human Services Administration Program, Rider University, Lawrenceville, New Jersey*

FORENSIC SOCIAL WORK: LEGAL ASPECTS OF PROFESSIONAL PRACTICE, SECOND EDITION by Robert L. Barker and Douglas M. Branson. (2000). "The authors combine their expertise to create this informative guide to address legal practice issues facing social workers." *Newsletter of the National Organization of Forensic Social Work*

HUMAN SERVICES AND THE AFROCENTRIC PARADIGM by Jerome H. Schiele. (2000). "Represents a milestone in applying the Afrocentric paradigm to human services generally, and social work specifically. . . . A highly valuable resource." *Bogart R. Leashore, PhD, Dean and Professor, Hunter College School of Social Work, New York, New York*

SOCIAL WORK IN THE HEALTH FIELD: A CARE PERSPECTIVE by Lois A. Fort Cowles. (2000). "Makes an important contribution to the field by locating the practice of social work in health care within an organizational and social context." *Goldie Kadushin, PhD, Associate Professor, School of Social Welfare, University of Wisconsin, Milwaukee*

SMART BUT STUCK: WHAT EVERY THERAPIST NEEDS TO KNOW ABOUT LEARNING DISABILITIES AND IMPRISONED INTELLIGENCE by Myrna Orenstein. (2000). "A trailblazing effort that creates an entirely novel way of talking and thinking about learning disabilities. There is simply nothing like it in the field." *Fred M. Levin, MD, Training Supervising Analyst, Chicago Institute for Psychoanalysis; Assistant Professor of Clinical Psychiatry, Northwestern University, School of Medicine, Chicago, IL*

CLINICAL WORK AND SOCIAL ACTION: AN INTEGRATIVE APPROACH by Jerome Sachs and Fred Newdom. (1999). "Just in time for the new millennium come Sachs and Newdom with a wholly fresh look at social work. . . . A much-needed uniting of social work values, theories, and practice for action." *Josephine Nieves, MSW, PhD, Executive Director, National Association of Social Workers*

SOCIAL WORK PRACTICE IN THE MILITARY by James G. Daley. (1999). "A significant and worthwhile book with provocative and stimulating ideas. It deserves to be read by a wide audience in social work education and practice as well as by decision makers in the military." *H. Wayne Johnson, MSW, Professor, University of Iowa, School of Social Work, Iowa City, Iowa*

GROUP WORK: SKILLS AND STRATEGIES FOR EFFECTIVE INTERVENTIONS, SECOND EDITION by Sondra Brandler and Camille P. Roman. (1999). "A clear, basic description of what group work requires, including what skills and techniques group workers need to be effective." *Hospital and Community Psychiatry* (from the first edition)

TEENAGE RUNAWAYS: BROKEN HEARTS AND "BAD ATTITUDES" by Laurie Schaffner (1999). "Skillfully combines the authentic voice of the juvenile runaway with the principles of social science research."

CELEBRATING DIVERSITY: COEXISTING IN A MULTICULTURAL SOCIETY by Benyamin Chetkow-Yanoov. (1999). "Makes a valuable contribution to peace theory and practice." *Ian Harris, EdD, Executive Secretary, Peace Education Committee, International Peace Research Association*

SOCIAL WELFARE POLICY ANALYSIS AND CHOICES by Hobart A. Burch. (1999). "Will become the landmark text in its field for many decades to come." *Sheldon Rahan, DSW, Founding Dean and Emeritus Professor of Social Policy and Social Administration. Faculty of Social Work, Wilfrid Laurier University, Canada*

SOCIAL WORK PRACTICE: A SYSTEMS APPROACH, SECOND EDITION by Benyamin Chetkow-Yannov. (1999). "Highly recommended as a primary text for any and all introductory social work courses." *Ram A. Cnaan, PhD, Associate Professor, School of Social Work, University of Pennsylvania*

CRITICAL SOCIAL WELFARE ISSUES: TOOLS FOR SOCIAL WORK AND HEALTH CARE PROFESSIONALS edited by Arthur J. Katz, Abraham Lurie, and Carlos M. Vidal. (1997). "Offers hopeful agendas for change, while navigating the societal challenges facing those in the human services today." *Book News Inc.*

SOCIAL WORK IN HEALTH SETTINGS: PRACTICE IN CONTEXT, SECOND EDITION edited by Toba Schwaber Kerson. (1997). "A first-class document . . . It will be found among the steadier and lasting works on the social work aspects of American health care." *Hans S. Falck, PhD, Professor Emeritus and Former Chair, Health Specialization in Social Work, Virginia Commonwealth University*

PRINCIPLES OF SOCIAL WORK PRACTICE: A GENERIC PRACTICE APPROACH by Molly R. Hancock. (1997). "Hancock's discussions advocate reflection and self-awareness to create a climate for client change." *Journal of Social Work Education*

NOBODY'S CHILDREN: ORPHANS OF THE HIV EPIDEMIC by Steven F. Dansky. (1997). "Professional sound, moving, and useful for both professionals and interested readers alike." *Ellen G. Friedman, ACSW, Associate Director of Support Services, Beth Israel Medical Center, Methadone Maintenance Treatment Program*

SOCIAL WORK APPROACHES TO CONFLICT RESOLUTION: MAKING FIGHTING OBSOLETE by Benyamin Chetkow-Yanoov. (1996). "Presents an examination of the nature and cause of conflict and suggests techniques for coping with conflict." *Journal of Criminal Justice*

FEMINIST THEORIES AND SOCIAL WORK: APPROACHES AND APPLICATIONS by Christine Flynn Salunier. (1996). " An essential reference to be read repeatedly by all educators and practitioners who are eager to learn more about feminist theory and practice: *Nancy R. Hooyman, PhD, Dean and Professor, School of Social Work, University of Washington, Seattle*

THE RELATIONAL SYSTEMS MODEL FOR FAMILY THERAPY: LIVING IN THE FOUR REALITIES by Donald R. Bardill. (1996). "Engages the reader in quiet, thoughtful conversation on the timeless issue of helping families and individuals." *Christian Counseling Resource Review*

SOCIAL WORK INTERVENTION IN AN ECONOMIC CRISIS: THE RIVER COMMUNITIES PROJECT by Martha Baum and Pamela Twiss. (1996). "Sets a standard for universities in terms of the types of meaningful roles they can play in supporting and sustaining communities." *Kenneth J. Jaros, PhD, Director, Public Health Social Work Training Program, University of Pittsburgh*

FUNDAMENTALS OF COGNITIVE-BEHAVIOR THERAPY: FROM BOTH SIDES OF THE DESK by Bill Borcherdt. (1996). "Both beginning and experienced practitioners . . . will find a considerable number of valuable suggestions in Borcherdt's book." *Albert Ellis, PhD, President, Institute for Rational-Emotive Therapy, New York City*

BASIC SOCIAL POLICY AND PLANNING: STRATEGIES AND PRACTICE METHODS by Hobart A. Burch. (1996). "Burch's familiarity with his topic is evident and his book is an easy introduction to the field." *Readings*

THE CROSS-CULTURAL PRACTICE OF CLINICAL CASE MANAGEMENT IN MENTAL HEALTH edited by Peter Manoleas. (1996). "Makes a contribution by bringing together the cross-cultural and clinical case management perspectives in working with those who have serious mental illness." *Disability Studies Quarterly*

FAMILY BEYOND FAMILY: THE SURROGATE PARENT IN SCHOOLS AND OTHER COMMUNITY AGENCIES by Sanford Weinstein. (1995). "Highly recommended to anyone concerned about the welfare of our children and the breakdown of the American family." *Jerold S. Greenberg, EdD, Director of Community Service, College of Health & Human Performance, University of Maryland*

PEOPLE WITH HIV AND THOSE WHO HELP THEM: CHALLENGES, INTEGRATION, INTERVENTION by R. Dennis Shelby. (1995). "A useful and compassionate contribution to the HIV psychotherapy literature." *Public Health*

THE BLACK ELDERLY: SATISFACTION AND QUALITY OF LATER LIFE by Marguerite Coke and James A. Twaite. (1995). "Presents a model for predicting life satisfaction in this population." *Abstracts in Social Gerontology*

BUILDING ON WOMEN'S STRENGTHS: A SOCIAL WORK AGENDA FOR THE TWENTY-FIRST CENTURY edited by Liane V. Davis. (1994). "The most lucid and accessible overview of the related epistemological debates int he social work literature." *Journal of the National Association of Social Workers*

NOW DARE EVERYTHING: TALES OF HIV-RELATED PSYCHOTHERAPY by Steven F. Dansky. (1994). "A highly recommended book for anyone working with persons who are HIV positive. . . . Every library should have a copy of this book." *AIDS Book Review Journal*

INTERVENTION RESEARCH: DESIGN AND DEVELOPMENT FOR HUMAN SERVICE edited by Jack Rothman and Edwin J. Thomas. (1994). "Provides a useful framework for the further examination of methodology for each separate step of such research." *Academic Library Book Review*

CLINICAL SOCIAL WORK SUPERVISION, SECOND EDITION by Carlton E. Munson. (1993). "A useful, thorough, and articulate reference for supervisors and for 'supervisees' who are wanting to understand their supervisor or are looking for effective supervision." *Transactional Analysis Journal*

ELEMENTS OF THE HELPING PROCESS: A GUIDE FOR CLINICIANS by Raymond Fox. (1993). "Filled with helpful hints, creative interventions, and practical guidelines." *Journal of Family Psychotherapy*

IF A PARTNER HAS AIDS: GUIDE TO CLINICAL INTERVENTION FOR RELATIONSHIPS IN CRISIS by R. Dennis Shelby. (1993). " A welcome addition to existing publications about couples coping with AIDS, it offers intervention ideas and strategies to clinicians." *Contemporary Psychology*

GERONTOLOGICAL SOCIAL WORK SUPERVISION by Ann Burack-Weiss and Frances Coyle Brennan. (1991). "The creative ideas in this book will aid supervisors working with students and experienced social workers." *Senior News*

SOCIAL WORK THEORY AND PRACTICE WITH THE TERMINALLY ILL by Joan K. Parry. (1989). "Should be read by all professionals engaged in the provision of health services in hospitals, emergency rooms, and hospices." *Hector B. Garcia, PhD, Professor, San Jose State University School of Social Work*

THE CREATIVE PRACTITIONER: THEORY AND METHODS FOR THE HELPING SERVICES by Bernard Gelfand. (1988). "[Should] be widely adopted by those in the helping services. It could lead to significant positive advances by countless individuals." *Sidney J. Parnes, Trustee Chairperson for Strategic Program Development, Creative Education Foundation, Buffalo, NY*

MANAGEMENT AND INFORMATION SYSTEMS IN HUMAN SERVICES: IMPLICATIONS FOR THE DISTRIBUTION OF AUTHORITY AND DECISION MAKING by Richard K. Caputo. (1987). "A contribution to social work scholarship in that it provides conceptual frameworks that can be used in the design of management information systems." *Social Work*

Order Your Own Copy of
This Important Book for Your Personal Library!

FORENSIC SOCIAL WORK
Legal Aspects of Professional Practice

_____ in hardbound at $49.95 (ISBN: 0-7890-0867-X)

_____ in softbound at $29.95 (ISBN: 0-7890-0868-8)

COST OF BOOKS_____

OUTSIDE USA/CANADA/
MEXICO: ADD 20%_____

POSTAGE & HANDLING_____
(US: $3.00 for first book & $1.25
for each additional book)
Outside US: $4.75 for first book
& $1.75 for each additional book)

SUBTOTAL_____

IN CANADA: ADD 7% GST_____

STATE TAX_____
(NY, OH & MN residents, please
add appropriate local sales tax)

FINAL TOTAL_____
(If paying in Canadian funds,
convert using the current
exchange rate. UNESCO
coupons welcome.)

☐ **BILL ME LATER:** ($5 service charge will be added)
(Bill-me option is good on US/Canada/Mexico orders only;
not good to jobbers, wholesalers, or subscription agencies.)

☐ Check here if billing address is different from
shipping address and attach purchase order and
billing address information.

Signature_____

☐ **PAYMENT ENCLOSED: $**_____

☐ **PLEASE CHARGE TO MY CREDIT CARD.**

☐ Visa   ☐ MasterCard   ☐ AmEx   ☐ Discover
☐ Diner's Club

Account #_____

Exp. Date_____

Signature_____

Prices in US dollars and subject to change without notice.

NAME _____

INSTITUTION _____

ADDRESS _____

CITY _____

STATE/ZIP _____

COUNTRY _____ COUNTY (NY residents only) _____

TEL _____ FAX _____

E-MAIL_____

May we use your e-mail address for confirmations and other types of information? ☐ Yes   ☐ No

Order From Your Local Bookstore or Directly From
The Haworth Press, Inc.
10 Alice Street, Binghamton, New York 13904-1580 • USA
TELEPHONE: 1-800-HAWORTH (1-800-429-6784) / Outside US/Canada: (607) 722-5857
FAX: 1-800-895-0582 / Outside US/Canada: (607) 772-6362
E-mail: getinfo@haworthpressinc.com
PLEASE PHOTOCOPY THIS FORM FOR YOUR PERSONAL USE.

BOF96